MW01142264

WORLD WAR II
The Story of a German Boy's Survival

Based on a True Story

By Sherry Malunat

Terry Ojala

Enjoy!

Thank you ♡

Sherry Malunat

Word Unlimited Publishing
Since 1985
Vancouver, WA – Indio, CA – Temple, TX – Portland, OR

WORLD WAR II
The Story of a German Boy's Survival

USA ISBN 978-0-9818470-6-1

Word Unlimited Publishing
Copyright© by Sherry Malunat, Author

All rights reserved. No part of this publication may be reproduced, stored in a retrieval system or transmitted in any form or by any means, electronic, mechanical, photocopying, recording or otherwise, without the prior permission of Sherry Malunat.

Printed in the United States of America

Table of Contents

Dedication

This book is based on a true story with an incredible journey of a child named Alex born in 1940 in Germany. This child, along with his older brother Ralph and younger sister, Renate, lived through the horrors of World War II and survived the problems and fears of living in the Communist East Germany after the war ended.

This book is dedicated to my husband, children, and grandchildren. Thank you to my husband and his family for sharing their stories that inspired this book.

Thank you to my dearest friend Dr. Wendy Flint owner of Word Unlimited Publishing who helped me publish.

Life will always bring us many tests and trials; it is in the mist of these test and trials that our faith must stand and have hope for a better tomorrow. Sometimes life's disappointments can turn into God's appointments.

Never give up faith and hope, for it is these that will sustain us in our darkest moments of life.

In Honor

In honor of those both dead and alive whose stories are in this book.

Karl born in 1989 - died in 1999
Josephine born in 1912 - died in 2002
Ralph, son of Karl and Josephine born in 1936 - died in 1995
Alex, son of Karl and Josephine born in 1940
Renate, daughter of Karl and Josephine born in 1942

Proverbs 3:5-6
"Trust in the Lord with all your heart, and lean not on your own understanding; in all your ways acknowledge Him, and He shall direct your paths."

Prelude   Fall 2014

Alex sat at the kitchen table with his aged hands wrapped around a warm cup of coffee looking out the window at the beautiful fall day that was just beginning. The sun moved slowly up the mountain where just a halo of brightness could be seen at the mountain top. He let out a big sigh as his eyes drank in the wonders of the mountain range with all its many different colors of leaf-bearing trees that were sprinkled among the tall Evergreen trees. Watching the sun move higher up over the mountain, the sky became stunning with the many different colors of reds and oranges that streaked across the horizon. Alex always enjoyed these quiet moments at the beginning of his day, before anyone else was up. Just to sit at the table enjoying God's beauty as he leaned back in his chair with his morning cup of coffee in his hands. Alex let all his cares roll upon the mountain range.

Many mornings the cares did not just melt away and this was one of those mornings where Alex's mind drifted back to his childhood in Germany. His thoughts went to the memories in his mind of what it was like growing up as a very young boy during World War II; or living in the aftermath of this war-torn Country when the war ended. He has tried over-and-over again to push back and forget what he saw as a child; but the painful memories would flood back into his mind again and again, even after all these years.

Alex's journey during the young years of his life was difficult. If he had the choice of his path in life he would have chosen a different path, but he was not given the choice. It is only God who knows each of our paths and the journey we take during our time on earth. When we are adults we are given the free will of choice. With each choice in life, we must live with the consequences, whether good or bad. But a young child lives with the consequences of the adult choices around him.

Alex's hands tightened around his coffee cup as the memories begin to pour out of his mind in picture form. The memory stopped and he saw himself as a young boy sitting with his brother and sister around his mother as she held a picture of their father and shared a story. This time mother was telling us the love story of her and father. She did this many times while father was missing in the war because mother hoped we would not forget father. A smile spread across Alex's face as he remembered the story. The stories mother told Alex were good memories and he cherished them.

Alex's parents had a strong love for each other and their children. His mother was a woman of great courage and a strong faith in God. But his parent's love story had taken a turn and became one filled with fear. Then other images of Alex's childhood flooded his mind as if he was watching a movie of his life.

Chapter 1 The Beginning 1898-1933

Karl was born in 1898 into a hard-working middle class family. He lived with his parents and sister in a small town in Germany near East Prussia. Karl's parents were very strict Lutheran's and he had to attend church and follow all the rules that his parents had set for him and his sister. At seventeen-years old, he was drafted into the German Army and sent to fight in World War I.

Since Karl's parents were strict with their children, he appreciated the disciplined life of the army. When his two years of service in the army were up, Karl decided to stay in the military and take the schooling and training they had to offer him. He excelled and soon began to move up in rank. By the time he was twenty-five years old he was an officer. His parents were proud of their son and this made Karl work even harder to obtain his parents continued acceptance.

Josephine was born in 1912, into a very wealthy family in the heart of Germany. Her father owned a transportation business that moved food and supplies all over Germany. She lived in a large elegant home, filled with beautiful furnishings. They had servants who did all the cleaning and cooking. Her parents were very kind to all their employees and every year they would have a Christmas party for their employees and families. Josephine's family was highly esteemed in their community. It was into this affluent culture that Josephine was born. Her family was considered upper class; and they were involved in all that high society life had to offer.

Josephine was four years younger than her brother Hans. Her parents told Hans that he was always to watch out for his little sister, since they were both very busy with the family business. The family transportation business was doing very well and employed a great number of people. Hans and Josephine's family was highly respected and her mother was invited to all the upcoming social events. This wealth allowed the children to be raised with the best of everything a child and young person could imagine.

Josephine attended the best schools that Germany had to offer. However, there was one problem for her as she grew into a young woman; her parents would not allow their children to be with people who were not within their upper-class circle. As she became a teenager her parents would not hear of her seeing anyone outside their upper class.

Josephine had one very special friend during her childhood named Margate; they were the same age and attended the same schools. Josephine was given permission to ride her bike the two miles without her brother to be with her friend Margate. When both girls were twelve years old, Margate's mother hired a seamstress to come in and give the girls sewing lessons. Josephine loved to sew and became a very good seamstress. While Josephine was sewing, she could be creative and make something she designed on paper into a beautiful garment. She made her dress for her sixteenth birthday party without telling her mother.

The day before her party she wanted to show her mother the calf length, cap sleeved pink dress that was adorned with flowers and lace. Josephine put on the dress and walked down stairs to the sitting room where her mother was reading. When Josephine's mother saw the dress, she asked, "Where did you get that lovely dress?" Josephine smiled and shyly spoke, "I made it." Her mother raised her eyebrows in surprise and replied, "Well it doesn't look that good, let's go down to the dress shop in the morning and get you a new dress for the party." Josephine just looked down as she shook her head "'yes'." Her heart was sad as she turned to leave the room, because she knew it was not worth arguing with her mother over a dress.

Josephine was raised in a Lutheran home where they followed the traditions and attended church regularly. Her faith was the one thing that was hers and she became very strong in her faith. Sometimes she would sit on the window bench in her bedroom and look out the window wishing she had more freedom from her parent's strict guidance and that she would be able to find her very own adventure in life. She dreamed of meeting a handsome young man someday, the one who would fill her with love and make her heart whole.

When Josephine became dating age, her parents needed to approve all the young men she met before she could go out with them. Her parents thought it was only proper that the young man fit into their family way of life. They loved their daughter so much and all they wanted to do was protect her and find her a husband that would be able to provide well for their daughter. This frustrated Josephine, so she decided not to date. She prayed daily for the right person to come into her life and that her parents would like him.

Josephine had permission to go to a medical lab technician school in the next town where they had room and board. She completed her school and graduated at the top of her class. In 1933, jobs were very hard to find and only the very best were hired right out of school. By the time Josephine was twenty-one years old, she was offered a job at a medical lab without even applying. This was a well-known medical lab in the same town as the school. She felt blessed and was very happy to be able to get this job even though she did not need to work because this job gave her some freedom from her parents' control. Being successful gave her a sense of pride.

After being offered the job Josephine moved back home. She planned to tell her parents about the new job that evening at dinner, since she was to begin her new job on the following Monday. Her parents listened and then Josephine's mother barked out orders, "Hans will be driving you to and from work." Josephine protested and after much persuasion and her father's agreement she could ride the bus each way. Josephine worked hard and loved her job; it was a great feeling being independent from her parents. She decided to save her money so she would be able move out into an apartment close to her work within a year. She had so many plans and dreams that she desired for her future.

Karl and Josephine grew up in two separate worlds - one in the middle class and the other in the upper class. Their worlds were never meant to collide and for sure the possibility of marriage was inconceivable. This kind of marriage would bring a disgrace on Josephine's family. During this time in Germany's history, it was unthinkable for the classes to mix in marriage. The only thing they had in common was both were raised in the Lutheran Church. But God had another plan for Karl and Josephine that had nothing to do with their classes in which they were born.

Most people living in Germany in 1933, were like people everywhere in the world; they went to work and enjoyed being with their families. The people did not pay too much attention to politics unless it was an election year. Josephine and her family were busy working and had no idea what was happening in the political realm. Karl, an officer in the German Army, did not know that Hitler was building a secret group of hand-picked military from the very elite of each member of the armed forces – Army, Navy, Marines and Air Force. This group that was being formed was called the SS Elite and they reported directly to the Head of State.

By 1933, the German military had begun quietly splitting into two military forces following the direction of Hitler's plan. One part of the military was those who attended to regular military duty; the other part was built of those who protected Hitler and did his bidding – the SS Elite. The SS Elite were body guards to the Head of State and protected him at all cost. The SS Elite – or Secret Service – were involved in private meetings with Hitler.

Those who did not belong to this Elite group of soldiers, were kept in the dark and did not know the evil plans that were being formed for Germany's future. Karl was part of the regular army and did his duty with a thankful heart that he had a paying job since the economy was in crisis and people were desperate to find work.

The German people were looking for an answer to solve the economic crisis that was facing Germany; they needed jobs. Hitler arose and began to speak at the rallies proposing change and jobs. He promised the people jobs in the auto industry and in road construction. With Hitler's power, he could make his promise come to past. Germany began building the Volkswagen (People's Car) and building up the highways throughout Germany. People were being put back to work and a sense of joy came upon the people. But they did not know that very soon Hitler would begin his evil plans.

Before World War II began, Karl was assigned the post in the army where he would travel from factory to factory inspecting weapons. Each year Karl's job of inspecting weapons became busier with more traveling. His job was to inspect weapons to ensure that the quality of weapons met the military's specs that were given him. Once the weapons had passed inspection, they would be ready for sale to the armed forces. Over time Karl had become the expert in the field of weapon inspection and was assigned a new position to be head weapon inspector. Due to the increase of weapons that were built to be sold to the military, Karl was assigned the responsibility of training all new weapon inspectors with the knowledge he had obtained over the years.

There were so many secrets going on within the German military where the Head of State was involved. The regular army did not know what the Special Forces or the SS Elite were up to, but they had a feeling something wasn't right. None of the regular army soldiers would dare ask questions or they would face disciple for stepping out of line. Karl kept to himself and focused on doing his job well.

Driving from factory to factory became tiring and occasionally Karl would be able to go on leave to see his family. One day on Karl's drive to one of the weapons' factories, he pulled his jeep over to the side of the road and looked out over the city that was below. He was tired and needed a change; he wanted to get away from all the busyness and perhaps he would visit his friend Michael. Turning the jeep back onto the road he affirmed to himself he would take some time off.

There were so many changes taking place in Germany prior to Karl and Josephine meeting. There was a new political party rising and rallies that were taking place in the big cities. These rallies were led by the SS Elite. The rallies were orchestrated to get the German people pumped up and to give them hope for a change in the economic crisis they were in. There were small groups of handpicked people that would attend the rallies and stand in the crowd to help pump up the people for change. These people were handpicked by the SS Elite and told what to do when they attended the rallies and if they did what they were told they would be rewarded.

Most German people thought it was all politics and were not interested in the movement. Most the people were not aware that there was a hidden undercurrent of evil moving within the political environment. This movement would undermine the German people and make changes that would horrify most of them. Germany would never be the same once the evil plans were in place.

The world as Karl and Josephine knew it was about to change drastically and never be the same again. Yet there was something happening outside of their control; something divinely orchestrated. Love filled Karl and Josephine hearts the moment they met and it was this love that went deep into the depths of their hearts that sustained them for a lifetime. A love so strong it gave them strength. There was nothing that could stop the destiny of their meeting, nor stop the love that would fill their hearts. Karl and Josephine did not know at the time they met and fell in love just how much their love would be tested. But the testing of their love would stand strong in the face of every adversity.

Magdeburg Germany 1933

Karl had earned his time off from his military duty and decided to go and visit his friend Michael in Magdeburg instead of going to visit his family. Karl just needed some time away to relax and not listen to his father complaining about the economy or politics. Early Friday morning, Karl rose from bed and pushed back the curtains to look out to see what the weather was like. "The sun rise is beautiful this morning," Karl said to himself as he walked to the closet to get dress in his uniform. "What a wonderful day this is going to be," then he thought to himself, wishing he could just wear regular clothes when he traveled. But the military forbid any soldier to travel in civilian clothes.

Karl arrived at the train station with his duffle bag slung over his left shoulder. Karl had booked the first train that was heading to Magdeburg; he was excited to see his friend Michael. It seemed strange that Michael had the same leave from the military as him. He took two steps at a time as he boarded the train; he walked down the train aisle until he found an empty seat next to the window.

The train was not very crowded this early in the morning, so Karl was able find a seat where he could stretch his long legs across the aisle. He put his bag in the overhead shelf above the seat and sat down next to the window. Karl took off his hat and placed it on his lap. He looked out the window as the train pulled away from the station. Even though it was the beginning of the day he felt tired and all he wanted to do was clear his mind and relax. There was tension in his neck and he told himself to relax and enjoy your time off as he leaned his head back against the seat.

Karl sat staring out of the train window and watching the scenery outside move by quickly. He could hear the rhythm of the continual clicking of the train wheels as they moved along the track. The sound and movement of the train began to lull him to sleep and he closed his eyes and allowed sleep to engulf him.

Karl woke with a start as the train slowed down to a stop and he heard the voice of the conductor announcing, "Next station, Magdeburg." He had not realized just how tired he was from his traveling to different factories every day. He took a deep breath and stretched his arms over his head before springing to his feet to depart the train and reached up and grabbed his bag before walking toward the train door. He hoped that his friend would be there waiting for him; it had been a long time since he had seen Michael.

Michael paced back and forth on the train podium as he waited with excitement; looking at the train doors for Karl to get off the train. The moment Karl stepped off the train Michael walked up behind him and gave Karl a slap on the back. Michael reached over and took Karl's bag and threw it over his shoulder. Then Michael stepped back and took a long look at his friend before saying, "It has been a long-time Karl, I am so glad you have decided to visit. Come on let's go." Karl smiled down at his friend who was a few inches shorter than him and said, "Thank you for letting me come and relax at your home for the week."

As they walked along the cobblestones street towards Michael's house, Karl looked over at Michael who had a silly grin on his face. Karl stopped and asked, "What's going on?" Michael stopped, swinging around he looked at Karl and said, "Oh! I wanted to surprise you, but I can't wait to tell you. I have arranged a blind date for you to meet my cousin Margate best friend Josephine." Karl raised one eyebrow and thought to himself, "Now what has Michael gotten me in to!" Karl's throat had suddenly turned dry and he had to clear it before he spoke, "Well that is a surprise alright!" Michael gave him a wink and said, "We need to hurry and get home, I know mother will have some food set out for us when we get there."

They quicken their pace and Karl looked in shop windows as he listens to Michael tell him about his duty in the military, his family, and how amazing it was that they both would be on leave at the same time. Karl listened to Michael, nodding his head and smiling at the appropriate time while Michael shared. But Karl's thoughts were somewhere else, on the blind date Michael had arranged for him.

Suddenly Michael stopped talking and came to an abrupt stop in front of his parent's home; Karl bumped into Michael bringing him back from his thoughts. Michael's mother had been watching for them from the window and as soon as she saw them, she threw open the front door. She had a sweet smile on her face as she gave them each a warm hug as they walked through the open door. "Hello Mrs. Rendell." Karl said as he hugged her back. Mrs. Rendell looked pleased to have them both in her home as she led the way to the kitchen.

The house was filled with the aroma of homemade soup and fresh bread. They entered the small cozy kitchen; the table was already set with fresh crusty French bread sliced and placed in the center of the table. Mrs. Rendell pointed to the table and said, "Please take a seat." Karl did not realize how hungry he was until Mrs. Rendell filled his bowls with the sausage soup.

The smell of food and the warmth of the kitchen gave Karl the feeling of being home. When lunch was over both Michael and Karl rose to help with the dishes. Mrs. Rendell objected. Michael walked over and gave her a hug and said, "Mother, you prepared such a lovely meal, Karl and I would count it a privilege to clean up the kitchen." Mrs. Rendell patted her son on the cheek and say, "Thank you son that would be wonderful." She turned and left the kitchen.

Mrs. Rendell came back into the kitchen just as they finished putting away the dishes, a smile spread across her face. Michael gave a sheepish smile back and said, "Well, what do you think? Did we do okay?" Then Michael walked over and gave his mother a hug and a kiss on the cheek and said, "Karl and I are going to go sit out in the garden and relax for a while."

Michael's mother was still smiling as she watched the two young men walk out the back door, she shook her head as she was remembering her son as a young boy. The path that leads to the garden was made up of heavy hewed stones that were lined with all sorts of flowers. Karl took in a deep breath to inhale the sweet aroma of the fragrances the flowers expelled. The path curved around the house and at the end of the path there was a covered patio full of outside furniture and surrounded by more flowers and colorful shrubs. For the first time in month's peace entered Karl's heart.

Michael led the way onto the patio and they both found a chair and sat down. "What a beautiful day!" Michael said as he leaned back in his chair. "Yes indeed, such a lovely day, thank you for allowing me to stay with you", Karl said as he placed his locked fingers behind his head and leaned back in his chair. They talked for hours catching up and before long Michael could hear his mother's voice, "Son it's time for dinner." Karl looked at his watch and said, "Wow, the time has just flown by." Michael got up and holler toward the house, "We will be right there."

The dinner that Mrs. Rendell prepared was just as tasty as the lunch; it has been such a long time since Karl had a home cooked meal. Once dinner was over Mr. Rendell stood and invited them into the living room to visit over a glass of wine. They entered the living room which was filled with rich dark furniture that had lace on the arms; and crystal decorations throughout the room. The floors were dark cherry hardwood that had an oval shaped tapestry rug in the middle of the room. Mr. Rendell walked over to the crystal wine holder and glasses and poured four glasses of wine. Karl took the glass of wine that Mr. Rendell offered him and walked over to a large overstuffed chair next to the fireplace to sit down. The conversation was warm as Mr. Rendell shared stories of his past. The wood crackled in the fireplace which sent out soothing warmth that filled the room. Karl ran his hand back and forth on the smooth wooden arm of the chair as he listened to Michael tells his parents about his job. Mr. Rendell filled their glasses with more wine and for the first time in a long-time Karl allowed himself to completely relax.

The warmth of the fire and being relaxed caused Karl to become even more tired, so he decided he would excuse himself for bed before he fell asleep in the chair. Karl rose to his feet and looking at Michael's parents and said, "Thank you, Mr. and Mrs. Rendell, for a wonderful evening, but I am tired and need to be off to bed, goodnight." Mrs. Rendell smiled and said, "Karl we always enjoy it when you can come and visit, you are like family to us. Have a good night's sleep." Karl smiled as he walked over to embrace them both and said, "Thank you!" Michael rose and gave Karl a hug and said, "Get some rest; we have a big day tomorrow." Karl closed the door to the living room and walked over to the guest room.

Even though Karl was extremely tired he could barely sleep and kept tossing and turning. The ticking of the wall clock sounded louder than normal. His mind kept racing to what Michael had said about the blind date he was going to have tomorrow. His thoughts rambled on in his mind. Was she pretty like Michael had said, with her long wavy hair and stunning green eyes? Would she like him, would he like her? Karl heard the rooster crowing and even though it was still dark outside he decided to get up since he couldn't sleep anyway. He reached over and turned on the lamp that was sitting on the small table next to the bed so he could look at the clock and see the time. Five AM. Karl stretched his arms over his head and took a deep breath.

He slowly slid his feet over the edge of the bed and sat up. The wooden floor felt cold to his feet. He ran his hand through his thick dark hair as he looked over at the clock on the wall, shaking his head as if to command the tired feeling to leave. He sat on the edge of the bed trying to decide if he wanted to take a shower now or wait until the others were up. He stood up and took a deep breath. The smell of coffee filled his nostrils and the aroma of coffee was calling him. Karl moved quickly to the bathroom and thought to himself, "Well someone else is up."

He got ready and headed to the kitchen where he found Michael sitting at the table sipping on a hot cup of coffee and reading the newspaper. Karl and Michael decided to surprise his parents by making breakfast. They were setting the kitchen table just as Mr. and Mrs. Rendell entered the kitchen. Mrs. Rendell wrapped her arms around both of their waist and said, "I could get use of this you know."

After breakfast, Karl and Michael went for a walk before they got the bikes ready for their day's adventure. Michael poked Karl in the ribs and said, "What a day you are going to have?" Karl gave him a puzzled look as they went back into the house to finish getting ready for their bike ride. Karl's busy military life of traveling gave him very little time to date. But the older he became the more he thought about having a wife and children. These thoughts were always present in his mind. Today these thoughts pushed in loud and clear. Sometimes when he lay in bed at night his heart would wish and hope that he would find the right woman - woman he was destined to be with, his "soul mate."

Michael had been trying for years to set Karl up with a date, but had been unsuccessful. He kept telling Karl that he works too hard and needed to go out and have some fun. For some reason this blind date intrigued him and he could not refuse Michael's plan. But now that the time was here to meet her, he wished he would have said, "No" to Michael as the fear of being rejected filled his mind.

Karl walked over to the mirror for the third time to adjust his tie; he studied himself in the mirror for a long moment, taking in his six-foot four-inch solid and lean frame. He was in his late thirty's but looked ten years younger. He adjusted his tie one last time and turned from the mirror and slowly walked over and looked out the open window. Staring out the window he said to himself, "I don't know why I am so nervous, I am just meeting a girl and having a good day with my friend and that's all it will be." He ran his fingers through his hair as he looked out at the trees branches swaying in the light breeze and listened to the birds chipping. He could not stop thinking about what Michael had said about Josephine being pretty.

Karl was still staring out the window deep in his thoughts when heard a knock on the bedroom door that brought him back to reality. Karl let out a big sigh as he turned and walked towards the door. When he opened the door, he saw Michael standing there with a big grin on his face and he said with a twinkle in his eye, "Well my friend, are you ready to go for our wonderful bike ride?" Karl looked at his friend and thought this girl must be either something very special or an ugly duckling, then Michael would have a great laugh afterwards.

Michael slapped Karl on the back and said, "What are you waiting for let's go!" Karl smiled at him and said, "Okay, let's go, just give me a minute to grab my jacket."

Chapter 2 The Meeting 1933-1934

Josephine was twenty-one years old and had completed her education which gave her the new job at the medical lab. Josephine wanted to prove to her parents that she was old enough to take care of herself and make her own choices. She works and spends time with her dear friend Margate. Margate wanted Josephine to meet other men besides her parent's pre-arranged dates.

Now that Josephine was working and had a little more freedom Margate had to figure out a way to get Josephine to meet someone. A perfect opportunity came up when Margate's cousin Michael, who was on leave from the military, told her that his friend Karl was coming to visit for a week. Margate devised a plan that she just knew would work and had to talk to Michael about.

Right after work that day Margate decide to ride her bike over to Michael's house and tell him her plan of getting Josephine and Karl together. Michael thought it was a grand idea to have Josephine and Karl meet since he wanted Karl to meet someone also. A joint bike ride would be perfect, which would not actually be a date since they would be with them.

In the past when Margate tried to suggest that Josephine go on a date with someone other than her parents pre-arranged dates, she would always turn her down and say, "No, I don't want to meet anyone." So it was a surprise that evening when she mentioned to Josephine about going on a bike ride with her cousin Michael and his friend Karl, Josephine quickly said "yes." Margate was hoping that Josephine and Michael's friend Karl might be attracted to each other. Margate thought to herself, "Josephine needed to get out and have some fun."

The next day on Josephine's bus ride home from work she thought to herself, "Margate was right. She needed some adventure and fun in her life." She was thankful that Margate talked her into going on a bike ride with her cousin Michael and his friend Karl. She was glad that she had agreed to go. All she wanted was to feel some freedom and meet new people, have a good time and enjoy a bike ride with her friend.

It was two days before the bike ride. Margate and Josephine sat on the back porch looking out into the back yard and noticed that flowers were just beginning to bloom. They chatted about the bike ride and how much fun it is going to be. Margate turned toward Josephine and said, "You know I met Karl a few years ago and he is a very handsome man, tall with deep blue eyes." Margate batted her eye lashes at Josephine when she repeated, "Deep blue eyes." They both started laughing and joking around about the bike ride and how it wasn't "really" a date, just friends getting together. "The bike ride is going to be great fun even if you don't like Karl," Margate said with a wink.

The thoughts of what Margate had told her about Karl, with his deep blue eyes kept coming to her mind over and over. These thoughts of Karl were stuck in her mind like glue and no matter what she did or how she tried to distract herself, she could not get Karl out of her mind. These thoughts frighten Josephine, since she was not sure how her parents would feel or how upset they would be if she wanted to see him again. It was hard to concentrate at work and she had to keep forcing the thoughts of Karl to the back of her mind in order accomplish her Friday work load.

Riding the bus home staring out the window and watching the city go by, the thoughts of Karl came back to her mind in full force. Josephine reprimanded herself saying, "You don't even know the man and you are acting like you are already in love with him." Josephine knew in her heart that it would never work, but deep inside there was a hoping that Karl was all that Margate had said he was.

That night before the bike ride, Josephine could barely sleep with the excitement and anticipation of meeting Karl. The sun was just coming up as she pulled up the blinds and looked out the window on the new day. She took a deep breath and thought to herself, "This is going to be a beautiful day for a bike ride."

Josephine stood in front of the mirror looking at her petite four-foot-ten inch' stature; she kept turned from the left to the right trying to decide if she should change into something else. Josephine decided the full skirt and sweater would do, it only needed a hat; she went to the closet to find the perfect one.

Since Josephine was a small child her mother was in the habit of walking into her room without knocking. In her mother's eyes, she still thought of her as her little girl. Usually Josephine could hear her mother enter the room, but this time Josephine was so deep in thought she did not know her mother was standing behind her looking in the mirror at her as she was trying to put on her hat.

When her mother asked, "Where are you going child?" Josephine was so deep in thought about meeting this handsome man named Karl, she jumped at the sound of her mother's voice, which caused the hat to slip from her hands and glide to the floor.

Josephine turned to look at her mother and said with excitement in her voice, "Oh mommy! I have been invited to go over to Margate's; we are going on a bike ride and have a picnic lunch in the country by the lake." Josephine bent down and picked up her hat from the floor, she wrapped her hair in a bun and tucked it up under the hat, a few strands of hair curled down the back of her neck.

Her mother stood with her hands on her hips and looked Josephine up and down taking note that the skirt was to the middle of her calf and acceptable for bike riding, then she said, "Oh that will be nice for you to get out on this beautiful day. I will have the cook pack you a picnic lunch to take with you to share with Margate." She turned and walked out of her room without another word. "Thank you mommy," Josephine quickly said, "I will pick up the lunch from the kitchen before I leave." Her mother yelled up from the bottom of the stairs, "Be safe today my dear child and be home before dark." Josephine replied, "I will," as she wished her mother would stop treating her like a little girl since she was a grown woman after all.

Josephine hurried down to the kitchen to ask the cook to make enough lunch for four people. The cook smiled and gave her a wink as she obeyed Josephine's request. The cook had always been kind to Josephine and would make her favorite meal at least once a week. The cook finished filling the picnic basket and place in on the counter top.

Josephine gave the cook a quick hug and thanked her before picking up the picnic basket and walked outside to her bike. "Wow this is heavy, there must be lots of food in here," she said to herself as she lifted the picnic basket up to place it on the back of the bike. She had to get her balance as she started pushing the bike peddles to make sure the weight did not tip the bike. Her heart felt light today and she whistled as she rode her bike to Margate's house.

Josephine took in the beauty of the day as she rode her bike along the side of the road; the sun shone bright making everything look brighter or was it that she was so excited that everything just looked brighter. She was nervous about the day and hoped that she would arrive at Margate's house early. Josephine wanted to have time to ask some more questions about Karl before the others got there.

Once Josephine arrived at Margate's house she looked around and did not see any other bikes. Josephine let out a sigh of relief as she parked her bike next to the house and quickly walked up the steps to the door. She gave the door a light knock. Margate swung open the door with a big smile on her face giving her a hug as she pulled her into the house. Josephine gave her a hug back and said, "My cook has prepared a picnic lunch for all of us today."

Josephine looked nervously into Margate's eyes and asked, "Tell me more about what your cousin told you about the gentleman he is bringing with him today." Margate tried not to laugh as she looked at her friend's serious face. Taking Josephine's hand in hers to comfort her, she could feel Josephine's hand trembling in hers. Margate realized just how nervous and freighted Josephine was; she knew Josephine like a book. They had been good friends since childhood and Margate loved Josephine as a sister.

She led Josephine to the sofa to sit down. Taking both of Josephine's hand into hers and looking her dear friend in the eyes Margate said, "Everything is going to be great today, don't worry, I will be there with you and we can leave if you hate Karl."

While Margate sat waiting for Josephine to respond she wondered why she would pin up her beautiful long flowing wavy brown hair and put it up under her hat. Josephine cleared her throat and said in a quiet voice. "I know, and I am not quite sure why I am so nervous." Margate smiled and said, "Okay here is what I know, Karl is in the Military, I think Michael said Army. He has kind eyes and acts like a gentleman." Josephine suddenly stood and looked down while she straightens her skirt then looked up and said, "Do I look alright?" Margate replied, "You look beautiful."

The compliment embarrassed Josephine and she looked down at the floor. She looked up again at Margate and asked, "Do you think they will arrive on time?" Margate gave a little chuckle and said, "I think they will, don't worry you look very pretty and I am sure everything will be fine. Besides, remember, I will be there with you, so you don't have to be so nervous."

There was a loud knock on the door. Margate looked at Josephine and gave her a smile as she turned to open the door. Josephine stood in the back of the room looking wide eye towards the door. Margate opened the door and said, "Hello Michael and good to see you again Karl?" She extended her hand to give Karl a handshake. Michael spoke, "Yes, Karl this is my cousin Margate, you met her a few years ago when you were here."

Karl acknowledged and extended his hand out to shake Margate's hand. "Come in, come in, this is my friend Josephine," Margate said as she pointed towards Josephine. "Hello," both Michael and Karl said at the same time. Josephine walked towards them and they reached out their hands toward her to shake her hand. She extended her hand first to Michael and then to Karl and said softly, "Glad to meet you both." Margate said with excitement in her voice, "Let's go!" Josephine seemed frozen in place staring up at Karl, who was also staring down at her. Margate grabbed Josephine by the arm and started towards the door,

Margate lead Josephine out the door and both men waited and then followed them out. Michael pulled the door closed behind him and walked over to the bikes. Margate walked over to her bike and pointed at the large picnic basket on the back of her friend's bike and said, "Josephine brought our lunch today."

Karl walked over to Josephine and said, "May I carry the basket on the back of my bike for you?" Josephine was speechless as she looked up at Karl. Margate walked over and took the basket off Mary's bike and gave it to Karl and said, "Thank you that is very thoughtful of you."

Josephine blushed as she continued to look at Karl's deep blue eyes; they were like a pool on a hot day that you were drawn to. Karl could not keep his eyes off Josephine and drank in her beauty as he took the basket from Margate. Once the basket was in Karl's hand the spell that held both him and Josephine in was broke and they both walked over to their bikes.

It was a beautiful spring day with a light breeze blowing through the trees making a swishing sound. The birds were chirping in the tree tops, singing out to their hearts content. The four of them rode their bikes for quite some time without much conversation, just enjoying the beauty of the day. Each of them lost in their own thoughts as they rode the couple of miles down the winding road that lead to the park. Michael pulled to a stop at the park entrance and the others followed suit.

The park was breath-taking, as the sun reflected on the spring colors that filled the park. The fragrances of the flowers floated through the air. Josephine was always amazed at how the park ground keeper arranged all the flowers into such a beautiful array. This was the first-time Karl had been to the park; getting off his bike he was amazed at how much the park looked like a picture postcard. Margate let out a big sigh as she said, "This is the reason I always love coming to the park in the spring."

Walking their bikes into the parking area, they put their bikes in the bike rack. Margate pointed to a large maple tree that stood in the center of the park and said, "That will be the perfect spot for our picnic lunch." Everyone agreed. Karl took the picnic basket off the back of his bike and waited for Josephine before following Margate and Michael towards the maple tree.

Michael carried a large blanket under his arm and he and Margate were just far enough ahead of Karl and Josephine so they could not hear their conversation. Josephine looked over at Karl and notice just how strong and handsome he looked in his uniform. He turned and smiled down at her and said, "I am glad that Michael arranged this bike ride." Josephine smiled back and then quickly looked away toward Margate and Michael. Margate looked up after she had finished spreading the blanket out in the perfect spot under the tree. Michael hollered, "Come on you two my stomach is growling."

Karl set the basket down next to the blanket. Margate and Josephine busied themselves arranging the food on the blanket, while Karl and Michael talked about when they both had to report back to duty. Margate looked over at the men and said, "Okay enough of that talk, let's eat and enjoy the day." Josephine was already seated on the blanket and looking up she patted the blanket and said, "Come, sit down and enjoy our lunch." Michael rubbed his stomach before he sat down and said, "The sandwiches look great Josephine."

With a slight flush in her cheeks, Josephine replied, "I did not make the lunch, my cook prepared the picnic lunch for us." Margate said, "Isn't that wonderful." After only a couple bites of his sandwich Karl said, "These are really great sandwiches; your cook out did herself. We must make sure to thank her." The rest of the lunch was spent enjoying the wonderful food, the beautiful setting of the park and the light conversation between the four of them.

Karl had not been able to keep his mind on anything but Josephine. He wanted to get Josephine by herself, so that he could ask her out on a real date, just the two of them. Oh, he could listen to the conversation over lunch but his mind was on Josephine. He could not believe just how beautiful she was, with a shy spirit and a kind gentle heart. Karl just had to get to know her. Josephine kept stealing glance at Karl during the conversation over lunch. She thought to herself, "he is as handsome and the perfect gentleman that Margate had said he would be."

Once they had finished enjoying the lunch, Josephine reached into the picnic basket and pulled out a small cake for desert. The cake would have to wait; everyone was too full to eat it. Michael stretched and lay down on the blanket staring up at the blue sky. Margate began cleaning up the remains from the lunch. Karl turn towards Josephine and looked deeply into her green eyes.

They stared into each other eyes for a long moment before Karl asked, "Would you like to take a walk with me before we eat the cake and finish our bike ride back home?" Margate who had been watching them looked away and crossed her fingers behind her back. Josephine continued to stare into Karl's eyes and a flush of heat came to her face as she thought how different Karl was from all the others men she had met. He did not brag about himself and yes she wanted to get to know him better.

Josephine broke the stare and looked over to Margate to see what she thought and if she needed help. Margate smiled and gave her a nod and a look that said, "it's ok." Josephine looked back into Karl's deep blue eyes and answered, "Yes, I would like that." Josephine was so happy that he asked her to go on a walk. Karl stood up and he gave Michael a quick wink before he extended his hand to help Josephine to her feet. Josephine brushed off her skirt and said to Karl, "I truly love this park and I am excited to show you all its beauty while we walk." Margate looked up and said, "Off with the two of you, go walking all ready."

Josephine lead the way as the two of them walked down toward the creek that was about 500 yards away from the Maple tree. Karl noticed how well kept the park was and commented, "I understand why you love this park, it is beautiful here." Josephine pulled her sweater across her chest to keep warm in the cool spring breeze. After a moment of holding the sweater so it wouldn't blow open, she decided to button her sweater up dropping her hands down to her side. It surprised her when Karl reached over and took her hand and said, "I am enjoying the time we are spending together. I would like to know if you would like to go out to dinner with me on Saturday." Josephine's hearts leaped as she looked down at the ground to gather her composure.

She thought he was so handsome and was hoping that he would ask to see her again. Josephine stopped walking and looked up into his eyes which radiated so much kindness and said, "Yes, I would to like to see you again and dinner on Saturday would be wonderful." Karl smiled, taking her hand up to his lips and giving it a light kiss saying, "It will be a great pleasure spending more time with you." Josephine's heart melted at the warmth of his lips on her hand.

They continue to walk towards the creek taking in the beautiful park setting. Josephine felt his strong hand wrapped around her hand, she liked the way it felt and hoped this could lead to more. They walked quietly as she kept thinking how very handsome Karl is and how when he smiles his blue eyes twinkle. She smiled to herself and Karl noticed the smile and wondered what she was thinking about. Karl stopped walking and turned towards Josephine with a smile on his face and said, "What was that smile about?" She blushed and said, "I was just enjoying our time together." A big smile came across Karl's face as he agreed, "Me too."

Once they arrived at the creek, they both stood at the edge staring at it and marveled at the peace and beauty the creek brought to the park. The creek was full from the melted winter snow. The water bubbled softly over the rocks and filled the air with music that only a creek can make. The sun was bright and reflected off the crystal-clear water. A bird sat on a nearby tree branch chirping out a song. Karl and Josephine were content to just stand together hand in hand taking in all the beauty and peace. Something was at work in both of their hearts and at that very moment they fell in love and they both knew that they would someday marry.

They continued to enjoy the quiet moment listening to the sound of the creek and the chipping bird. The beauty of nature surrounded and enveloped them. Just to stand there, being in each other presence, neither one wanted to disturb what seemed to be a perfect moment of peace that flooded them both.

Josephine finally broke the silence and turned towards Karl, looking up at him she said "We really need to be getting back, eat the cake and finish our bike ride with Margate and Michael." Karl turned towards her and looking down without saying a word he lifted her chin with his hand and tilted it up towards his face, he leaned down kissing Josephine softly on the lips. Josephine was surprised but glad at the same time and she kissed him back.

The two of them walked back hand in hand to where Margate and Michael were still sitting under the Maple tree waiting for them to return. Both Margate and Michael had smiles on their faces as Karl and Josephine approached. Josephine blushed slightly as she wondered if they saw the kiss between her and Karl. Josephine and Karl joined them on the blanket and enjoyed the piece of the rich chocolate cake that Margate set before them. Michael quickly devoured his piece of cake and then said to Josephine, "Wow, this is the best cake I have ever eaten." Josephine smiled at Michael and said, "I will let my cook know."

Margate began wrapping up the dirty dishes in the towels and placing them back into the picnic basket. Josephine quickly folded up the blanket, while Michael picked up the picnic basket to carry it. They walked slowly up the hill back toward their bikes. Once the basket was loaded they got on their bikes and continued their bike ride back home. Michael and Margate rode ahead to give Karl and Josephine more time to talk.

Margate looked back and saw Josephine and Karl peddling slowly behind and talking softly. Margate turned towards Michael and said, "Looks like this is working out just the way we had planned." Michael chuckled and said, "Perfectly." They both smiled at each other as they peddled on to keep well ahead of their two friends. By the time they finished their bike ride and returned to Margate's house it was late afternoon.

Josephine felt the day went by way too fast as they all were saying their goodbyes. Karl turned towards Josephine and said, "I will pick you up Saturday at your house, what is your address?" Josephine panic inside for a moment at the thought of how she was going to tell her parents about Karl, but smiled at him and gave him the address. Josephine and Margate stood waving as they watched Karl and Michael get on their bikes and ride down the road.

Margate turned towards Josephine with a big smile on her face and said, "Wow, looks like you two really like each other." Josephine blushed and smiled at her friend and said, "Yes, Karl is a gentleman and I am looking forward to getting to know him better, just not sure what my parents are going to say."

Josephine looked down at her watch and said, "I need to go so that I can get back home before dark." Margate smiled and shook her head in agreement giving Josephine a hug. All the way home Josephine thought about Karl and his deep blue gentle eyes and his soft kiss. She pulled the bike up to the house and prayed as she put away her bike for words to tell her parents about Saturday night.

Josephine could barely eat her dinner and decided to just tell her parents. Hans was telling their parents about his day, so Josephine had to tap her fork on her plate to get their attention. Josephine cleared her throat before saying all in one breath, "Mommy and Papa, I met someone today and he is in the military, his name is Karl and he has asked me to go to dinner with him on Saturday."

Her mother stood up from the table and said, "No! You will not see this man again." Her father reached for her mother's hand and gently pulled her to sit back down, then he turned towards his daughter and said, "Tell me more about this Karl." Josephine took a deep breath and shared how amazing she thought Karl was. Her father looked over at her mother and said to Josephine, "I would like to meet this young man." Her mother sat with her arms crossed and did not say a word.

Chapter 3 The Wedding 1934-1936

The days went by rapidly from the time Josephine and Karl met. They would see each other as often as Karl could get time off. Josephine hated the time they were apart and wrote him long letters. Karl came to see his beloved Josephine and did not want to leave when he had to return to duty. By the end of summer Josephine and Karl's hearts became one and they had fallen deeply in love with each other. Josephine was so happy all she could talk about was Karl and how wonderful he was. While on duty Karl counted the days until they could be together again.

Josephine's parents were concerned that Karl was not the right person for their daughter, because he was not from the upper class and would not be able to provide for her the way they thought best. But when they saw how happy their daughter Josephine acted and how her face lit up every time she talked about Karl, they decided not say a word against him. Josephine's brother Hans liked Karl and told her that he hoped all her dreams would come true. Joy filled Josephine's heart knowing that her family approved of Karl and she dreamed of a wonderful future with him.

It was a crisp October morning and today Karl would propose to Josephine. Karl had been planning the proposal for weeks now and could hardly contain the excitement he felt as he rode the train to see Josephine. The train came to a stop and Karl departed the train and began walking toward Josephine's house. Karl's mind kept replaying what he was going to say and do when he proposed to Josephine; he wanted everything to be perfect. He stopped at the bottom of the steps that lead to her parents' front door and said a quick pray before going up them. Taking in a deep breath he knocked on the door.

Hans open the door and said, "Karl, great to see you, come in and take a seat, Josephine will be down in a minute." Hans hollered up the stairs, "Josephine, Karl is here." Karl stepped into the living room and took a seat on the sofa. One of the servants came into the large room and sat a tray with hot coffee and cookies on the deep cherry wood table that was in front of where he sat. Karl thanked her and poured himself a cup of coffee. He looked around the room as he sipped his coffee, with its chandelier, elegant furniture with lace on the arms, and crystal vases. Hans came in and poured himself a cup of coffee and chatted with Karl while they waited for Josephine.

Josephine knew Karl was coming today at ten in the morning but she was still deciding on what to wear when she heard her brother call up the stairs letting her know Karl had arrived. Her heart leaped at the mention of Karl's name. She decided to wear a long warm black skirt that went down past her mid calves and a deep red sweater. She stood in front of the mirror and tied a ribbon around her hair pulling it away from her face, but allowing the soft brown curls to fall around her shoulders. She put on a pair of boots and a little lipstick before grabbed her warm coat, hat and gloves, and heading downstairs.

Karl was excited as he thought about his plan. He had decided to go back to the park where they shared their first kiss to propose to Josephine. Karl heard Josephine's shoes on the wooden steps as she walked down the stairs. He looked up towards the stairs, his heart jumped, and he held his breathe for a moment at the sight of his beautiful Josephine. Karl got up and met her at the bottom of the stairs taking her into his arms and giving her a warm kiss. Hans said. "Okay break-it up you two; Josephine's mother said not to be late for dinner." They both turned to look at Hans and Josephine said, "We will be back on time."

Karl helped Josephine with her coat and told her that he would like to take a bike ride back to the park today. Josephine turned to Hans and asked, "Would you mind if Karl borrowed your bike today?" Hans replied, "No problem, see you at dinner." Josephine loved going to the park and with the weather turning to winter soon, this might be the last time this year she would be able to bike ride to the park. Josephine went to the kitchen and asked the cook if she could put together a little something for them to take to the park. The cook winked at them both and said, "I would love to, just give me a few minutes and I will have the butler bring it out to you." Josephine gave the cook a quick hug and said, "Thank you." Then she took Karl's hand to lead him out to where the bikes were stored.

It was proving to be a perfect fall day. There was a slight breeze that tugged at the red and orange leaves on the trees which lined the road and every now and then a leave would float down to the ground. The sun was bright and warmed the air as they rode their bikes to the park. They parked their bikes in the bike rack, then Karl lifted the small basket and blanket off the back of his bike as Josephine pointed over to the same oak tree and said with excitement, "Let's eat lunch under the Maple tree again today."

Josephine pulled the blanket away from Karl and raced down to the Maple tree. She spread out the blanket and Karl put down the basket and said, "Why don't we take a walk before lunch." Josephine looked at Karl and thought to herself, "Why is he acting so nervous today?" but she chose to ignore it and reaching out she slid her hand into his and replied, "Okay, I would love to walk with you."

Walking hand in hand through the park where they first fell in love, that same magical feeling filled them both. The breeze kicked up and the fall leaves were blowing down from the trees, floating and swirling around in the wind before falling gently to the ground. Once they had arrived at the brook, Karl stopped and looked out over the brook for a long time, but did not let go of Josephine's hand. They both stood there for a long moment as they quietly listened to the melody of the water rushing over the rocks. Josephine could not stand the silence any longer and turning she look up at Karl and said, "I will never grow tired of coming to this place and feeling the peace it always brings to my soul."

Karl smiled as he turned towards Josephine, then he knelt down on one knee before he stated, "I love you Josephine more than life and want to spend the rest of my live with you. Will you marry me?" Tears of joy began to trickle down her face as she looked down into Karl's deep blue eyes, shaking her head and softly said, "Yes!" Karl rose and taking her into his arms he kissed her deeply. Karl pulled back from Josephine to look down on her and asked, "I want to ask your father for your hand in marriage before I give you your engagement ring, I hope that will be okay with you?" Josephine smiled up at Karl and said, "That would make me and my father very happy."

Karl and Josephine spent the day at the park laughing and planning their future. Both knew in their hearts that the future would be wonderful because they had each other. On the bike ride, back to Josephine's house Karl got real quiet. Josephine looked over at him and said, "What's the matter? You look so serious." Karl turned and gave her a half smile and said, "I am nervous about asking your father for permission to marry you." She smiled and said, "I will pray and trust God that He will give you the words you need." Karl gave her a wink and smiled back saying, "Thank you." But inside he still felt anxious at the thought of talking to her father.

That evening after dinner Josephine and her mother went into the kitchen to talk to the cook about tomorrow's menu. Josephine's father walked over to the overstuffed chair in the small room off the dining room and pulled out his pipe. Karl thought to himself, "It is now or never," as he followed her father into the small room. Karl took the chair next to the window and watched him stuff his pipe.

Karl cleared his throat and said, "Sir, I would like to ask your permission to marry Josephine." Her father immediately put down his pipe and stood up in front of his chair. Karl rose to his feet also not knowing what Josephine father was going to do. Her father walked over and gave him a vigorous handshake and said, "Of course son, I have never seen Josephine happier."

Karl looked at her father in surprise at his answer and spoke softly, "Thank you sir, you have made me the happiest man in the world. I have a special dinner planed in the city tomorrow night for Josephine; I will give her engagement ring to her there." Josephine's father smiled and gave Karl a wink, then set back down, lit up his pipe and took a deep puff; slowly he released the smoke into the air which made a circle around his head.

Karl excused himself and went into the kitchen where he found Josephine listening to her mother talk to the cook about tomorrow's menu. She looked up and walked over to him. Karl greeted his mother-in-law-to-be and the cook. He thought it best if Josephine's father tells her mother about the engagement. Turning towards Josephine he asked, "Would you like to sit on the porch for a little while before I head back over to Michael's?" Josephine reached out for his hand and led the way to the porch. They sat on the porch bench without talking for a long time, both staring out at the stars reflecting in the sky on this crisp clear fall evening. Karl looked over at Josephine with the light of the moon shining down on her and thought, "She is so beautiful, she takes my breath away."

Karl took her hand in his and said, "Your father gave us his blessing." She smiled up at him at the same time a shiver ran through her from the chilly air. Karl wrapped his arm around her shoulder and she snuggled into the warmth of his body. Everything seemed perfect and they both felt content sitting there together. Karl finally asked, "Would you go with me to the city for dinner tomorrow?" Josephine turned to him with a peaceful look on her face and answered, "Yes, of course I will."

Karl had planned a very romantic dinner at one of the best restaurants in the city. In his pocket was the single diamond engagement ring he bought the day after their first kiss in the park. That kiss told him that Josephine was the soul mate that he had been longing for and that she would become his wife.

Michael drove Karl and Josephine to the train station in the late afternoon so that they could catch the train to the city. Karl wanted them to get to the city early enough to be able to walk around the city and look at the sites before dinner. As they walked past the large fountain in the middle of the city, they stopped to throw in a couple of coins each making a wish. Karl thought to himself, "What a beautiful city." As they crossed the street to continue window shopping they noticed that one of the shop windows was boarded up. Neither of them could figure out why as they both looked at each other with puzzlement.

Time went quickly by and before they knew it the sun was setting and they were sitting in the restaurant enjoying their meal. The food was exquisite and once they finished eating, the waiter brought a bottle of Champaign along with two glasses. He then cleared the dishes from the table and left. Karl stood and poured Champaign into each glass. He sat down and reached across the table to take Josephine's hand. He looked deeply into her beautiful green eyes and asked her again, "Josephine will you marry me?"

A glow of happiness filled Josephine's face and a smile crossed her lips as she said, "Yes, I will." Karl picked up his glass to toast their engagement before he reached into his pocket for the ring. Karl got a twinkle in his eyes as he knelt again and slid the engagement ring onto her finger. She watched with awe at how romantic he was as he kissed her hand. Karl sat back down, this time Josephine held up her glass for a toast.

They sat there for the longest time holding hands across the table and staring into each other eyes. Karl cleared his throat and said, "Sweetheart, I have to tell you something very important. Within six months I am being transferred by the army to another post further away." Josephine sighed and a sad look came into her eyes, then she thoughtfully asked, "Can we get married as soon as possible?" Karl squeezed both of her hands slightly as he answered, "That is what I hoped you would say. We must talk to your parents' tomorrow." Josephine softly bit her lower lip as a worried look came across her face.

The next afternoon it was raining, Karl knocked on the door to Josephine's parents' house. Josephine had already told her parents that she and Karl needed to talk to them, so everyone was awaiting Karl's arrival. The butler opened the door and led Karl into the sitting room where everyone looked up as he entered the room. Karl walked over and took a seat next to Josephine.

All eyes were on the two of them as they explained Karl being transferred and their plans of wanting to get married soon. Josephine's mother stood up and walked over to the window and began to express the many obstacles they would face being from different classes and with Karl being in the military. She feared that the military alone would bring a hardship on a family. Her father stood up and walked over to the window and wrapped his arm around his wife's shoulder and said, "They will work it out and look how happy Josephine is." Her mother looked over at Josephine and agreed.

The wedding date was set for February 10, 1934. Karl's parents both passed away five years earlier and would not be at the wedding, so this made him happy that Josephine's parents had finally accepted him into their family. After lunch Karl sat with Josephine's father as he smoked his pipe, listening to him tell stories of Josephine when she was a young girl. Karl had to leave first thing in the morning, he stood up from the chair and thanked Josephine's father for accepting him into the family. Then he excused himself to go spend some time with Josephine before he had to get back to Michaels'.

Josephine, her mother, and the cook were busy talking and making wedding plans when Karl walked into the kitchen. Josephine looked up and said to her mother, "Thank you for all your help, I know the wedding will be wonderful." Her mother just patted her hand and smiled as she walked out of the kitchen, pausing to say, "Goodnight Karl and have a safe trip tomorrow."

Karl walked over to Josephine and kissed her lightly on the forehead. She began bubbling with excitement about all the plans for the wedding. Karl listened with a smile on his face watching the animation of her arms and hands and she explained everything. Josephine stopped and smiled up at Karl and said, "I am so glad my family has accepted you." Karl drew her to himself in a big hug and in a deep tone of voice agreed, "Me too."

The next morning Josephine met Karl at the train station to say goodbye. They stood hand in hand on the platform waiting for his train, both dreading the separation. The train pulled into the station and Karl took Josephine into her arms lifting her off her feet as they kissed good bye. Setting her back down, the tears was already stinging Josephine's eyes; she blinked to stop the tears from falling.

Karl picked up his bag and boarded the train. Josephine stood and watched for him to wave out the window. He found the first seat next to the window, open the window and his eyes locked with her eyes. The train began to move as they both waved good bye until they could no longer see each other. The tears that Josephine had held back ran down her face as if a damn had broken. Wiping her eyes, she slowly walked away from the train station to Han's car and headed home.

The months between October and December flew by for Josephine, keeping busy with wedding details her mother was arranging. Josephine's mother was planning every detail to make sure Josephine and Karl's wedding was the talk of the upper society, which would give praise to her for such an elegant and wonderful wedding celebration. Josephine agreed with all her mother's wedding plans. It was wonderful to see her mother so filled with joy and acceptance of Karl. Josephine preferred to day dream about Karl when he was away and allowing her mother freedom to plan the wedding.

Karl had not been able to get leave for over two months, but was looking forward to getting some time off for the holidays. Christmas was in two days; Josephine could hardly wait to see him. The cold of winter was setting in, but they had not had their first snow fall. She was praying for snow this Christmas, making their celebration together perfect. All Josephine could think about since she got word last week of Karl's coming, was how wonderful it would be spending their first Christmas together.

Josephine was counting down the days until she could see Karl again. Christmas Eve is tomorrow and he would be coming to celebrate it with her family. Since his parents died, he and his half-sister Anna didn't feel they had a reason to celebrate Christmas, so there was an excitement within him that he hadn't felt for years as he prepared to go on leave.

The train pulled into Magdeburg train station just before noon. Karl stepped off the train just as the snow began to fall. He smiled to himself as he began walking towards Josephine's house. He loved the snow and how everything took on a wonderful glow.

Josephine kept looking at her watch as she paced in anticipation of Karl's arrival. She walked over to look out the window again and said to herself, "It's almost 1p.m." Karl was going to leave the day after Christmas and Josephine's parents had agreed that he could stay in the guest room. "There he is!" Josephine shouted as she grabbed her coat and ran out the door to meet him. The whole family seemed complete now as she felt his arms wrap around her in a warm welcome. Josephine's family stood in the door way watching as they walked arm in arm into the house.

Magdeburg Germany February 10, 1934

Josephine and Karl's courtship has been short, but very romantic. Karl was always the perfect gentleman and Josephine loved that about him. The day of the wedding was finally here and the weather was cold with a fresh new dusting of snow on the ground. The sun shone brightly in the sky this February day as Josephine's father drove her to the church. To Karl and Josephine everything seemed brighter and their hearts were filled with the promise of a wonderful future together on their wedding day.

The wedding was held in the Lutheran Church where Josephine and her family attended with the reception to follow at the country club. The car pulled up to a stop in front of the church and Josephine looked up at all the stain glass windows of the church. She smiled thinking to herself, "how beautiful it will be as the sunlight flowed through the stain glass windows into the church and fill her wedding with all the colors of the rainbow." Josephine's father helped her out of the car and up the church steps. He went back to the car to carry in her dress.

Karl was already at the church waiting in a back room, dressed in his formal uniform. He wore his uniform just for Josephine, since she always would tell him how very handsome he looked in it. Karl's best man, John, one of his dear friends from his childhood, knocked on the door and said, "It's time to get married." Karl walked out and stood at the front of the church with John at his side as he waited for his bride and watched as people filled the church. Karl prayed that his nerves would calm down. Then he saw his sister Anna came into the church; she waved and smiled at him. Knowing Anna was there, gave him some peace and he took a deep breath as he continued to wait for Josephine at the altar.

Josephine's hands were shaking with nervousness as her mother helped her step into her wedding gown. The wedding gown was full of lots of lace and pearls that shimmered in the light; the gown made her feel like a princess. Her mother stood back and admired her and said, "Josephine you are a beautiful bride," then she walked over and adjusted the veil around her shoulders and gave her a kiss on the check.

There was a soft knock on the door and her father entered the room. He gasped as he looked at his beautiful daughter, "You look amazing Josephine." He walked over and took her by the arm and said, "Are you ready?" Her mother pulled the veil down over her face and Josephine replied, "Yes, papa, I am ready." Her mother went to get seated so the wedding could begin.

The music sounded for the bride to enter; Josephine's father patted her hand and then led her down the aisle. Karl caught his breath and tears stung his eyes at the sight of his beautiful bride. He took a deep breath to calm his pounding heart, their eyes met. Everyone in the church was standing watching Josephine, but her eyes were fixed on Karl as she walked toward him.

The wedding was beautiful and something sealed inside of both Karl and Josephine's hearts, it was at that very time they knew this was a once in a life time love. Neither of them knowing at that moment of joy and happiness what their future would hold, nor did they know how their love would be tested. Walking hand and hand down the aisle after the ceremony, the sun shone through the stain glass windows and rainbows of colors danced around the room, just as Josephine had imagined.

Karl and Josephine boarded a train to spend their four-day honeymoon in Venice. Walking hand in hand through the city, Josephine thought that Venice was the most beautiful city she had ever seen. Nothing in the world mattered to them except being with each other and sharing their deep love for one another. As they walked through the streets of Venice everything in the store windows looked so inviting in hopes to draw visitors into their shops.

Josephine stopped in front of a jewelry store and her eyes widened as she saw all the jewels and stones twinkling in the sunshine. Karl looked at his beautiful new wife to see what had her transfixed. He could see her looking longingly at a necklace and bracelet set made of a stone called "Bernstein." Karl reached out and took his wife by the hand and led her into the store. She looked up at Karl with a puzzled look on her face as she followed him.

Karl asked the store keeper if he could see the set of Bernstein stones. He handed them to Josephine to try on and thought to himself, "Wow, they look beautiful on her and make the green in her eyes stand out." He turned to the store keeper and said, "We'll take them." Josephine touched the stones on the necklace as they left the store. Karl took both of her hands in his and said, "Josephine I want you to always have good memory of our honeymoon. This is my wedding gift to you and every time you wear your Bernstein stone jewelry I want you to remember just how much I love you."

Josephine was speechless and tears filled her eyes as Karl pulled her to himself and kissed her deeply. They stood there wrapped in each other arms in front of the store for the longest time. Then they walked hand in hand back to their hotel. Even though the air was cold and they could see their breath, great warmth filled them both and that moment in Venice would forever be imprinted on their minds.

On the third day of their walk through the city they looked in the many shop windows dreaming and making wishes for their future. That evening was crisp and cold and the city lights filled the streets as they left the restaurant from dinner. Walking along the canal that ran throughout the city they notice the boats with young couples wrapped in each other's arms. It was so romantic with the soft lights from the street reflecting in the water.

Josephine turned to Karl and said, "I know it is cold out, but I would like to take a boat ride on the canal before we leave." Karl squeezed Josephine's hand and led her towards the small docking area where the boats pulled in next to the street. The ride in the boat was a wonderful memory to add to their honeymoon.

Everything seemed perfect and the four days in Venice went by too quickly. The next day they boarded the train to go back home to Germany. This was the first time they had snow since they arrived; it was as if the city of Venice was saying goodbye. Josephine snuggled next to Karl in the seat and said, "Thank you for a wonderful trip, I wish it would never end."

The first month of their marriage was wonderful, because Karl had taken a thirty-day leave from the Army. During that time, they found an apartment not far from her family; it was small with only one bedroom. Her parents help to furnish the apartment with a bed, kitchen furniture, sofa and table in the living room.

Josephine placed the wedding gifts around the apartment to help make it feel like her home. Josephine sat on the sofa and she carefully un-wrapped the beautiful crystal vase they purchased in Venice; she held it for a moment before setting it in the center of the table. In the evening after dinner they would sit on the sofa looking at the vase and reminisce about their trip to Venice.

Josephine and Karl's love for one another grew deeper with each passing day. As they dreamed their dreams for the future, neither of them could have known that the depth of their love for one another is what would sustain them when all their hopes and dreams would be shattered. For very soon the world as they knew it would change forever. Some of these changes were already taking place in the German government at that time.

Karl was called back to duty a few days early, his assignment had changed and he was to travel to nearby cities weapon factories to inspect the weapons for quality. Karl told Josephine about not being moved far away, but he would be close enough to where they lived that he could be home every night. Josephine was thankful that Karl would be able to be home for dinner each night. She gave him a big hug and said, "This is the best news." He smiled down at her for he knew the military's ways that they could move you any time anywhere.

The weather warmed and the spring showers began to bring things back to life after the cold winter. Karl came home for dinner the beginning of April and said, "Josephine I am being transferred to other cities further away and I won't be able to be home every night." Josephine stuck out her lower lip in a little pout before saying, "I'm sorry, it will be difficult, but I know you must do your duty and we'll make the best of it."

Karl and Josephine decided to have children right away since he was fourteen years older than her. In September, Josephine found out that she was pregnant with their first child. She could hardly wait until Karl got home to tell him. She had purchased a baby nightgown and decided that after dinner on the first night he could come home, she would put the baby gown in the center of their bed to surprise him with the news. Josephine wanted to be a mother ever since she played dolls as a young child and now her dream had come true.

Karl was exhausted after a long week of work and happy to be coming home. The smell of dinner filled the house as he came through the front door with Josephine standing there to greet him. During dinner, she seemed distracted and ate her dinner fast. Karl looked over at her and said, "Are you alright?" Josephine smiled at Karl and took a deep breath calmed herself before she said, "I am wonderful, just really glad to have you home."

 Karl finished his dinner in silence as Josephine sat with her hands folded in her lap watching him. Karl helped Josephine with the supper dishes. Once they were done Josephine draped the dish towel on the hook and took Karl by the hand, leading him towards the bedroom. Karl looked at Josephine with surprise that she wanted to go to the bedroom so early in the evening. As soon as she opened the door she suddenly stopped in the doorway, Karl almost ran into her. Josephine just stood there and stared into the bedroom. Karl looks around trying to figure out what she was looking at.

Karl's eyes roamed around the room and at first he could not see the small gown lying on the bed. Then he saw the baby gown; he turned grabbing Josephine up and twirling her around as he asked, "Are we going to have a baby?" Josephine shook her head "yes" with tears of joy running down her cheeks. Karl picked her up into his arms and carried her to the bed. He sat down on the bed with Josephine on his lap and they kissed passionately. Great joy filled both of their hearts with the news of having a baby; they were happy beyond measure. Josephine thanked God every night for bringing Karl into her life and allowing all her dreams to come true.

Both Karl and Josephine were extremely happy and in their own private world all was well, but not in the world around them. The next week Karl was transferred to Berlin. Karl said to himself, "why now?" He hated to tell Josephine and hated to leave her now that she was having their first child. After much discussion they decided it would be best if Josephine stayed near her parents until after the baby was born. Being apart was very difficult for both Karl and Josephine; it was their love letters that sustained them while they were separated.

One bright sunny day in the middle of June, Josephine went into labor. Her father took her to the hospital while her mother sent word to Karl to come home as soon as possible. He was unable to get leave for the birth of his first child. Karl tried everything to get the General to let him go home for the birth of his baby. Josephine was greatly disappointed that he was not there to hold his new son, but glad her parents were there with her. Ralph was born in early summer of 1936, with lots of dark hair like his papa. Josephine sent word to Karl and told him how handsome their baby son was. She missed Karl and longed to go to him, but the doctors said she needed to wait until the baby was a little older.

Chapter 4 The Move 1936-1939

A month after Ralph was born the doctor finally told Josephine that she could move to Berlin to be with her husband. Josephine was excited as she sent a telegram to Karl to let him know that she and Ralph would be taking the train to Berlin the first week of August. It was a difficult time for Josephine's parents as they packed up and moved the things from the apartment to her parent's home. Having their daughter move away to Berlin was something they dreaded and frightened them. This was the first-time Josephine would be so far away from home.

The night before Josephine and Ralph were to leave, her mother began to cry as she helped Josephine pack the bags. Josephine stopped and looked up at her mother; sadness filled Josephine as she walked over to give her mother a hug. Holding her mother close she whispered in her ear, "Mommy, everything will be alright, you know that Ralph and I need to be with Karl." Her mother stepped away from Josephine's arms, wiped the tears from her eyes and without a word continued to pack where she had left off.

The sun was already warming up the air and it looked like it was going to be a hot day. Josephine and her parents stood on the platform at the train station waiting for the train to arrive. She watched as her mother cuddled her son, and the thought of taking Ralph away from his grandmother pained Josephine's heart. The train whistled as it pulled into the station startling Ralph and he began to cry. Josephine kissed both her parents' goodbye; tears ran down both her mother and her cheeks as she took the baby from her mother's arms.

Her mother wrapped her arms around Josephine and the baby in a long embrace. Josephine looked up as she heard her father say, "You better get moving if you want to catch this train." Her father picked up the suitcases and carried them as he led the way to board. One last hug and Josephine followed her father onto the train. Before leaving the train, her father wanted to make sure Josephine and the baby were settled into a seat. Turning to walk away she could see tears glisten in her father's eyes. "Goodbye papa," Josephine said as she watched him walk towards the exit. Her father stopped at the exit and looking back he said, "Remember you can always come back home."

The train ride was difficult with a small baby and two suitcases, since she had to change trains before her final stop in Berlin. Josephine was thankful that people around her were so very kind and thoughtful. When she needed to change trains someone always stepped up to give her help on and off the trains. Ralph was a little angel and slept most of the trip. On the last train toward Berlin Josephine changed and fed Ralph before humming to him as she rocked him in her arms. The warm air and the steady movement of the train lulled them both into a sound sleep.

The train whistle sounded loud and startled Josephine awake as she heard the conductor said, "Berlin next stop." Josephine suddenly felt alert and an excitement fill her heart. She looked down at her baby as the train pulled into the station and quietly said to him, "You are going to meet your papa today."

As the train came to a stop, Karl stopped the pacing he was doing while he waited and longed to see his beautiful wife and new baby. This would be the first time he would be able to see and hold his new born son. He looked up and down the train doors to see which one Josephine would exit. Then he saw her step down from the train followed by two young students who helped her with her suitcases.

The students sat the suitcases down next to her and hurried on their way. Josephine thanked the students as they departed and begun to look for Karl in the crowd. Turning around she saw him walking towards her. With his over six-foot height, he stood a head above most people. Their eyes met and locked as he continues to walk through the crowd. Karl was happy beyond measure to see Josephine. As soon as he got close enough to her he wrapped his arms around her and the baby, pulling them into an embrace. Josephine stood up on her tiptoes and kissed him. Karl then looked down at his son, who lay quietly in Josephine's arms looking at the two of them. Karl thought to himself, "How wonderful it was to have a beautiful wife and now a son."

Karl took his son into his arms and kissed Ralph on the forehead. Karl had a smile of contentment on his face as he wrapped the other arm around his wife shoulder. He looked down at Josephine and gently kissed her on the lips. Suddenly Karl looked up remember where he was and knew he had to leave the train station as soon as possible.

He quickly gave the baby back to Josephine, picking up the suitcases he quietly said, "I have rented us an apartment not far from here and have furnished it with what I could for you and the baby." Josephine looked up at him and smiled saying, "All we really need is to be here with you." Karl said, "Come we must go." Josephine for the first time saw all the SS Elite soldiers standing watching people; she quickened her step as she followed Karl away from the train station.

Hitler become more powerful in the German government as he continued building his secrete German military called the SS Elite. The activities of the German SS Elite became more secretive and the execution of their plans was increased day by day. The rest of the regular military all the way up through the officers had no idea what Hitler's SS Elite squad activities were. Concerned filled the hearts of the regular military once they saw the SS Elite making raids on homes, arrest people and taking them to secrete locations. Any soldier who questioned the SS Elite was shot on the spot. Fear set in deep throughout the military in Germany.

Karl began to be concerned for his small family's safety in the big city of Berlin. Even as an officer in the Army, he was not invited to the secret meetings and had no idea what was happening with these Secret Service Elite Members of Hitler. He wished he could find out why these raids were going on, but dare not let on that he had any question or show concern because anyone who questioned what was happening or tried to find out what the SS Elite were doing had to report immediately to the commanding officer. These soldiers did not report to duty the next day, they would disappear without trace. Like his fellow-officer Jorgen, who had not been heard from in over a month.

Since the raids on homes and soldiers disappearing, Karl prayed for his family every day and did what he was told, keeping to himself to protect his family. With more and more raids taking place on the homes in Berlin, he decided to move his family back to Magdeburg with Josephine's parents. Karl asked his commanding officer for a few days leave to take his wife and child back to her parents' home. The commander granted Karl his leave request.

On the way home to their apartment that day, Karl purchased train tickets and sent a telegram to Josephine's parents. He headed for his Berlin home feeling that he had made the right decision for his family. But his heart was sad knowing that he would not see Josephine and Ralph every day. Josephine was playing blocks with Ralph when she heard Karl came in the door; she got up and gave Karl a kiss. He walked over to pick up Ralph and give him a hug before taking him over to the sofa where he could set him on his lap. Josephine watched Karl with concern on her face, then followed and sat down next to Karl wondering why he looked so sad.

Karl cleared his throat and said, "I have requested time off to take you and Ralph back to Magdeburg tomorrow, it is for both of your safety." Josephine looked deep into Karl's eyes and said, "I understand, but I really don't want to leave you." Karl wrapped his arm around Josephine and said, "I know, I would prefer also you to be here with me, but it is not safe." Ralph looked up at his parents as he chewed on a block and with drool running down his little chin he said, "Da," as if to agree with them.

Karl looked at his son, who looked so much like him with dark hair and deep blue eyes. Karl stood Ralph up on his lap and said, "Good boy Ralph." Ralph giggled and began bouncing up and down on Karl's lap.

The December early morning air was cool and crisp, they stood waiting for the arrival of their train to Magdeburg. Ralph was bundled up in his snow suit to keep him warm. The train pulled into the station; they boarded and quickly found a seat. This was the shortest train ride they had ever been on, even with the train change the hours flew by as they snuggled and talked while Ralph slept. The four months they had together went by too quickly and now they would have to be apart again. Sadness filled both of their hearts as the train pulled into the Magdeburg train station. Josephine's parents were there to greet them as they got off the train.

Josephine's mother gave both Karl and Josephine a hug before taking Ralph from Josephine arms. She pulled Ralph into a big hug and then held him out to look at him as she exclaimed, "My have you grown, you are such a big boy!" Both of Josephine's parents were glad to have their daughter and grandson back home. Now they could be an "opa" and "oma" to their grandson.

Karl could only stay one night in Magdeburg and had to take the train back to Berlin the next day to report to duty. Early the next morning Josephine asked her mother if she would watch Ralph while she went to the train station with Karl. Her mother smiled and said, "Of course." Before leaving, Karl went to the Ralph's crib and picked up his sleepy son. As he hugged and kissed Ralph goodbye tears began to sting his eyes. He laid Ralph back down in his crib and blinked away the tears. Josephine's heart felt like it was being torn in two as she watched.

Josephine's father drove them to the train station and then waited in the truck as he watched the two of them walk hand and hand to the train platform. Within minutes the train whistled and pulled into the station. Karl took his wife in his arms and they held each other for a very long moment before he kissed her goodbye. He boarded the train just before the door closed and quickly found a window to wave out at Josephine.

They waved at each other with tears running down their cheeks until they could no longer see each other. Karl found a seat and his heart was heavy and torn on his way back to Berlin. He knew he had to report to duty, but all he wanted to do was to be with his family. Josephine stood there as tears continued to run down her cheek. She watched the train disappear around a bend before pulling out her tissue to wipe her eyes. She turned and slowly walked back to her father's truck.

Josephine's brother Hans had married his childhood sweetheart and moved to Leipzig with his wife. She was pregnant with their first child when he got drafted into the military. Hans and his wife Lisalota lived about two hours from Magdeburg so that Lisalota could be close to her family. Josephine was happy for Hans and Lisalota to have their first child, but sad that Hans had to leave before the birth. It seemed like all the young men were being drafted into the military. Josephine's niece was born in January 1937. She and her sister-in-law would visit each other often.

Josephine and Karl exchanged love letters frequently. Everyday Josephine would watch for the postman and then run out to check the mail box for a letter from him. Karl's letters seemed to get further and further apart, it had been over three weeks since Josephine got a letter. Worry filled her heart as she checked the mail, but today was her lucky day when she reached into the mail box and pulled out the mail. There was a letter from Karl. Josephine ran into the house and set the other mail on the table before going to her room to read her precious letter. The letters always began as a wonderful love letter and then he would tell her limited news of what was happening where he was at.

He wrote in his letter that the SS raids were moving out of some of the large cities into the smaller ones. Josephine held the letter to her heart and let out a big sigh and gave thanks that SS had not yet come to Magdeburg. That evening as Josephine rocked Ralph to sleep; she decided that she needed to let her parents know what was happening with the SS raids.

Josephine looked down at her baby, who looked restful as he slept in her arms; she rose from the rocking chair and laid Ralph in his crib. She went to the writing desk in her room and sat down and wrote Karl a long love letter. She told him that she would speak to her parents about the SS raids. Sealing up the letter Josephine went to bed but did not sleep well.

After breakfast Josephine asked her parents if she could talk to them for a few minutes. Josephine began to tell her parents about Karl's letter and what he said about the SS raids on homes in the large cities and how they were moving out to smaller cities. Her parents had a shocked look on their faces at some of the stories she told about when she lived in Berlin.

Josephine's father stood up and paced the floor for about five minutes before turning to his wife and daughter and saying, "I have an aunt that lives in a very small town in the woods, I think we need to move to Suderode and move away from the cities. We can set up the business there. We will need to let the servants go and I will pay them a month's salary." Both Josephine and her mother looked at each other but understood and agreed that this would be for the best.

That night after putting Ralph to bed Josephine wrote Karl a letter to let him know of their plans to move. As Josephine sealed the letter her heart was heavy, she wanted to go be with Karl but instead she was helping her family move. Josephine's father had gone ahead to Suderode to find a house and set up his transportation business just outside of the small town. He had to lay off many employees that did not want to transfer. Those who could not transfer he gave them a large sum of money to help them until they could find another job. Within a month, the rest of the family was packed up and moved to Suderode. Josephine wrote Karl to update him on all that had transpired since her last letter and letting him know their new address.

Suderode is a little town in the heart of Germany nestled up in the woods. Josephine's father purchased a large house close to town. Suderode, a beautiful little town that was quiet and had many trees and well-maintained houses lined along the very narrow cobblestone streets. Since the move and the change of address it was almost two months before the next letter arrived from Karl. Josephine was so happy when she got the letter; while Ralph napped, she read it over-and-over again. Josephine missed Karl and prayed for his safety daily. Ralph woke from his nap and stood in his crib. Josephine looked over at her son; he was growing up so fast and she wished Karl wasn't missing so much of their son's life.

Josephine missed his wonderful kisses and warm hugs. She sat on the sofa watching Ralph play with blocks; he would build them up and then knock them down. Ralph laughed and then started all over to build his tower of blocks. She thought how easy it was for little ones to entertain themselves; sitting there watching Ralph made her miss Karl even more and thinking about all he had missed in not being able to watch Ralph grow up.

Karl longed to see his family, but was unable to get leave from the military to see them again until the Christmas that Ralph was two-years old. It was only the love letters between Josephine and Karl that sustained them until they could be together. Josephine worried when a letter did not arrive at least once a month.

Every evening before putting Ralph to bed Josephine would take Ralph up onto her lap and show him a picture of his papa in hopes that he would recognize his papa when he saw him again. Then she read Ralph a short story before snuggling with him and singing a lullaby to him until he fell asleep. Josephine sat there in the quietness with Ralph asleep in her arms, she thought about Karl's last letter and a smile spread across her face. He was coming home for Christmas.

It was only two weeks until Christmas and Karl would soon be home for a week. For the past six months when Josephine wrote to Karl she would asked if she and Ralph could move to where he was, but he never answered her question. A smile crossed Josephine's face as she thought about her husband and hoped this time when she saw him he would say she could go back with him.

It was snowing heavy as Karl stepped off the train in Magdeburg; he walked the few blocks to the bus stop that would take him just outside the town of Suderode. Karl was covered in snow by the time the bus pulled to a stop. He boarded the bus and found a seat next to the window. The closer he got to see his wife and son the longing for them increased. Karl patted his bag that was sitting on the seat next to him thinking about Josephine's warm embrace. No trains went into the small town of Suderode and the bus ride was over an hour, but today the bus ride would be longer, since it was driving slower than normal due to the heavy snowfall.

Karl looked out the bus window watching the snow fall and thinking about the gifts he had brought his family. The slow movement of the bus caused his eyes to slowly shut. The bus sliding to a stop woke Karl and he heard the bus driver said, "Last stop." Karl picked up his bag and stepped off the bus, the snow was so deep it went above his boots.

The snow was blowing in the wind and causing drifts along the road. With this heavy snow and wind Karl hoped he could see the road signs to find the house. He had a five mile walk from the bus stop to the town where his family lived. Karl pulled his coat collar up to keep the wind from blowing snow down his neck; it was his thoughts of Josephine that warmed him as he walked.

Christmas Eve and the snow had been falling all day and now it looked almost like a blizzard out. Josephine looked at her watch every five minutes in anticipation for Karl's arrival; Karl could not tell her what time he would be there on Christmas Eve. Josephine walked to the window too many times to count during the day looking for him to walk up the path to the house.

As the day moved on the snow became deeper and it was almost dark, Josephine became worried and prayed that her husband would arrive safely. Josephine's mother interrupted her prayer when she came into the room and said, "We can hold supper for another fifteen minutes and then we will need to eat, Ralph is hungry." Josephine turned from the window to look at her mother as she replied, "Okay."

Retuning to look out the window Josephine noticed that the wind had picked up and the snow was blowing into large snow drifts. The snow was getting deeper all the time. She frowned as she looked out into the white snow in the dusk of the evening; she began to pray again as she stared out the window. Then she saw something moving at the end of the path, her heart leap in her chest as the figure moved closer, it was Karl covered in snow and walking up the path. Josephine let out a big sigh and said aloud to herself, "With Karl being home, this was going to be the best Christmas ever."

Josephine turned from the window and walked over to the kitchen and said, "Karl's home," then she took Ralph by the hand and walked towards the front door and said to him, "Your papa is home." Ralph looked up at her with a puzzled look on his two-year old face; he thought the picture Josephine showed him every night was his papa.

Josephine stood by the front door holding Ralph by the hand, her son looked wide eyed at the door and was not sure what was going to happen. Then Josephine heard Karl pounding the snow off his shoes on the porch. Ralph's eyes got wider as Josephine began jumping up and down and said to him, "Your papa is here!" Josephine let go of Ralph's hand and opened the door. Karl was a sight with wet snow all over him. It did not matter to Josephine she wrapped her arms around him as she pulled him into the house.

Karl felt warmth go through him as he held his wife before setting down his wet bag next to the door. Josephine would not let him go until he leaned down and kissed her gently on the lips, all the while Ralph was staring up at them both. Karl took off his jacket and hung it on the wall rack next to the door. He looked down and saw his wide eyed little boy looking up at him in wonderment.

Karl bent down and picked Ralph up into his arms and gave him a kiss on the check and said, "Ralph, I am so glad to see you, look at what a big boy you are." He sat his son back down as Josephine's parents came into the room, and greeted him. Ralph pointed up at Karl and said, "Papa." Everyone smiled and then Josephine's mother said, "Come in and warm up, dinner is ready."

After dinner was finished they all walked into the living room where the small Christmas tree sat in the corner with a few gifts under it. Josephine mother lit the candles on the tree and the Christmas tree glowed. They all watched the flicker of the candles until Ralph pulled on Josephine's skirt and pointed at the tree. Karl excused himself and said, "I will be right back." He went over to his bag and pulled out four gifts. He entered the living room and placed the gifts under the tree with the other gifts. Josephine's father led them in some Christmas carols before they exchanged gifts.

Ralph got a gift from each of them, but it was the toy horse that Karl had gotten him that interested him the most. Ralph pulled the string on the toy horse and the legs would move up and down as he giggled. Karl sat down and played with his son. After a while Josephine walked over to Ralph and said, "Ralph it is time for bed, would you like your papa to read you a story?" Jumping up and down Ralph said, "Yes, papa." After tucking Ralph into bed, Josephine sat on the end of the bed watching Karl as he read a story to Ralph. Before the story was finished Ralph was fast asleep. They both gave him a kiss on the cheek before quietly leaving the room.

Karl was happy to once again hold his loving wife and son in his arms daily. It seemed like time stood still while Karl was home and he wasn't looking forward when it came time to leave. Karl, Josephine and Ralph had a wonderful time during the Christmas Holiday, laughing and just being a family. Karl took time to play with Ralph every afternoon and the bond between father and son was beginning to blossom. Josephine enjoyed having her husband home more than anything in the world and seeing Karl playing with their son filled her heart with joy. She wished this time would never end, every night when they were wrapped in each other's arms she hoped that Karl would tell her she could go back with him and they could live together again.

New Year's Eve was the first day without snow fall; the sky was clear and bright blue, the air crisp and cold. Karl, Josephine and Ralph spent a few hours playing out in the snow; they laughed, threw snow balls and built a snowman. Ralph was fascinated with the snow as they played. For this small family, time stood still, they were filled with joy, happiness and the world for them was at peace.

Josephine kept pushing back the thoughts that Karl had to report back to his duty the day after New Year; she refused to allow these thoughts to steal her joy of this wonderful moment. She cherished each moment in her heart as she watched father and son laughing and throwing snowballs. Josephine hoped that her two-and-a-half-year-old son would be able to hold on to some of these memories with his papa.

That evening after giving Ralph a warm bath and tucking him into bed, Karl and Josephine sat on the sofa wrapped in each other's arms, simply watching the fire flicker in the fire place. Josephine's parents had gone to bed early to allow them some alone time. The warmth of the fire was making Karl tired, so he stretched his arms over his head as he cleared his throat to speak. Josephine thought she knew what Karl was going to say, so she sat up straight in anticipation for whenever Karl cleared his throat he had something important to say.

Karl turned toward Josephine taking both of her hands in his and cleared his throat again before quietly saying, "I know you were hoping you and Ralph could go back with me this time, but I must tell you that it is still not safe for you to go. I will let you know as soon as I know you will be safe to come." Josephine wanted to be brave even though her hopes were crushed, a crooked smile came to her face and tears began to flow from her eyes as she looked up at Karl. Josephine took a deep breath to calm her tears. Karl pulled out his handkerchief and offered it to her; she took it and wiped her tears before looking up into his face.

Karl looked deeply into Josephine's beautiful eyes that glisten in the firelight and said, "This is hard for both of us and I pray you and Ralph can come where I am soon." Karl wrapped his arms around Josephine and pulled her close, they sat there in the quiet just staring into the smoldering fire that was about to burn out. Josephine's voice was so quiet that Karl barely heard what she said, "Karl, I love you and I am so glad we have this time together." Karl leaned down and kissed her lips lightly and said, "I love you too and by the way Happy New Year!" Then Karl kissed his wife again as they began their new year.

Early New Year's Day there was a loud knock on the door; everyone looked at each other with puzzlement, since they were not expecting anyone. Josephine's father got up and answered the door as the rest watched from behind. A man dressed in postman clothes with a small bag slung over his shoulder looked in to the living room and said, "I have a telegram for Karl, is he here?"

Karl stepped forward and said, "I am Karl." The postman reached into his bag and handed Karl the telegram, then he turned abruptly and went on his way down the snowy path. The room was very quiet as Karl read the telegram, then he looked up from the telegram and said, "I am being transferred to another city and I am to report to duty in Hamburg tomorrow."

Early the next morning Josephine looked out the window, squinted her eyes as the bright sun reflected off the snow. She turned towards Karl and said, "It is not snowing and the sun is out, I think we can take Ralph with us to the train station to see you off." Karl walked over and stood next to Josephine, wrapping his arm around her waist as he looked out the window.

Pulling Josephine into a hug Karl said, "That will be wonderful and I know Ralph will love being out in the snow again." They walked together over to Ralph's bedroom to get him dressed and tell him that papa was going to take the train station today." Ralph rubbed his sleepy eyes, then jumped up with excitement and said, "Train!" Josephine knew at two-and-a-half he did not understand about his father's leaving; he was just excited to go and see the train.

Right after breakfast Karl set up the stroller, Josephine bundled up Ralph and sat him in it. Josephine's father said, "Josephine, I will drive the truck into town in about an hour to get you and Ralph." Josephine smiled at her father and said, "Thank you." Josephine wrapped a warm blanket around Ralph's little legs to make sure he would not get too cold. Karl and Josephine gave themselves plenty of time to walk down the cobblestone path. Karl looked down at the path that was cleared and wondered who had cleared it. He pushed the stroller and Josephine tucked her hand under his arm as they slowly made their way to the bus stop to wait for the bus which would take them to the train station.

On the train platform Karl bent down and lifted Ralph from the stroller; he gave him a kiss on the cheek just as the train pulled into the station. Ralph pointed at the train with a big smile on his face, at the same time Josephine reached to take Ralph from Karl. Karl pulled them both into his arms and kissed Josephine deeply before he boarded the train.

The train ride to Hamburg was long and all Karl could picture in his mind was Josephine's tears running down her cheeks and his little boy crying, "Papa." as he boarded the train. He already missed his family and his heart was breaking at the thought of being apart from them again. He wished he could leave all this behind and stay with his family to protect them and make sure they were safe. But he knew that if he did leave the military without permission the SS Elite would come looking for him and he would put his family in danger. Karl lived in daily fear for his family safety, which is why he needed to continue with his military duty even when his heart is not in it.

There was division in the Army and every soldier could see the split. The SS Elite soldiers were getting special treatment, while the rest of the soldiers were working twice as hard to keep up with the assignments. The SS Elite were sent off to rallies in civilian clothes to where Hitler was speaking. Karl could not figure out why there was a double standard, but kept it to himself as he thought about his family's safety.

The SS Elite were in the crowd to help rev up the people as Hitler spoke about his hope for a better future for Germany and promising jobs to all who were willing to work. Many of the people were out of work and without hope for a job, so they became mesmerized by Hitler's charismatic speeches and began to believe Hitler had the answers to Germany's economic crisis.

Chapter 5 The Reunion 1939

It has been ten long months of being apart from his family and Karl longed for Josephine and Ralph. Hamburg was a beautiful city nestled up by the North Sea, he was glad he got stationed here. His job assignment kept him so busy he could not get time away to visit his family. The city of Hamburg was a large city and quiet most of the time, which surprised Karl. There was some SS Elite present on the streets of Hamburg, but no raids on homes.

Karl began to think this was a safe place to bring his family. Every night for the last week he dreamed of them; they were walking together holding hands along the boardwalk by the North Sea. Karl awoke from these dreams and disappointment would fill him as he realized it was only a dream.

The sun was just going down over the horizon on Karl's way back to Base from one of the factories near Hamburg. Instead of going to the Base he drove his military jeep to the North Sea. He said to himself, "I need a quiet place to think and pray." As he looked out over the North Sea the sky was filled with red and deep purple as the sun was touching the sea about to descend below it. Karl gave out a huge sigh and began to pray; he missed his family; Ralph was now over three years old. The longing in Karl's heart was so great he felt as if there was a physical pain in his chest.

Karl was so torn on the inside as he lifted his prayers up to God, he did not stop until he was filled with peace. It was dark as he drove back to the Army Base. He knew the answer he was seeking in prayer - Josephine and Ralph would come to Hamburg to live and they could all be together again.

Karl was so excited he could not sleep, so he pulled out a pen and paper and began to write one of his many love letters to his sweet Josephine. He ended his letter by telling her what she desired to hear most, that she and Ralph could come and live in Hamburg as soon as she could get there. Excitement filled Karl as he sealed the letter and his thoughts of getting an apartment set up for Josephine and Ralph's arrival.

Josephine sat next to Ralph reading his favorite story, The Three Bears, when she heard her mother come into the house. Josephine looked up at her mother and got excited as she watched her mother pull Karl's letter from the pile of mail and hand it to her. Ralph looked up from the book and said, "What's that?" His "oma" (grandma) took him by the hand and said, "I want to play cars, will you play with me?" Ralph looked at his oma's smile and then followed her to get the small box of car toys.

Josephine held the letter to her heart for a moment and then walked to her bedroom to read it in private. Tears welled up in her eyes as she read the love that poured from the pages of her letter. She had to read the last paragraph twice, "What?" she said to herself, thinking she read it wrong the first time. Josephine held the letter to her heart as tears of joy ran down her cheeks, she was so happy. She said to herself, "I have to begin to make plans right away. I will send a telegram to let Karl know once I have all the plans in place." Thoughts of what do next filled her mind as she sat there with the letter pressed against her heart.

Ralph came into the bedroom and climbed up onto the bed to sit next to his mother. Ralph was a smart child and perceived a lot for a child under 4-years old, he looked up at his mother and said, "Was that letter from papa? What did papa say? Is he coming home soon?" Josephine wrapped her arm around her son and replied, "Papa loves you very much and told me to give you this big hug from him. Papa hopes we can see him soon."

She kept the part about going to see his papa from Ralph because she did not want to get Ralph's hopes up before talking to her parents about leaving to go to Hamburg. Josephine asked Ralph, "Would you like to draw your papa a picture that we can mail to him?" Ralph jumped down off the bed and ran over to the writing table. He pulled out the chair and got up on his knees ready to draw a picture for his papa. Josephine pulled out a piece of paper and dipped the feather pen in the ink and gave it to her son, "Remember don't push too hard or the pen will rip the paper I will be back in a minute, I need to go and talk to your oma and "opa" (grandpa)."

Josephine slowly walked out of the room, she already knew her parents would be upset with her decision to leave, but she needed to be with her husband. She asked her parents to sit down as she explained to them her plans to move to Hamburg so she could be with her husband. She could see in her parents' eyes, that both did not approve.

Her mother stood up and vocalized her disapproval by saying, "I will not allow my daughter and grandson to leave and be put in danger," and then she burst into tears. Josephine's father pulled out a handkerchief and gave it to his wife. Josephine took in a deep breath and tried to explain to her parents how a wife needs to be with her husband and a boy needs his father. Her father wrapped his arm around his wife and said, "You know she is right and we have to let them go." Her mother looked at him and sniffed as she slowly shook her head in agreement.

Early the next morning the sun seemed brighter and the sky bluer as Josephine's father drove her into town to make the arrangements to take the train from Quedlinburg to Hamburg, which left in two days. Josephine tucked the tickets into her purse as they walked down the street to the telegraph office. She needed to send Karl a telegram letting him know the train arrival information. They sat in silence as Josephine's father drove back home. She looked over at her father and he had a sad faraway look on his face with his eyes fixed on the road ahead. Even though she was excited to see Karl, she decided to contain her joy for fear it would cause her father more pain about her leaving.

All Josephine could think about as she packed the two suitcases was how much she longed to be with her husband. She decided it was best not to tell Ralph about the trip until the morning they were going to leave for the train. For she knew all too well that he would be so excited he would be unable to sleep the night before and she need a well-rested child for the long trip.

Josephine packed after Ralph went to bed. After she finished packing the last items, she asked her parents if she could store her remaining items with them until she could have them sent. Even though her parents were reluctant to have their daughter and grandson so far away, her mother knew if she had some of Josephine's things with them then Josephine would always come back home.

Karl was called into his Commanders office as soon as he got back from one of his factory inspections. As Karl walked over to the Commanders office his heart was filled with dread, since he did not know why he would be called. Karl knocked on the door and waited until he heard the Commander say, "Come in." Karl walked over to the desk and stood at attention. The Commander looked up and said, "At ease soldier this came for you today, read it in your quarters."

A smile came to Karl's lips as he looked at the telegram and said, "Yes sir." He saluted his Commander then turned to leave the office. Karl walked quickly towards his quarters looking down at the telegram he decided to open it immediately. He continued to walk as he read that Josephine and Ralph were coming in two days. Karl leaped in the air and shouted "Yahoo!" The soldiers who were standing nearby looked over at Karl and gave him a puzzled look while he hurried into his quarters.

Two days did not give Karl much time for preparation of his family coming to Hamburg. Karl asked some of the other soldiers if they knew of any small apartments near the base. With the gathered information, he could find an apartment not too far from the base. Once he secured the apartment he bought a few pieces of furniture for the apartment and other kitchen and bathroom essentials.

After arranging everything, Karl took in a deep breath as he looked out the apartment window. Peace and an overwhelming sense of joy filled him as he thought about tomorrow and seeing Josephine and Ralph again. He put in his request to have the day off and it was approved. He wanted to make sure they all got settled into the apartment before he went back to work.

After a restless night's sleep, Karl arose bright and early. While he sat drinking his cup of coffee, he decided he would go to the market and fill the house with groceries prior to picking up his wife and son from the train station. He brought home the groceries and put them away just in time to go and pick up Josephine and Ralph. Even though Karl's body was tired from lack of sleep, his mind was racing with excitement that gave him the energy he needed as he waited on the train platform for the train to arrive.

Josephine rolled over and shut off the alarm on the clock; it was four in the morning. She stretched and went to get prepared for her long trip. The train would leave for Hamburg at six am. She got ready and then took the suitcase to set them by the front door. She walked back up the stairs and opened her son's bedroom door. Ralph looked so peaceful with his rosy cheeks and his dark hair lying across his forehead, she sighed and thought how much he looks like his father.

She walked over and set on the edge of the bed next to her son. She pushed his hair off his forehead and gave her son a kissed her on the forehead to wake him up. Ralph stretched, opened his eyes and gave his mother the sweetest smile. Josephine smiled back down at him and said, "Do you want to go and see your papa today?" Ralph jumped out of bed, his little feet hit the ground and he started dancing around the room.

Josephine's parents took her and their grandson to the train station to see them off; both Josephine and her mother shed tears as they hugged goodbye. Josephine's father picked up her bags and helped her find a seat with a window on the platform side of the train, so they could see and wave as their daughter and grandson left. Josephine settled Ralph into the seat next to the window. Her father looked at his daughter in a way that made her want to cry, but instead she hugged him goodbye and said, "Thank you papa for everything, I love you."

When Josephine pulled away and looked in her father's eyes she could see him blinking back a tear, he turned and left the train. Ralph got up on his knees to look out the window and said, "Look mommy, there is oma and opa." She stood by the window with her arm wrapped around Ralph's shoulder as they both waved goodbye. Her parents stood waving as the trained pulled away from the station and out of sight.

On the train ride Ralph stayed up on his knees to look out the window; all he could talk about was seeing papa again. It wasn't until the train changed halfway that he settled down and let his mother read him a story. As she read, the train lightly bounced on the tracks, Ralph laid his head against Josephine's arm and was lulled to sleep. Josephine put away the book and laid her son's head on her lap and thought about how happy Karl would be to see his son again. She looked out the window watching the scenery go by and thinking about Karl. Her eyes felt heavy and she fell asleep dreaming of being in Karl's arms. The train whistle sounded and Ralph jumped up and said, "Are we there yet?" The conductor said, "Next stop Hamburg." Josephine smiled at her son and said, "Yes we are."

Karl paced up and down the train platform as he waited for the trains arrival, he was so excited to see his family again. The train whistle sounded as the train pulled into the station; he looked down at his watch and said to himself, "Right on time." He was in his dress uniform, remembering how much Josephine liked to see him in it. With his over six-foot fame he stood a head above the rest of the crowd and could easily see the train. Anticipation filled him as he watched the train pull to a stop.

Ralph kneeled on the seat and looking out of the window as the train came to a stop. Josephine gathered up her things and said to Ralph, "It's time to find papa." Ralph jumped down off the seat and began to walk away from Josephine, she quickly yelled, "Ralph STOP!" Ralph stopped and looked at his mother with a question of "why?" on his face. With a suitcase in each hand she instructed Ralph to hold onto her skirt; he complied and they walked slowly toward the exit door. They exited the train just as the train conductor yelled, "All aboard." Josephine set down the suitcases and took Ralph's hand as she looked out into the crowd of faces for Karl.

Looking to the right Josephine saw Karl a few feet away, their eyes locked as Karl made his way towards his family. When Ralph saw his papa, he wanted to see him so he pulled his hand free from his mother's hand. The moment his hand was free he ran towards his father yelling, "Papa, papa!" Karl looked down at Ralph and gathered him into his arms. Ralph wrapped his little arms around his father's neck in a big hug. Karl then took the few steps left to reach Josephine. He leaned down and wrapped one of his arms around Josephine and pulled her into a long kiss, with Ralph squished between them. Ralph brought Karl back to reality when he took his little hands and pushed against his cheek saying, "Papa, please put me down, I am a big boy you know." Karl did not want to stop kissing his wife but stepped back to set Ralph down on the platform. Looking up he remembered where they were.

Karl bent down and picked up the suitcases to leave, looking up he saw a couple of SS Elite walking through the crowd. Karl said in a quiet voice, "We need to get going now; I have rented us an apartment not far from here." Josephine looked up and saw the SS Elite and quickly picked up Ralph to carry him. Ralph wiggled in her arms and started to complain, but stopped when he saw his mother's eyes. Josephine had a look in her eyes that Ralph did not recognize, so he decided to comply with his mother and let he hold him tightly.

Josephine noticed that everyone was in a hurry to leave the train station as SS Elite watched everyone's movements. The SS Elite had machine guns slung over their right shoulder as they walked through the crowd. Karl led the way as they walked quickly away from the train station towards the apartment. Seeing the SS Elite again made Josephine very nervous, she quickened her step to be able to keep up with her husband's long stride. Ralph looking around with big eyes taking in the city sites and was not aware of any danger This was the first time he could remember being in a large city. It seemed like a long walk, but they finally came to the apartment. Josephine let out a sigh as they entered the building and closed the door behind them.

They had settled into their apartment and it became a place of refuge for Karl. Josephine loved having Karl home and when he was there her whole world felt safe. Over the next few months Karl continued to work long hours and sometimes was called away to be gone for weeks at a time. Ralph wanted his papa home to play with him and read him stories. Karl had been gone for two weeks now and every day Ralph would ask, "Mommy is papa coming home today?"

Josephine turned to her son and wrapped her arms around him and said, "Not today son." She could see the tears well up in his eyes, but he crossed his arms and chose not to cry. Seeing the pain in her little boy's eyes broke her heart. Ralph walked over to play with his cars. She stood there watching him. She knew how Ralph's little heart was filled with disappointment every time Karl had to be away. She put her hand on her chest as the pain for her son stabbed at her heart like a knife. She prayed every night that Ralph would not be affected by his father's absence.

The streets of Hamburg began to fill with more SS Elite, but there still had not been any raids on homes. Karl was gone most of the time, coming home a few days a month. Josephine kept inside the apartment; she would only venture out once a week to purchase food. She chose the middle of the week to go shopping since there seemed to be less SS Elite walking up and down the street than.

It was raining and Josephine did not want to go out in the rain with Ralph, but knew Wednesday was the best day to go shopping and she was almost out of food. Josephine pulled rain boots from the closet for her and Ralph. She put all her hair under a scarf. Josephine stood by the front door and called, "Ralph, come it is time to go shopping."

She dressed her son first in his rain jacket and boots, and then she put on her coat and grabbed the umbrella that stood by the door on the way out. Josephine took him by the hand and said, "You must remember to always hold my hand or coat pocket when we are outside. Ralph held tightly to his mother hand and said, "Okay mommy. Why does the sky cry?" Josephine looked down at her three-year-old son with a smile on her face as she answered, "I think sometimes, God feels sad too." They quickly walked to the nearby store, finished shopping and headed home. They passed three SS Elite smoking and talking on the corner near their home. After Josephine walked by the men she thought to herself, "That's strange," she hurried up the steps to her apartment.

After living in Hamburg for eight months Karl got word that he was being transferred to yet another city, Leipzig. The commander told him that families were not yet allowed to travel to Leipzig. His heart dropped like a rock in his chest when he heard this news. He did not want to tell Josephine the news, for he knew her heart would break. He became angry with the military for keeping his family apart. He knew when he told Josephine both her and Ralph would be disappointed. Over the next week he planned how he would tell Josephine about the transfer.

The day came for Karl to head home for the weekend before his transfer. Sadness filled him as he drove home, he did not look forward to telling his wife the news that he was being transferred to Leipzig and his family could not go with him. "Why did life have to be so difficult," Karl thought to himself as he slowly walked up the stairs to his apartment. He paused at the door and pulled his keys out of his pocket, putting the key into the lock, he opened the door taking in a deep breath for courage. The smell of dinner filled his nostrils as he entered the house and his stomach growled with hunger at the same time.

Josephine was in the kitchen finishing up the dinner and Ralph was playing with his cars when he heard the key go into the front door lock. He jumped and ran to the door to greet his father. Karl barely stepped over the threshold when Ralph wrapped his little arms around his father's legs and exclaimed, "Papa!" Karl sat down his bag and scooped Ralph up into his arms giving him a kiss on the cheek. Ralph wrapped his arms around his father's neck as Karl walked to the kitchen.

Looking at Josephine standing on her tiptoes so she could reach dishes from the cupboard, Karl said, "Something smells mighty good in here." Josephine spun around with surprise at the sound of his voice and almost dropped the dishes she had just pulled from the cupboard. Putting the dishes down on the counter she walked over and kissed him deeply. Karl responded to the kiss and Ralph scrunched his face and said, "Eeew." They parted lips and Josephine smiled at Ralph. Karl put Ralph down and patted him on the bottom and said, "Go get into your chair, it looks like dinner is ready."

Josephine cleaned up the dinner dishes while Karl played cars with Ralph. She walked into the living room and watched the two of them playing. She thought to herself, how much Ralph adored his father and how could a little boy look so much like his father? Karl looked up at Josephine and his heart melted at the sight of her. Josephine looked at Karl and then cleared her throat before asking Ralph, "Son, can I play cars with you and papa?" Ralph smiled and shook his head 'yes.' Karl patted the floor for her to sit next to him. They all sat on the living room floor together, allowing Ralph to lead the play time until his bedtime.

When the clock chimed seven times Ralph knew it was his bedtime, he looked up at his mother with a pleading look and said, "I don't want to go to bed, I want to play." She looked over at Karl with sympathetic eyes and then back at their son. Karl stood up and gave her the 'not tonight look' as he said to Ralph, "Son you need to go and get ready for bed. When you are done, I will read you your favorite story before you go to sleep."

Josephine got up and took Ralph by the hand and said, "Okay son, let's get your pajamas on so papa can read to you." Ralph looked up at both of his parents and since they both seemed excited about reading a story, he jumped up and walked hand in hand with his mother to get ready for bed.

After a few tickles on the tummy Josephine tucked Ralph into bed and Karl began to read from Ralph's favorite book. Ralph's eyes were heavy with sleep as Karl finished the story. He closed the book and said to Ralph, "Okay it is time for you to go to sleep." Karl kissed his son on the forehead and walked over to the door. Josephine tucked the covers up under Ralph's chin and gently kissed his cheek and said, "See you in the morning big boy." She turned off the light and closed the bedroom door.

Karl took Josephine by the hand and led her into the living room. Karl stopped and turned towards Josephine, his voice sounded very serious as he spoke, "Josephine, I have something I need to discuss with you, come sit with me on the sofa so we can talk." A worried look crossed her face; she could tell by the tone in his voice that this was going to be a serious conversation.

Karl stood by the entry way and stared as if in deep thought while Josephine walked over towards the sofa and took a seat. She looked over at her husband and patted the place next to her on the sofa and quietly said, "Karl come sit and tell me what it is you have on your mind." Karl slowly walked over to the sofa and sat down next to Josephine. He reached over and took both of Josephine's hands into his. He was nervous so he cleared his throat before speaking, and then blurted out, "I have been transferred to the city of Leipzig and my family is not allowed to come until further notification." There was a long pause as Josephine stared into Karl's eyes and tried to process what he just said. Karl continued, "I think you should go back home and stay with your parents until you and Ralph can come to Leipzig."

Josephine looked down and did not say anything for a few minutes, she blinked away tears. Josephine had thought about this very scenario many times in her head and what she would do if Karl got transferred again. Karl did not say a word as he waited for Josephine's response. She gathered her courage before looking up into Karl's eyes and stated with strength and determination, "Karl, I am not going back home! I want to wait here in Hamburg until I can come be with you."

Karl was surprised at her boldness and raised his eyebrow as Josephine continued, "Do you have any idea how long it will take before Ralph and I can come and live with you in Leipzig?" Karl took a deep breath and ran his fingers through his hair before turning and looking deep into Josephine's eyes. He took Josephine's hands and said, "You know I love you but this is a crazy idea, since I don't know how long it will take before you can come."

Karl wrapped his arm around Josephine's shoulder and stared across the room. Neither of them spoke and it was quiet until Karl continued, "I will be worried about you and Ralph, remember the only form of communication we will have is our letters." He paused yet again and then said, "I always look forward to your letters and I'll write as often as I can." Josephine reached up and touched his cheek and said, "I love you."

Karl turned towards Josephine and said, "If staying in Hamburg is what you really want to do, then I will trust you into Gods hands. Karl kissed Josephine then said, "I will come home whenever possible. I will miss you and always feel empty without you." They sat quietly wrapped in each other arms enjoying the moment they had.

Karl rose early the next morning to get the coffee ready and make breakfast for Josephine and Ralph. He sat at the table drinking a hot cup of coffee and planning the day; since this was his last day home he wanted to spend as much time with Ralph as possible. The thought of his three-year-old son not understanding why his papa had to leave again, made his heart sad. He pushed aside the thought as he heard Josephine getting up.

The smell of fresh brewed coffee gently woke up Josephine; she stretched and looked over and saw Karl was no longer in bed. She put on her bathrobe and headed for the kitchen. Karl's back was to her and he was pouring coffee into two cups when she entered the kitchen. A smile spread across her face at the sight of Karl and a warm feeling filled her heart.

Karl turned and handed Josephine a cup of coffee then said, "I have plans for all of us today." She sat down in the kitchen chair and looking at him and said, "Tell me about your plans." Karl sat down in the chair next to his wife, "I want to do all the cooking today, I thought we would take Ralph to the park and play ball, and do whatever we want to do." Josephine looked at the enthusiasm in her husband's eyes and said, "Why don't we let Ralph make the choices for us today, that way we will make it his day and build memories for him." Karl smiled and leaned over giving her a kiss on the cheek before getting up to prepare the breakfast. Josephine said, "Sounds like we will have a busy day, I better get ready and then wake up our boy."

Ralph could barely contain his excitement as Josephine put on his coat. The weather was perfect for a day in the park and she thought to herself, "What a wonderful day this will be." Karl dropped the soccer ball down on the lawn at the park and said, "Ralph, let's play ball." Ralph picked up the ball and ran with it. Josephine walked over to a nearby park bench and sat down; the sun was warm on her face as she sat watching Karl trying to show his three-year-old how to play soccer.

Ralph would run after the ball and kick it, then call out, "Mommy, mommy look at me." The next time he would kick the ball and fall over it as he kicked. Ralph sat on the ground and laughed until his father picked him up and swung him around in a circle before setting him down. Then the game would begin all over again. Josephine closed her eyes for a moment so she could treasure up these precious memories of Karl and Ralph in her heart. She opened her eyes and saw two SS Elite watching them. Josephine prayed that they would leave them alone. Suddenly the SS Elite turned and walked the other direction.

The day flew by; they went out to lunch and then back to the park for more play time. Ralph wanted ice cream on the way home. Karl prepared a quick dinner of open face sandwiches with peppermint tea to drink. After dinner Ralph took his father by the hand and led him into the living room to play cars. It was only six in the evening and Josephine looked over at Ralph who was lying on his side holding a car but very still. She looked at Karl and said, "Ralph is falling asleep I think we better get him ready for bed." Josephine put away the cars while Karl picked him Ralph to carry him to bed; Ralph suddenly woke up and said, "Where are we going?" Josephine chuckled and said, "It is time for your bedtime stories."

After a warm bath Karl began to read Ralph's favorite story and before he finished the first page Ralph was fast asleep. Both parents kissed their son goodnight and then walked slowly out of the room. Karl reached over and took Josephine's hand and led her to the living room and they sat down on the sofa. Neither of them spoke, they just sat there in each other's arms wishing the night would not end. This was their last night together before Karl had to leave for Leipzig.

Early the next morning Karl and Josephine got up together, it was still dark outside as Karl packed his bag. He went to make coffee while Josephine went to wake up Ralph. They ate breakfast and Karl tried to explain to Ralph that his papa had to go away for a while. Ralph began to cry and said through his sobs, "No papa, please stay." Tears ran down Josephine's cheeks and Karl blinked away his tears as he picked up his son to comfort him. His heart felt torn wanting to stay and run somewhere safe with his family, but knowing he must report for duty in Leipzig.

It was decided that Karl would go to the train station alone and say his goodbye at home. Ralph did not want to get out of his father's arms, so Karl pulled Josephine in wrapping his free arm around her to kiss her goodbye. The three of them stood huddled together until Karl heard the clock strike six am, he knew he had to head for the train station. Karl handed Ralph to Josephine and Ralph pulled back. Josephine said, "Ralph papa needs to go now." His little lower lip quivered as he tried not to cry again and went into Josephine's arms. Karl kissed Josephine goodbye before he picked up his bag. He kissed Ralph on the forehead and said, "You need to be brave until I get back okay?" Ralph through his sniffles shook his head 'okay.' Karl opened the door and was gone. Josephine stood in front of the closed door cuddling Ralph until he fell back to sleep.

Chapter 6 Alex's Birth 1939-1941

Karl's transfer and having to stay behind in Hamburg was more difficult than Josephine thought it would be. She was alone in a big city and far away from her parents. Sometimes during the lonely times, she would think back about her life as young women before things got complicated and wished her life now could be that simple again. Ralph would play with his cars but the joy he once had seemed to be depleted. Josephine missed Karl and wasn't feeling well and decided she needed to find a doctor.

Karl had been gone for six weeks; Josephine sat in the doctor's office and heard him say that she was pregnant with their second child. Fear and joy flooded her at the same time as she shook the doctor's hand and headed home. On the way home from the doctor's office Ralph looked up at his mother and said, "Mommy, are you okay?" Josephine squeezed his hand and said, "Yes, son everything is okay."

After putting Ralph to bed that evening Josephine sat down to write Karl. She had mixed feelings as she wrote him a long love letter filled with how much she missed him and longed for his arms. After three pages Josephine stopped to think about how she would tell Karl that he was going to be a father again, she decided to be direct and just tell him.

Setting the letter aside Josephine picked up Karl's picture off the nightstand and pressed it to her chest and prayed that Karl could change jobs and be near home. Placing the picture back down, Josephine completed the letter, sighed and placed the letter in its envelope and sealing it with a kiss. As Josephine prepared for bed she thought about how all the men were being drafted and it was not very hopeful that Karl would be able to leave the military any time soon.

The mail was being randomly searched by the SS Elite, so mail took longer than normal to get to its destination. Josephine's letter arrived to Karl two weeks after she had put it in the mail. Every day Karl would go out to mail call and there was nothing. As the days went by he began to worry about his family. He stood again with the other soldiers as the names were called out. He finally heard his name called out and his heart leaped with excitement as he walked over and took the letter from the sergeant. The love that poured out of Josephine's letters always filled his heart with a sense of peace. He whistled a tune as he walked over to the barracks visualizing his beautiful wife.

Karl walked into the barracks and went straight to his bed. There were a few other soldiers in the barracks sitting on their beds reading their letters. He held the letter to his heart before opening it. As he read the letter, a longing for Josephine filled his heart. A smile spread across his face as he savored every written word. He read the last paragraph of the letter and then had to read it again. He had conflicting thoughts as he read the paragraph for the third time. He wanted to be there with Josephine, to hold her in his arms and let her know how happy he was. But then those thoughts were invaded by the practical of not being with her very much during her pregnancy as he was not sure when he would be able to get leave. He wanted to be with Josephine for the birth of their new baby in October. Then he thought about Ralph and how great it would be for him to have a sibling to grow up with.

Karl sat quietly for a moment allowing his thoughts to settle. Then he stood up and turned to the soldier sitting on the bunk next to his with excitement in his voice said, "I am going to be a father again." The soldier stood up and slapped Karl on the back and said, "Congratulations!" Karl said, "Thank you." Then they both sat back down on their beds to write letters back to their loved ones. Karl pulled out his stationary and pen from the draw in the table beside the bed and laid them on his lap. He stared across the room at the wall trying to formulate his words before he began to write.

Once he put his pen to the stationary the words spilled out onto the page like a flood. After five pages Karl put down his pen and placed the letter into the envelope and sealed it. As he wrote the address on the envelope he hoped it would go out in the morning mail. He got up to put the letter in the mail, as he walked over to the mail drop a longing for his family filled his heart with heaviness. He wished things were different and he could be home with his family. But for now, all he had was the love letters to sustain him while he was apart from his beloved Josephine.

New and more advanced weapons were being built every day. Not only was Karl expected to inspect the old weapons, but he had to study the new specification for the new weapons prior to their inspections. With so much time doing his military duty he had less and less time to go home. The summer of 1940 was hot and steamed with high humidity. Karl's military truck had no air conditioning and it was almost unbearable to be traveling in the heat, but he had to keep a schedule. There were many times during the hot summer that he would have to stop, get out of his vehicle to cool off and check the water level of the truck before he would continue his travel toward the weapons factory where he needed to do his inspection.

Cologne was the furthest location that the Army sent Karl for weapons inspections. The factory had an urgent need of inspection and wanted the best weapon inspector, so they requested Karl. It was a long drive to Cologne and even though the weather was beautiful for the first day of fall, it was still quite warm. Traffic was light, so Karl allowed his mind to wonder. He thought about the last time he was home, three months ago for Ralph's fourth birthday. He smiled to himself as he could still hear Ralph say, "Papa look how big I am getting." The hardest part of leaving home was when it was time to leave Ralph would cry and beg him to stay.

Karl hoped the new baby would help Ralph not feel so alone. The new baby's due date was in a little over six weeks and Karl hoped to be home with Josephine for the delivery. Last week Karl checked again with his commander about families coming to Leipzig and the answer was still no.

He pulled off the highway into the town of Cologne driving towards the weapons factory. He drove past a park where he saw a gathering of people who were standing around a stage. Karl was hot and decided to stop and get out into the air. He pulled over and got out of the truck, wiping his brow with his handkerchief.

As he walked up and down the street, his eyes were drawn over to the park where he saw lots of the SS Elite milling through the crowd of people. The people looked like they were waiting for someone to speak. Karl got back in his truck to leave when he heard a voice over the loud speaker – it was Hitler's voice. He drove off wondering why people even listened to that man.

Even though it was the end of September the weather was warmer than normal. The sun was bright in his eyes as he drove to his next weapon inspection location. Karl had a hard time keeping his mind off his family as he drove; he still had not been able to go home. The time approached for the birth of his second child. Josephine mentioned in her last letter that the doctor told her the baby could come any time. Karl needed to be there for his wife and for Ralph. He told himself that once he gets back to the base he would talk to his commander and ask again about time off.

Three days later as Karl drove back to the base, the weather had cooled and it rained all the way back. The drumming of the rain on the windshield and the dark clouded sky felt like his mood. He had word today that the SS Elite were stepping up their raids all over Germany. This news caused him to worry more about his family. All he wanted was to leave this crazy military life and be with them.

October came with cool air and windy weather; leaves blew from the trees and glided through the air. Karl had to wait over two weeks to get an appointment to talk to his commanding officer about time off. Most soldiers were not able to get time off so he was unsure if he would be able to get any time away for the birth of his new baby. He pulled to a stop by the factory he was to inspect and he just sat there for a few minutes just looking at the leaves hitting the windshield before getting out. Karl's heart was heavy and longed for his family.

The morning of Karl's appointment the sun made the sky look deep blue with not a cloud in sight. The sun felt warm on his face as he walked over to his commander's office. The rays of the sun warmed his heart and he prayed for favor as he pleaded his case before his commanding officer. "Lord, help my commander have an understanding heart and allow me time off for the birth of my child, Amen." Karl stood at the office door and took a deep breath before knocking on the door, after a few minutes he heard a gruff, "Come in."

Karl was nervous as he stood at attention in front of his commander. This was the third time since summer he had come to his office and ask for time off to be with his family. He began to explain about the birth of his new child and wanting to have time to be there with his wife, when the commander without looking up from his paperwork blurted out, "You've got three days and you will leave tomorrow morning."

Karl just stood there in shock staring at the commander for just a brief minute. The commander looked up from his paperwork and said, "Is there anything else?" Karl saluted him and said, "No sir and thank you." The commander pointed to the door and said, "Then you are dismissed." Karl turned on his heels and walked out of the office with a spring in his step as he whispered a prayer to thanks to God. With such short notice, he had no time to write and let Josephine know he was coming home tomorrow. He had to quickly make travel arrangements to leave first thing in the morning.

Josephine knew it was close to the time to having this baby; she had carried her baby the full nine months. This last month was very uncomfortable and she was having trouble sleeping. Ralph was now four-years old and a big help to Josephine. Every night after she read Ralph his bedtime stories he would place his small hand on Josephine stomach and asked her, "Will our baby come out of your tummy soon?" Josephine would rub her tummy and with a big smile on her face say, "I hope so." Tonight, Ralph reached for his mother's hand and asked, "Mommy, when is papa coming home?" Josephine tucked Ralph into bed, kissed him goodnight and whispered in his ear, "I hope your papa will be coming home very soon." Ralph smiled and closed his eyes. She pushed herself up off the bed and turned off the light.

Josephine had a hard time sleeping the last few nights. This baby seemed to be the most active at night and it felt like the baby was playing soccer inside her. She sat in a chair by the kitchen table rubbing her belly to calm down the kicking baby inside her. She lifted her eyes up towards the ceiling and prayed out loud, "Lord, you know I need my husband here with me during the birth of this baby and I have not heard a word if he will be able to come or not, would you please provide the way for him to be here? Thank you for your watchful care over my family. Amen."

Josephine turned her thoughts toward her husband and how much they have been apart since they were first married. As Josephine's mind wondered back in time she smiled as she remembered the joy of being married to Karl, he had such a kind and generous heart. Memories filled her mind of the time she first met him and how nervous she was, and then when they were first married and moved into their very own apartment. Longing again flooded her heart for the days when her beloved husband and father could be home every night again after work.

Then everything changed and now there is so much uncertainty of what the future held for them and she wondered if having Karl home every night would ever happen again. The whole world which she had known seemed so upside down to her now. The separation became more and more difficult with each passing day. The only thing that felt right about her circumstance was their son and the precious baby growing inside her. The love letters that flowed between them gave her the strength to go on. Josephine let out a big sigh and decided to go to bed and try and get some sleep before morning and her active four-year old son would wake-up.

Josephine awoke with sharp labor pains, she looked over at the clock and it was four in the morning. She laid there trying to breath and counted the contractions wishing Karl was there. Josephine did not have to worry about the hospital or who would care for Ralph, since she befriended an older couple who lived in the upstairs apartment. Josephine had made advanced arrangements with them a few months ago to take care of Ralph and the husband would take her to the hospital.

It was such a relief when they had agreed and gave her peace knowing that she would not have to worry about Ralph while she was in the hospital. As she laid there counting the contractions and thinking about how thankful she was for this sweet couple who had had taken her and Ralph under their wings, keeping an eye on her and her son.

Josephine looked over at the small clock that sat on the table next to the bed. It was almost five in the morning and the contractions were getting closer together and more painful. She decided to get up and get dressed so that she could wake-up Ralph and take him to the neighbors upstairs. Just as she finished getting dressed she heard a noise in the kitchen; fear gripped her which started another strong contraction. Holding her belly with one hand and the other hand on the wall, she slowly walked down the hall toward the kitchen.

As she neared the kitchen door she could hear the whistle of her husband as he was preparing coffee. He was so happy to be home and wanted to surprise Josephine with breakfast in bed. Just then another contraction hit hard she bent over holding both hands on her belly and letting out a loud moan.

Karl turned towards the kitchen door and saw his wife bent over in pain. He quickly walked over to help Josephine walk to the kitchen chair. Karl gently asked, "How far apart are the contractions? It looks like I made it home just in time for our baby." Josephine responded with a slight smile despite the pain and whispered, "They are less than five minutes apart."

Karl turned off the stove and bent down to kiss his wife and said, "I think it is time to go to the hospital, I'll go and get Ralph up; do you have your bag packed?" Josephine just shook her head 'yes' as another contraction hit. Karl went to get Ralph. When he entered Ralph's bedroom Karl softly called his name, "Ralph, son." As soon as he heard his father's voice he immediately opened his eyes and smiled at the sight of his papa. He leaped out of bed and jumped into his father's arms. "Good morning son, I am glad to see you too, but we need to get you dressed right away because mommy needs to go to the hospital to have our new baby." He sat Ralph down on the bed and took the clothes Josephine had laid out for him on the foot of the bed. Ralph looked at his father and said, "We are going to the hospital to get our baby today, right papa?" Karl just smiled at him and carried him into the kitchen.

When they got back into the kitchen Josephine said, "There is no need to wake the neighbors now that you are home." Karl went to get the bag for the hospital and gave it to Ralph. Then Karl helped Josephine out to the car that he had borrowed from a friend with Ralph following close behind. He thought to himself that he was so glad he had borrowed the car instead of taking the train. He got Josephine settled into the car then he took the bag from Ralph and helped him into the car. They headed towards the hospital. It was dawn and the sun was just beginning to rise with a few small lines of pink on the horizon. Josephine looked out at the sky and said, "I think it will be a beautiful fall day to welcome our new baby."

On the way to the hospital, every time Josephine had a contraction Ralph would take his mommy's hand and ask, "Why is our baby hurting you?" Karl explained, "The baby just wants to come out of mommy's tummy to meet us that is why mommy is hurting. Mommy will feel better once our baby is here." Josephine looked over at her husband and smiled as she said, "Thank you for being here, I love you."

The air was brisk and the sun was bright in the sky this October day in 1940, the day when Alexander was born. Josephine just finished feeding Alexander when Karl and Ralph came back into the room. Ralph loves it when the baby would wrap his hand around his finger. They all were quietly watching the baby sleep. Alexander had lots of light blond hair. Josephine studied her baby and she said, "I want to call him 'Alex' for short." Karl smiled as he reached down and lightly rubbed his finger across Alexander's face and said, "Hello baby Alex, welcome to your family." Ralph said, "Alex," and baby Alex opened his eyes and looked at his big brother.

Karl's heart felt discouraged as he drove Josephine and the baby home from the hospital, but he tried not to show it. Josephine's heart was also heavy for she knew Karl had to leave late that afternoon to go back to the base, but chose to be cheerful for Ralph's sake. Ralph said, "Mommy I am glad to have a little brother." Karl answered him, "You are going to be a wonderful big brother." After Alex fell sleep Josephine turned to Ralph and said, "How would you like papa and me to play cars with you while Alex sleeps." Ralph got excited and ran over to get the small box of cars, then sat down in the middle of the living room floor. Karl and Josephine looked at each other as they joined him on the floor. They both knew it was time to let Ralph know his papa had to leave again, but decided they wanted to wait until it was time and let Ralph enjoy himself until then.

The time they had all dreaded had come and Karl needed to leave. This was one of the hardest days in Karl's life to have to leave his wife, child and new born baby alone in Hamburg. Josephine knew in her mind that Karl had to leave, but her heart needed him to stay. She smiled and kept her heart-breaking thoughts to herself as she did not want to worry her husband. Karl kissed Alex on his chubby cheeks and laid him back down in his cradle. Then Karl picked up Ralph and said, "You are getting so big I am not sure I can pick you up next time I see you." Ralph wrapped his arms around his daddy's neck and did not want to let go. When Karl had to put him down, he sensed his papa was leaving again.

Josephine took Ralph's hand as Karl pulled her into his arms for a deep kiss. They stood in a long embrace; then Ralph let go of his mother's hand and wrapped his little arms around both of their legs. Saying goodbye was hard, not knowing when they would see each other again. Karl broke his embrace and looked down at Ralph. He was trying to be brave and not cry as he yelled, "Goodbye papa!"

Karl's heart was heavy as he closed the door and walked away leaving his family behind. He felt angry and cheated that he had to leave his family again. He decided that day, once the Army would allow people to leave the military, he would finish his duty time and not re-enlist. He would leave the military career behind, find other employment, and be with his family.

At the sound of the door closing, Alex began to cry. Ralph ran over to the cradle and reached in taking Alex's little hand. Josephine eyes stung with tears as she picked up her crying baby and held him tightly with one arm at the same time with her free arm pulling Ralph to herself since now he was also crying. Tears began to run down her cheeks as she tried to comfort her sobbing children. As she stood there she prayed a silent pray of protection over her husband and that she would have strength to be alone taking care of her children until his return.

Alex stopped crying and Ralph looked up at Josephine with a hiccup and sniffing and asked, "Can I hold baby Alex?" Josephine wiped her tears with her sleeve and smiled down at Ralph as she replied, "Yes son, go get a tissue to wipe your nose and wash your hands first, then come back and sit down on the sofa." As Josephine watched Ralph leave, she knew in her heart that he was going to be a good big brother. This made her heart happy as she changed Alex's diaper. Within a few minutes Ralph was back and sat down on the sofa with his arms stretched out towards her.

Josephine place Alex on Ralph's lap gently wrapping both of his arms around the baby. He looked up at his mother with a smile. She sat down next to Ralph and wrapped her arms around his shoulder. The two of them sat quietly watching Alex suck his thumb. Josephine let out a sigh and began to sing one of her favorite Hymns "Amazing Grace." A warm sense of peace filled the room and baby Alex fell asleep in Ralph's arms.

The SS Elite began to take more control over the military and they also began arresting anyone who did not agree with them. The SS Elite kept the regular soldiers busy doing the menial work. Time passed by somewhat quickly; but it had been almost a year since Karl was last home. The SS Elite continued monitoring the mail which caused delay in letters reaching the intended person. During their time separated, it was Karl and Josephine's love letters that sustained them during his long absence.

Early October in 1941, Karl got transferred to Berlin. The commander told all the soldiers with families that their families could come live with them in Berlin. Karl was so excited when he heard this news and the thought of seeing his family again filled him with great joy. He was to change his post immediately.

The next day after reporting to duty and inspecting the three weapon factories in the Berlin area, he drove to the telegraph office and sent Josephine a telegram. On his next day off he found a furnished apartment to rent. All Karl could think about was how wonderful it would be to see his family and have them near him again.

It was evening and Josephine had just finished feeding the boys. She tucked five-year-old Ralph into bed and laid her one-year old Alex in his crib with a bottle. Josephine was tired after a long day and missing Karl terribly that she needed some quiet time. She sat down on the sofa and began reading her Bible. Within a couple of minutes there was a loud knock on the door. The knock startled Josephine and she thought, it's late, who would be calling this late. She prayed it would not be the SS Elite.

Josephine set her Bible down and got up to answer the door. Alex began to cry and there was a pitter-patter of Ralph's feet across the floor. He burst into the living room and with fear in his little voice he asked, "Do you think it is those men with the guns?" Even the children sensed the fear of the SS Elite. There was a second even louder knock on the door. Josephine looked down at her son and softly said, "No son! You sit here and I will answer the door." She prayed that her children would be at peace as she walked towards the door.

After the third loud more urgent sounding knock, Josephine hurried to the door. She opened the door a crack and saw a postman standing outside the door. She slowly opened the door all the way. The postman stated in an irritated tone, "I have a telegram for Josephine, is that you?" Josephine looked surprised and quickly answered, "Yes that is me." The postman handed her a clip board that had a form on it and a pen. He pointed at the form and said, "Please sign here." After Josephine signed the form the postman gave her the telegram then turned quickly and left in a hurry.

Josephine turned and closed the door; she held the telegram to her heart. Alex was still crying and Ralph looked at her with his big blue eyes and asked, "Mommy is the man going to come back." Josephine walked over to her son and said, "Let's go and get Alex and let him know everything is okay and then I will read a story to both of you before you have to go back to bed. Ralph shook his head 'yes' as he ran ahead into the bedroom and tried to comfort Alex.

Josephine put the telegram on the table and followed her son into the bedroom. Josephine bent down and picked up Alex from his crib; she gently rocked him in her arms to calm his crying. Picking up his half drank bottle, she carried Alex to the living room with Ralph following close behind her. Ralph went and got his favorite book; he loved to hold the book and help read it. He had heard this story so many times he could tell the story without help since he had memorized most of the books.

Josephine began to feed Alex his bottle and Ralph was too tired to read tonight so he turned the pages as Josephine read the book. By the time she had finished reading the book; Alex was fast asleep in her arms. Josephine got up and said to Ralph, "Okay son, time to go to sleep." She carried Alex into the bedroom and Ralph followed her. Ralph climbed into his bed while Josephine laid Alex in his crib and covered him up. Then she tucked in Ralph and kissed him good night. Josephine quietly pulled the door shut as she left the bedroom.

Walking back into the living room, Josephine picked up the telegram off the table and walked over and sat down on the sofa. She sat there staring at the telegram for several minutes, not sure what to expect. She was nervous that it would hold some sort of bad news. Josephine took a deep breath as she tore open the telegram and began to read that not only was her husband alright, but she was going to be able to go to Berlin and be with him. Josephine couldn't believe her eyes and had to read the telegram several times for it to sink in. The last line of the telegram said, "Make arrangements and let me know via telegram when you will be able to catch a train to Berlin. Forever Yours - Love Karl."

Even though Josephine was exhausted she was too excited and could not sleep. Plans ran through her head on how to arrange everything quickly so they would be able to go and be with Karl. They boys would be so happy to see their papa again, especially Ralph. It had been almost a year since Josephine had seen her husband, baby Alex was just beginning to take his first steps. Josephine thought to herself, "Karl has missed so much of his children's lives." She thought about the things her husband would be able to enjoy with his children once they were together again. To be able to celebrate Alex's first birthday and Ralph was five years old and going to start school soon. These thoughts filled Josephine's heart with joy as she fell asleep dreaming of being in the arms of her beloved Karl.

Chapter 7 Berlin 1941-1942

Both boys slept in, which allow Josephine to get some much-needed rest. As Josephine opened her eyes to look at the clock she could hear Ralph talking to Alex. Eight o'clock, Josephine got out of bed to prepare for the day and even though she got a late start to her day nothing else seemed to matter but the thought of being together again with her husband. After breakfast, she took the boys upstairs to visit Mr. and Mrs. Meier. They had grandchildren which they had not seen since the trouble started in Germany and loved having the boys over.

Mrs. Meier opens the door with a smile on her face and was glad to see Josephine and the boys. Once Ralph was playing in the toy box and Alex was content playing with a ball, Josephine softly told Mrs. Meier about the telegram and asked her if she would watch the boys while she went out to make travel arrangements for her trip to Berlin and to send a telegram back to her husband. Mrs. Meier said, "No, problem child, I will make the children a snack while you are out." Josephine explained to Ralph that she needed to go out for a bit and Mrs. Meier wanted to give them a snack while she was gone. She kissed her boys' goodbye and quickly left.

Josephine walked to the train station with the crisp October wind blowing under her collar. She pulled her collar tighter around her neck and thought, "It is going to be a cold winter." It felt good to enter the warm train station building. She pulled off her gloves as she walked up to the tall window and asked the young lady who was attending to customers, "How much for one adult and two children one way to Berlin?"

After looking down at a very large book for a few minutes the young lady looked up at Josephine and said, "The price is thirty Marks. When would you like to leave? There is a train out at ten o'clock tomorrow morning." Josephine looked up from taking the money out of her purse and smiled as she replied, "That time would be wonderful, thank you." She exchanged the money for the train tickets and put them into her purse. Josephine stepped back out into the cold wind and headed across the street to the telegraph office. She was excited as she told the telegrapher what she wanted to say in her telegram to Karl.

That night after putting the boys to bed Josephine packed only what she thought she could carry on the train. Josephine had asked the Meier's to clean out the apartment and take whatever they wanted, since she would be unable to take it with her. She was exhausted as she checked on the boys before going to bed. She sat on the edge of the bed and took the clock to set the alarm for six in the morning. Since it was well past midnight and Josephine was exhausted, she fell asleep as soon as her head hit the pillow and began dreaming of Karl.

Early the next morning the alarm woke Josephine out of her peaceful dream. She quickly got ready and packed the last-minute items before carrying the bags to set them by the front door. Josephine prepared a light breakfast and then went to wake up her sons. She kissed Ralph on the cheek and said, "Good morning Ralph, I have a surprise for you today." Ralph jumped out of bed and said, "What is it mommy?"

Josephine did not answer as she walked over to Alex's crib to wake him and get him ready for the day. Ralph finished dressing and said, "Mommy, what is my surprise?" While Josephine dressed Alex, she smiled at her son's anticipation and replied, "We are going take the train to see papa today." Ralph jumped up and down with joy. Even though Alex did not understand, at the mention of papa he began to kick his legs making it hard for her to put on his pants.

After cleaning up from breakfast Josephine walked around the apartment one more time to make sure she had not forgotten any important stuff. She turned and walked over to Ralph and said, "Ralph, get your hat and coat on and button your coat all the way up, it is cold outside." Ralph complied as Josephine put on Alex's coat and hat.

There was a light knock on the door. Josephine opened the door and saw the elderly Mr. Meier standing there with a smile on his face. She put on her coat and hat, and then she put the backpack filled with baby supplies over her shoulders before picking up Alex. Mr. Meier had already picked up the suitcase and small bag while he stood waiting at the doorway. She took one last scan of the room before saying, "We are ready to go Mr. Meier." Ralph followed Mr. Meier and Josephine trailed behind as Mr. Meier led the way to his car. Mr. Meier put the bags in the trunk and then helped Josephine and the boys into the back seat. Turning around he helped his wife get into the front passenger seat.

The Hamburg train station was crowded with travelers; Mr. & Mrs. Meier walked Josephine and the two boys over to the train platform and waited with her for the train. The SS Elite stood watching the people as they departed and boarded trains. Josephine eyes filled with tears as she gave the elderly couple a hug and thanked them for all they had done for her while she lived in Hamburg. There was a loud whistle as the train bound for Berlin pulled up to the station. After the people departed from the train, Mr. Meier picked up the suitcase and bag and turned towards Josephine and said, "Better get you and the boys settled into a seat." He led the way to the train. Josephine with the backpack on her shoulder and baby Alex on her hip she gave Mrs. Meier one more quick hug before taking Ralph's hand and following him up the train steps.

They settled into a seat with Ralph sitting next to the window. Mr. Meier turns to depart, but before going he said, "Take care of yourself and the boys, if you are ever back in Hamburg please stop by and say hello." Josephine smiled up at him and said, "Thank you again for everything, and yes I will." Ralph waved goodbye to Mr. Meier and Alex just looked up at him from Josephine's lap, with drool running down his chin. Tears stung Mr. Meier's eyes as he quickly turned and walked away.

Josephine wiped the drool from Alex's face and stood him up on her lap so he could see out the window. Ralph was up on his knees waving at the Meier's as the train pulled out of the station. Within ten minutes of the train moving away from the station both children were fast asleep. Josephine took a deep breath and looked out the window watching the scenery go by for a few minutes before closing her eyes. She could picture Karl's face as the train swayed along the tracks. Josephine prayed that there would be another elderly couple like the Meier's in Berlin. With the soothing sound of her children sleeping and the swaying of the train Josephine fell asleep thinking about Karl and filled with hope to have him home more often.

The train whistle sounded jarring them all awake, as the conductor announced, "Berlin next stop." Alex began to cry and Ralph jumps up on his knees to look out the window as the train pulled into the station. Josephine tried to comfort her hungry baby while Ralph continued look out the window. The train began to pull to a slow stop. Ralph spotted his papa and pointed out the window yelling, "Look, mommy I see papa." Alex had finally settled down and began to suck his thumb as the train pulled to a full stop.

Josephine put Alex down on the seat so she could take down the suitcase and bag down from the overhead shelf. She gave Ralph the little bag and put the backpack on before picking up Alex. Josephine looked awkward wearing a backpack with a baby on one hip and a suitcase in the other as she explained to Ralph, "Make sure you hold onto my skirt as we leave the train, okay?" Just then she heard a man's voice, "Excuse me, do you need some help?" Josephine looked up into the steel blue eyes of an elderly gentleman and answered, "Oh yes, please, that would be very kind of you." The elderly man took the suitcase and Josephine took Ralph's hand as she followed him off the train.

Karl was waiting by the door of the train looking at every face as they departed the train. Then he saw his beautiful Josephine following an elderly man off the train. Karl smiled at Josephine as he took the suitcase from the elderly man and said, "Thank you for your kindness towards my family." The elderly man nodded and went his way. Karl took a few steps away from the train before setting the suitcase down. Ralph ran after his papa and sat his small bag down next to the suitcase and then he wrapped his little arms around his father's leg and shouted, "Papa, papa, I missed you soooo much."

Karl bends down and scoops Ralph up into his arms, kissing him on the cheek and giving him a warm hug. Then Karl looks over into Josephine's beautiful green eyes, she was standing next to the suitcase and bag watching Karl with his son. He put Ralph back down and took a step toward Josephine and baby, he leaning down and pressing his lips against hers. They were lost in each other's kiss until Alex poked Karl on the cheek and said, "No!" They both looked at their youngest son and laughed. Karl turned his face towards Alex and said, "Look at my big boy."

At the sound of Karl's voice Alex began to cry. The last time he saw his papa he was only three days old and did not know who his papa was. Ralph tugged on Karl's pant leg and said, "I a big boy too, I am going to school soon." Karl patted Ralph on the head and smiled as he said, "Yes son, you are a big boy and I am proud of how you have helped your mommy."

Josephine tried to comfort Alex with soft words, gently hugging and rocking as she said, "Alex, you are okay, this is your papa." In a few moments Alex stopped crying and looked over at Karl with his eyes still brimming with tears and pointed his small finger and said, "Pa." Ralph began to jump up and down singing, "Yes, pa is here!" Karl's face lit up with a huge smile as he reached out his arms towards Alex. Pulling back into Josephine's arms Alex looked carefully at his father. Karl smiled and encouraged him by saying, "It's okay Alex come."

Alex looked at his mother and then back at his father before leaning over and going into Karl's arms. A gentle peace came upon baby Alex who nestled his small head into Karl's neck. Warmth filled Karl's heart as he held his baby boy. Josephine took Ralph by the hand while she watched Karl with Alex; she stored these warm memories in her heart.

The happy family reunion was cut short when Karl looked around and noticed the crowd had thinned out and two SS Elite were standing nearby watching them. Even though Karl was in his uniform he knew he needed to get his family away from the train station as quickly as possible. The SS Elite uniforms were distinguished from the regular soldiers by the armband they wore on their right arm. Karl handed Alex back to Josephine and picked up the suitcase and bag as he said quietly with urgency in his voice, "We need to go now." Josephine also saw the SS Elite watching them and understood immediately what he meant; taking Ralph by the hand she followed Karl as he walked away from the train platform.

There was a known fear among the German people, that when they saw SS Elite around, they needed to go about their business as quickly as possible and stay out of the SS Elite's way. The people also knew never to look directly into the eyes of an SS Elite soldier and do not talk to them unless they talk to you first. As Karl and his family walked out of the train station he wished he would have never put his family into these circumstances with the SS Elite observing them. He had gotten caught up in the emotion of seeing his family again that he lost track of time. He looked back over his shoulder as they crossed the street away from the train station to make sure the SS Elite were not following them. Once they were a couple of blocks away from the train station a great relief filled both Karl and Josephine and they could relax.

The apartment Karl had rented was not too far from the train station. The October air was brisk against their faces as they walked towards the apartment. Josephine still had the backpack on and carried Alex on her left hip as she held tightly to Ralph's hand with her free hand. After they had walked a few blocks away from the train station Alex seemed to remember he was hungry and started to fuss. The streets this far from the train station was quiet and there were no SS Elite in sight. Josephine let out a sigh of relief. Karl tried to slow his pace down enough for a five-year old to walk and not get tired. Karl thought to himself, "The apartment is small but quite nice and only ten blocks from the train station, I hope Josephine will like it."

They turned a corner and ahead of them was a beautiful park. The trees in the park were still filled with most of their fall colored leaves; they looked amazing the way the October sun reflected off the leaves caused them to look like jewels hanging from the trees. When they walked past the park Ralph stopped suddenly, causing Josephine to jerk forward to a stop and she had to balance Alex so she would not drop him. Josephine was about to scold Ralph when her heart softened as he asked, "Mommy can we go to the park so papa can play ball with me?" She smiled down at him as she answered, "Not now son, we need to go with papa to see our new home and feed Alex first." Ralph stuck out his lower lip and reluctantly began to walk forward again.

Ralph looked toward his father who was walking just ahead of them carrying the small bag and suitcase. Then Ralph looked up at his mother and asked, "Can I walk with papa now?" Josephine looked down at her son with a worried look on her face, but did not answer. Karl had overheard Ralph request and said, "Let the boy come, we are almost there, only three more houses up the street." Josephine released Ralph's hand and he skipped towards his father. Alex stopped fussing and watched his brother skipping towards Karl and began to bounce up and down in his mother's arms pointing at his brother.

Karl stopped in front of a historic early 1600s, three story apartment building. He walked up the steps and let himself into the building with Ralph close behind him. Once everyone had entered the apartment building Karl pointed up the stairs and said, "Our apartment is on the second floor."

Josephine was tired and she was a little out of breath caring Alex and the backpack up the stairs. Stopping at apartment 210, Karl put down the suitcase and bag before reaching into his pocket to pull out the key. He had rented a furnished apartment this time and it was filled with beautiful antique furniture of the same era as the building. Josephine let out a sigh as she looked around the living room, then she turned towards Karl and said, "This is wonderful." Ralph wandered from room to room looking at his new home.

Josephine looked over at Karl who had been staring at her from the moment they entered the apartment and said, "Karl, thank you for making our arrival perfect." Alex began to cry again reminding them again that he was hungry. Josephine looked at her baby and said, "Okay my little one I know it is well past your feeding time." Josephine walked into a bedroom and sat on the edge of the bed to pull a bottle out of the back pack to feed her baby. Karl took Ralph to the kitchen to prepare lunch for the three of them.

That very next week Alex turned one-years' old and Josephine planned a birthday celebration, not only celebrating Alex birthday but their family being back together again. Having Karl home every night was such a wonderful blessing. Ralph played with Alex and was loving and kind with him. Alex began walking and climbing everywhere and Josephine had to keep a constant eye on him. Every time Karl came home after a long day of work; the boys would run to greet him. Such joy filled Josephine's heart as she watched him with his sons.

On Karl's day off he would take Ralph to the park and teach him soccer skills. It was the first of November and the trees were nearly bare. Josephine walked Ralph to Kindergarten every day. He was so happy to be in school. They seemed like a real family again with Karl coming home every night for dinner. Ralph and Alex looked forward to their papa sitting on the sofa with them and reading a bedtime story. Josephine stood back and observed the three of them as Karl read the boys a story. After the story time was over both boys would be tuck into bed. Karl and Josephine hearts were full as they sat and talked about their future till it was time for bed.

It was the end of November and Berlin had its first light snow flurry; the winter cold was beginning to set in. After work Karl came into the house, hung up his coat and said, "Burr, it looks like we will be getting some more snow tonight." Ralph looked up at his father and said, "Papa you are all wet, can we play in the snow?" Josephine was in the kitchen when she heard Karl's voice she quickly walked to the living room. She walked over to Karl and wrapped her arms around his waist and said, "I have some nice hot soup to warm you up." Ralph took his father by the hand and said, "Come on papa, I'm hungry." Alex was already in the kitchen sitting in his high chair banging his cup on the tray yelling, "Papa, papa."

After dinner dishes were done and the boys put to bed, Karl pulled his wife to himself and said, "I got orders today and I need to leave day after tomorrow for Frankfurt." Josephine pulled away; she tried to hide her watery eyes as tears threaten to fall and said, "Karl, you have only been home for six weeks." Karl pulled Josephine back into his arms and pressed her head against his chest as he said softly, "I know my love, but the Army needs me to move to another location for weapons inspection." Sadness filled both of their hearts that night.

The morning Karl had to leave, both Ralph and Alex began to cry, neither child could understand why their papa had to leave again. Josephine felt like crying also but held her tears until a time when she could be alone. Karl tried to button up his coat as Ralph kept pulling at his sleeve and saying through his crying, "Papa, please don't go." Karl kissed Ralph on the top of the head. Alex tried to run over to his papa but lost his balance right before reaching Karl and fell on his bottom. Alex being on years old and only able to speak a few words became frustrated and cried even louder as he looked up at his papa.

Karl did not say a word but his eyes stung with tears as he bent down to picked up Alex and kissed him before handing him to Josephine. Ralph reached up his arms to be held too, but Karl just knelt with one knee on the floor and pulled him into a hug and kissed him on the cheek. With both boys crying loudly he gave Josephine a goodbye hug and kiss. Turning quickly, he walked out the door and shut it behind him. Tears fell down Karl's cheeks and mixed with the soft falling snow on his face as he walked to the train station. The shutting of the door sounded louder than it should have to Josephine as the tears began to sting her eyes and threatened to spill out, but she held them back because she needed to be strong for her boys.

Josephine looked down at Ralph she pulled a handkerchief from her pocket and she wiped both boys' tears and running noses. She took Ralph by the hand and led him to the sofa. She held her sons close and gently rocked them back and forth. Ralph looked up at Josephine and said with his crying hick-ups, "Mommy, I don't want papa to leave." Kissing the top of his head she said, "I know son, I don't want papa to leave either, but he has a very important job in the Army and must leave for a while." Her words did not bring any comfort to the boys and they both continue to cry. Her mother's heart was torn; she did not know how to ease her children's heartache.

The tears that had threatened to fall from her eyes gently spilled out over her cheeks as she rocked her crying sons back and forth. Josephine began to sing hymns and allowed the tears to flow down her face. Soon a peace settled into all their hearts and the boys had stopped crying. The apartment was quiet as she continued to sing and rock her sons. The tears dripped down on her son's heads. Alex had cried himself to sleep in his mother arms. Ralph looked up at his mother and saw the tears running down her face. He reached his small hand up to wipe away the tears and asked, "Mommy, are we okay?" Josephine stopped singing and looking down at her five-year old and answered, "Yes, Ralph we are okay."

Ralph's eyes looked sad as he got up off the sofa, but he smiled at his mother as he asked "Can I play with my cars now?" Josephine shook her head yes before getting up to carry baby Alex to bed. The next three weeks went by quickly without a word from Karl. Christmas was next week and Josephine was not able to get the hope out of her heart that Karl would be home for Christmas. Josephine found a couple of new books to give to the boys for Christmas and the apartment was filled with the smell of homemade cookies.

On Christmas Eve, Josephine went out to check the mail as she did every day. After pulling out the mail of the box and looking through it she hung her head down in disappointment and all the hope in her heart that Karl would be home waivered as she said to herself, "No, letter."

Ralph and Alex were in the living room playing with their blocks. Josephine was in the kitchen finishing the Christmas Eve dinner she had prepared for her and the boys. As Josephine was putting the rolls on the table she heard the front door shut and Ralph yell, "Papa you're home." Joy bubbled up in Josephine's heart as she sent a pray of thanksgiving up to God for answering her prayers. Karl picked up Alex and followed Ralph into the kitchen. Ralph yelled, "Mommy look, papa is home." Christmas 1941 turned out to be a wonderful family celebration.

The day after Christmas Karl had to leave again. Before he left to go back to Frankfurt, he told Josephine the Army had promised him at least two days a month to come home for a family visit. They all stood at the door to say goodbye. Ralph was getting used to his papa going away, so he did not make much of a fuss this time. But Alex was too young and began to cry and for many days after his papa left, Alex would walk throughout the apartment looking for his papa and then go to the front door and begin to cry for his papa.

Kissing Karl goodbye was never easy for Josephine and she prayed every day while they were apart that God would sustain her by His grace. The day after he left, the sky opened and dumped a heavy load of snow all over Berlin. The radiator couldn't keep up with the cold outside and it was cool in the apartment. Josephine wrapped a blanket around her and the boys as she read one of the new books to them before putting them to bed. Once the boys were asleep, Josephine looked out the window at the bellows of snow and she longed for Karl, her heart was filled with heaviness. A chill ran up her spine as she worried about the safety of her husband. Josephine prayed that the day would soon come when Karl would be able to return home for good.

Chapter 8 Cherished Moments 1942

During the next few months Karl was only able to be home a couple days a month, just as the Army had promised him when he took his assignment. The times that he was home the apartment was filled with the joy and laughter of Ralph and Alex as they played with their papa. Josephine loved the quiet talks her and Karl would share after the children were in bed, or the touching of their hands as they passed by each other throughout the day. These were the things Josephine missed the most when he was away.

The spring air was warm and began to melt the snow and the first spring flowers were already trying to poke up through the white ground. Josephine opened the apartment window to let in some of the fresh spring air, looking down she noticed that there were SS Elite soldiers walking through the park. The soldiers had not been this close to the apartment before and the sight of them made her shudder and caused her to be nervous. She prayed that the SS Elite would not fill the streets of Berlin like they had in Hamburg. She decided to close the window and pull the drapes shut before walking over to check on the boys.

Karl was coming home tonight; he had missed being home on his birthday. Josephine was filled with excitement as she thought about her birthday surprise. She stood with her back pressed against the kitchen sink as she watched her children eating their breakfast. Ralph was getting so big; he was almost six and looked more like his father every day. Alex was a year-and-a-half old with thick white-blond hair he sat in his highchair trying to figure out how to get out of it. Josephine smiled as she thought about how much he looked like her baby picture. She walked over to Alex and said "Alex you can get down when you are done eating your breakfast." Alex began to finish his food.

Josephine began to clear the table; as she picked up Ralph's bowl she looked at him and said, "Tonight your papa will be coming home and I want to make a special supper for his birthday. Would you like you to help me bake a cake?" Ralph got excited, jumped out of his chair and began running around the kitchen with his arms out like an airplane shouting, "Yeah, papa's coming home." Alex watched him and began banging his hands on the highchair tray sending his bowl flying onto the floor as he shouted, "Papa, papa."

Josephine looked at her children with a smile on her face before bending over and cleaning up the cereal off the floor. The boy's joy and laughter filled Josephine with a warm sensation in her chest as she finished cleaning up the mess. Taking Alex out of his highchair Josephine said to her sons, "Go and play for now I will let you know when it is time to make your papa's birthday cake." Ralph took Alex by the hand and led him into the living room to play blocks. Josephine hummed as she cleaned the kitchen and set out the ingredients for the cake. Then she called the boys back into the kitchen to help.

Early that evening as they waited for Karl, Ralph sat and read Alex a story; he loved reading. Alex pointed at the pictures and turned the pages as Ralph read the book. Josephine had prepared Karl's favorite dish for dinner. She was in the kitchen finishing up the dinner when the front door opened and Karl stepped into the apartment closing the door behind him. Ralph put down the book and jumps to his feet, running over to him and Alex toddled behind just learning how to run.

Karl placed the flowers he had brought on the small table next to the door and knelt to scoop up both of sons into his arms. He looked at his children's happy faces and said, "I am happy to see my two boys," and kissed each of them on the cheek. He looked up and saw Josephine wearing her apron and holding a wooden spoon in her hand as she stood watching from the kitchen door way. Karl could not take his eyes off Josephine as he set Ralph and Alex on the floor. He grabbed the flowers from the small table he said, "Let's go and say hello to your mommy."

He walked over to Josephine with the boys trailing close behind. He held out the flowers presenting them to her, she smiled as she took them, then she brought the red roses up to her nose to smell their wonderful fragrance. Josephine looked up into Karl's eyes and at the same time he pulled her into a warm embrace before he bent down and kissed her. Ralph wrapped his arms around both parents to join in the hug. Alex's arms were too small to reach around both parents so he wrapped his arms around one of their legs. They both looked down at their sons and smiled. Josephine quietly said, "They have missed you so much."

Karl took a deep breath and said, "Something smells good, there is nothing better than your home cooked meals." Josephine blushed and said, "Well then I better get the food on the table." Karl bends down and lifts Alex into his arms and follows her into the kitchen placing his youngest son into the highchair. Ralph climbed up in the chair next to his papa as Josephine put the food on the table. The special time around the dinner table was delightful filled with laughter. Josephine looked over at her husband and said, "Did you get enough to eat?" Karl rubbed his stomach then reached across the table taking Josephine's hand and said, "Plenty, thanks for making this wonderful meal."

Ralph pulled on Karl sleeve to get his attention and then asked, "Papa, can you read us a story?" Karl took Ralph's hand in his and said, "I want to help your mother with the dishes first, why don't you play with your brother until then." Josephine stood up and said, "Not yet! I have a surprise for you. I know your birthday was two days ago, but I wanted to celebrate tonight as a family." Karl looked at her with a puzzled look on his face as she walked into the pantry. Ralph beamed as he looked at his father and said, "We got a surprise for you and I helped mommy make it."

When Josephine walked back into the kitchen, she had the birthday cake with one lit candle in the center and a small package tucked up under her arm. Karl stood up and walked over taking the cake from Josephine and gave her a light kiss on the cheek and said, "This is a wonderful surprise." Ralph and Alex both clapped their hands as he sat the cake down in the center of the table. They sang 'Happy Birthday' and Karl blew out the candle. Ralph asked with excitement in his voice as Josephine cut the cake, "Papa do you like the cake I made you?" Karl turned towards his son, patting his hand and said, "I like it very much."

Once everyone had eaten their cake Josephine handed Karl the small gift she had on her lap. Karl reached out and took the gift; the house was quiet as everyone watched him carefully open it. He held up three handkerchiefs each one having an initial from his family sewn on in the corner. Karl had a hard time containing his emotions and tears welled up in his eyes, but he blinked them away before looking up at his wife. He stood up and kissed the top of each boy's head before he went to Josephine and gave her a light kiss on the cheek. Karl cleared his throat, his voice was filled with emotion as he and said, "Thank you, I will carry these handkerchiefs with me everywhere I go." Josephine's was pleased as she stood up embraced and kissed her husband.

Ralph interrupted the moment between his parents by asking, "Papa can I help with the dishes?" Karl smiled down at his son and said, "Not this time son, I need you to play with Alex and when the dishes are done I will read to you, okay?" Ralph got down out of his chair and shook his head 'yes.' Karl lifted Alex out of the highchair and stood him on the floor. Ralph walked over and took Alex by the hand and led him into the living room to play. Josephine put away the cake and smiled as she watched her two young sons leave the kitchen.

Karl cleared the dishes off the table while Josephine filled the sink with water. Karl was helping put the dishes into the sink when Josephine reached over taking Karl's hand and softly said, "I have another surprise for you." She paused before adding, "I found out a few of weeks ago that I am pregnant again." Josephine looked deeply into Karl's eyes studying him, not sure how he would take the news of another child.

Karl stood staring at her for a moment before a huge smile spread across his face. He put his hands around her waist pulling her close; he picked her up and swung her. Setting her back down onto her feet, he kissed her and held her close. Still holding her and looking down into her eyes he said in a deep voice, "I love you and I am happy for us." Josephine relaxed in his arms this is the place where she always felt safe. She stood up on her tiptoes and whispered in his ear, "I love you." Reluctantly they release each other and then they quickly finish the dishes.

Karl walked into the living room and said, "Are my boys ready for a story?" Ralph jumped up and said, "Yes, papa," then he automatically began to put away the blocks. He then went into his bedroom to get some books to be read. Karl picked up Alex and carried him over to the sofa; he sat with him on his lap and Josephine sat down in the chair across from him as they waited for Ralph's return. Ralph came into the living room with his arms filled with every book he had. Josephine sighed and said, "Ralph it is getting late and you will need to pick only one book for your father to read and then it's time for a bath and bed." Ralph set the books on the floor and said, "But mommy." Karl interrupted Ralph, "No buts, you need to listen to your mother."

Ralph sat down on the floor next to the books and slowly looked through them having a hard time picking out just one. He stood and handed his father a book and said, "Okay papa, I found the best one for you to read." Ralph climbed up on the sofa and sat next to his father. Karl read the story and helped Alex turn the pages. In the quietness of listening to Karl's voice rise up and down as he read, there was a calming effect on the two boys. Alex began to suck his thumb and rubbing his eyes before the book was finished. Josephine walked over and took Alex from Karl. She headed towards the bathroom to draw the bath water for the boys. Ralph always had a hard time falling asleep when Karl was home. He knew his father had to leave the next morning so tonight he did not want to go to sleep.

After both boys were safely tucked in, Karl sat on the edge of Ralph's bed and held his hand until Ralph's eyes got heavy with sleep. Karl kissed him on the cheek before meeting Josephine at the bedroom door. Karl and Josephine walked hand in hand to the sofa and sat in each other's arms. Karl turned to Josephine and said, "I love you and I know how hard it will be for you with the two active boys and me being gone so much of the time. I am happy we are having another child. I do hope and pray I will be able to be here again for the birth of our new baby." Karl pulled Josephine close, he did not want to let her go. She snuggled into him and they sat quiet simply enjoying being in each other's arms.

Early the next morning Karl readied himself and now it was time for him to leave. Standing at the door to say goodbye, he knelt and said to Ralph, "Take care of your little brother." Ralph put his arms around father's neck hugging him and said, "I will papa." Alex reached over to give his father a hug and said, "Me papa." Josephine smiled down on the sweet scene and thought how wonderful her husband was with his children. Karl stood and kissed his wife goodbye. There were tears in her eyes as she closed the door and looked down at her sons. Ralph looked up and said, "Mommy, are we sad today?" Josephine tried to smile and said, "Just a little." Then she knelt and gathered her sons into her arms. Both boys began to cry and Josephine let the tears run down her face.

During the times Karl was away from his family he thought often of them, longing to be with them. Being together as a family was all any parent wanted, but with what was happening in Germany at the current time, being together as a family was impossible. Every time he had to leave his family behind, he wished he could stay and his heart was torn knowing that if he did not report back to duty they would come looking for him and that may put his family in harm's way.

There was so many secretes that were kept among the Hitler's SS Elite soldiers. Questions filled the minds of the regular soldiers but none of them would ever dare ask any questions for fear they would disappear, like the others soldiers had. There were now many SS Elite soldiers walking around the streets of the cities with guns strapped over their shoulder. They would stop people at will and ask them questions, if they did not respond the way the SS Elite thought they should the people would be arrested. A chill ran through Karl at these thoughts and concerns filled him for his family's safety while he was away on duty.

Karl and Josephine both began to sense that something was not right within their government and they prayed often for change and protection. Prayer was the only thing they had with the political power that were in control of Germany in 1942. Madness seemed to fill the leaders of the country and their focus seemed to be that they want to control everything and everyone. It was hard to see hope for change; all they could do was put their trust in God. The hearts of the people were filled with fear and sadness settled over the whole country.

Josephine wrote her parents with the news about Berlin and that she was with child again. She knew her parents wanted her and the children to move back home. Josephine missed her parents, but needed to keep her family close to Karl. It took over three weeks for her letter to get to her parents. Fear gripped their hearts and they sent a telegram immediately pleading with Josephine to come back home with the children. Josephine stared at the telegram and had mixed feelings about what she should do. That night after putting the boys to bed she sat on her bed and wrote a long letter back to her parents saying that she understood their concerns, but she needed to be near her husband and refused to leave Berlin.

Karl's leave time went from being able to go home once a month to three month or even more months apart. With the increase of the buildup of weapons Karl had to travel further and further away from home to the factory for inspections. This kept Karl away from his family most of the time and he did not like it. As Karl saw the increase in the stock pile of weapons a fear and concern entered his heart. He was not sure what was going on, but he had served in WWI and he knew something did not look right. Karl's greatest fear was that another war was about to begin.

Karl continued to pray daily that his fears of war would not come to pass and for the protection of his family. He knew he had no choice but to continue doing his job or be arrested. There were many times when he wanted to walk away from the army to take his family and hide them, but there was nowhere to be safe and if they were caught, he would be shot and who knows what would happen to his family, so that idea was impossible.

Most of the men in Germany were now drafted into the military, leaving the cities and towns with women, children and the elderly. The SS Elite soldiers began going door to door asking people for their identification papers and questioning them; some were arrested and taken away. Fear lay heavy on the hearts of the people in Germany. This kind of fear is so deep it causes people to do strange things trying to protect themselves. By the fall of 1942, there were so many SS Elite walking the streets and stopping people at will, most people did not go outside of their homes unless they had to for work or provision.

It was a warm day for October and the apartment felt stuffy. Josephine opened the window and sat on the window seat looking out, the warm sun felt good on her skin. The park and street below seemed quiet with only a couple of SS Elite soldiers walking around. Josephine looked over at her sons wrestling on the floor and decided that she would take them out for a walk in the park.

Josephine was eight-and-a-half months pregnant and trying to keep her six-year old and two-year old sons quiet was difficult and drained her energy. The boys seemed to have so much energy from being cooped up, it made her tired. She thought that taking the boys to the park for a short walk would hopefully release some of their pinned-up energy.

Ralph was excited as he carefully guided the stroller down the flight of stairs; it had been so long since they had gone to the park. Once outside in front of the apartment Josephine put Alex into the stroller, then she instructed Ralph to hold the side of the stroller while they crossed the street. A bird was chirping out a melody at the top of one of the trees and the air smelled fresh as they entered the park. The trees leaves had changed colors and now instead of green they were bright red, orange and yellow. Fall flowers were planted around the trees with their deep purple and red colors. Josephine spoke her thoughts out loud, "What a beautiful day." Ralph looked up at his mother and asked, "Mommy can I let go of the stroller now?" She answered, "Yes, but stay close."

Josephine pushed the stroller down the path enjoying the beauty of nature in the park which was situated right in the middle Berlin. Ralph skipped a little way ahead and sang one of his made-up songs. Alex pointed at a squirrel that scampered across the path in front of them and ran up a tree. There was a sense of peace as she pushed the stroller and watched her little boy skipping just ahead.

Josephine's mind began to wander to Karl and she wished he was here with them as they walked along the park path. She was so lost in thought she did not see the two SS Elite soldiers who were standing just further up the path leaning on a tree and watching as they came towards them. Ralph saw the soldiers first and he immediately stopped skipping, turned and ran back to his mother. Josephine looked and saw the SS Elite soldiers and slowed her pace. Ralph grabbed a hold of the stroller handlers and looked up at his mother with fear in his eyes. Josephine reached down and gently patted him on the head as she softly said, "It's going to be okay, stay close to me." Josephine squared her shoulders and kept walking forward with the determination not to fear.

The SS Elite soldiers watched as the eight-and-a-half-month pregnant woman waddled down the park path pushing a stroller with a small child and a young boy holding onto the stroller. One soldier elbowed the other as they both tried not to laugh at how strange a sight this was. Josephine took a deep breath as she neared the soldiers looking straight ahead not wanted to cause any problems. As she walked by the soldiers they did not move or say anything. Alex even at two-years old was outspoken and did not know about when it was the time and place to speak. He also had no fear nor did he have understood of danger.

Alex was watching the SS Elite soldiers and did not like the way they were looking at his mother. Alex pointed his little finger up at the soldiers and said loudly, "Why you look dumb?" Fear jumped into Josephine's heart at the words of her two-year old. She stopped walking and turned towards the soldiers who were both frowning at her. With a nervous laugh, hoping they would not be too upset, she said as cheerful as she could, "Children say the oddest things!" The soldiers stared at her looking down at her large baby bump for a few seconds before bursting into laughter. She smiled up at them but did not move as she waited to see what was next.

The SS Elite soldiers stopped laughing and with a smile on their faces one of the soldiers said, "Enjoy your day Frau." She gripped tightly the stroller handle and replied, "Thank you." The moment she started to walk forward the tension and stress she was feeling released, but fear still pulled at her heart. The soldiers continue to watch Josephine waddle away until she left the park. It was on this day that the joy of two-year old Alex left and fear entered his heart for the first time as his mother told him not to speak to the SS Elite soldiers again. Josephine did not go to the park again after that.

Chapter 9 A Daughter 1942

Letters from Karl were far between now since the SS Elite were checking all the mail of the regular soldiers, they wanted to make sure the regular soldiers did not know or share what they called classified information. Karl had warned Josephine a few months ago while he was home to only write personnel things and nothing about the government or her feelings about it. He feared every day for his family. He knew the time for the birth of the baby was soon, but still did not have the okay for leave. Karl thought to himself, "Why does everything seem so difficult and why was the SS Elite acting as if the people of Germany who did not do what they were told or spoke against them were their enemy?" Nothing made any sense, the world seemed upside down.

It was late October 1942, and Josephine was two days past her delivery date. She was hoping to hear from Karl, that he was coming home, but it had been over a month since his last letter. She longed for her husband to be there with her and the boys. Many nights she prayed and was unable to sleep knowing the baby would come any day now and Karl might not be there.

Ralph and Alex never asked to go out to play after that day in the park; they were content to play inside. Josephine had befriended an elderly couple in her apartment building. Mr. and Mrs. Groskauf, they were a wonderful couple who loved children, but had none of their own. The couple asked often to have the children come up for a visit. Josephine felt blessed to have such kind people living upstairs. Her prayer had been answered.

Josephine had felt "off" all day, but had energy to get things done. While the children were upstairs visiting, she cleaned and organized the kitchen cupboards. After supper, as she sat on the sofa between Ralph and Alex reading them a story, she felt her first labor contraction. Josephine stopped reading and laid her hand on her stomach. Both boys looked at their mother as she held her stomach and was taking slow deep breaths. Just as she began reading again another contraction came.

Once the contraction subsided Josephine looked at her oldest son and said in a very controlled voice, "Ralph, take your brother's hand we need to go upstairs to see if Mr. and Mrs. Groskauf are at home, I think we are going to have our baby today." Ralph jumped down off the sofa and obeyed by taking Alex's hand. Another contraction and this time Alex started to cry, he did not understand what was happening. Josephine patted him on the top of the head and said, "It is okay, we are going to see Mr. and Mrs. Groskauf. Alex stopped crying as Josephine led the way up the stairs. Josephine had to stop a couple of times with a contraction, holding her stomach and taking in a deep breath, she let out a quiet moan as the contraction got stronger.

Josephine lightly knocked on the door and Mrs. Groskauf asked, "Who is it?" No one answered their door until they knew who was there. She quickly opened the door when she heard Josephine's voice. She took one look at her standing there holding her stomach with her two young children looking wide eyed at her. Mrs. Groskauf called out to her husband, "Erich come quickly. You will need to take Josephine to the hospital." Mrs. Groskauf took Josephine by the arm and led her to the sofa. Mr. Groskauf came with car keys in hand. Alex looked confused when he saw Mr. Groskauf take his mother by the arm and walk her to the door. Alex began to cry and ran towards the door to follow his mother.

Mrs. Groskauf gathered Alex into her arms. Before going out the door Josephine turned to look at her two-year old boy stretching his arms toward her and crying, "Mommy, mommy." Her heart ached with compassion for her son and she said before Mrs. Groskauf closed the door, "Alex, it is going to be okay, I am going to bring you back our baby."

Alex cried harder as the door closed and his mother was gone. Ralph walked over and took Alex's hand to try and comfort him, but there was no comfort, he wanted his mother. Mrs. Groskauf still holding Alex went to the kitchen and found a box of crackers. Once she sat Alex down on the sofa next to his brother she held out a cracker, Alex looked up at her with big tears running down his face took the cracker and stopped crying. Mrs. Groskauf took out her hanky out of her skirt pocket and wiped off his little face. She gave the boys another cracker before she sat down to read them a story.

Baby Renate was born just after midnight without her father being there. Karl was unable to get leave. Josephine finished nursing her new born, pulling her new baby girl close, she looking down at her baby and sighed. Josephine's heart was filled with mixed emotions, the joy of a new baby girl and the sadness of not having Karl with her at the birth of their baby.

The nurse came into the hospital room to take the baby back to the nursery; she looked at the sadness in Josephine's eyes and said, "You need to get some rest before the next feeding." Watching the nurse carry baby Renate from the room a combination of worry and fear settled in on her heart as she thought, "Three children to keep safe until Karl returns." She laid her head back down on the pillow and tried to rest, but her mind was racing and she was unable to go to sleep. Lying there with her eyes closed a single tear slip out of the corner of her eye and ran down the side of her face onto the pillow.

Mrs. Groskauf stayed downstairs in Josephine's apartment with the boys while Josephine was in the hospital. Ralph remembered when Alex was born and knew mother would come home soon with their baby. But Alex being only two could not understand why his mommy did not come home and would cry himself to sleep at night. Mrs. Groskauf tried to comfort him by rocking him and singing to him, but nothing seemed to help. All Alex knew is that he wanted his mommy.

Three days later Mr. Groskauf brought Josephine home from the hospital. Ralph and Alex were building blocks or rather, Ralph was building the blocks and Alex was knocking them over. Both boys heard the front door opened and stopped what they were doing and looked up towards the door. The moment Josephine entered the apartment Alex ran over to her and wrapped his little arms around her leg saying, "Mommy, mommy!" Alex looked up at his mother bursting with joy to have her home, and then he noticed that his mother was holding a soft pink blanket in her arms.

A puzzle looked crossed Alex's face and a frown creased his little forehead. Ralph walked over and wanted to hold the baby, he said, "Mommy I am a big boy now, can I hold our baby?" Josephine looked down at her two sons and said, "Go wash your hands and sit on the sofa and I will bring baby Renate to you and you can hold her on your lap." Ralph turned walking as fast as he could to get ready to hold the baby. Mr. Groskauf standing by the front door with his hat in his hand chuckled as he watched the boys' reaction to baby.

Alex still had his arms wrapped tightly around his mother's leg afraid she would leave again if he let go. Josephine smiled down at Alex, and then she looked over at Mrs. Groskauf and asked. "Would you mind holding the baby?" Mrs. Groskauf replied, "With pleasure," and hurried over to Josephine and took the baby into her arms. Josephine knelt next to Alex taking his small hand in hers and looked in his eyes and said, "Alex you are such a big boy and I will need you to help me with your baby sister."

Josephine picked Alex up into her arms and held him close kissing him on the cheek before she carried Alex over to the sofa and sat him down next to his brother. Josephine walked back over to where both Mr. and Mrs. Groskauf who stood admiring the baby. Josephine thanked them for all their help and gently took baby Renate back into her arms. Mrs. Groskauf said, "No problem my dear, just let us know if you need anything else." Both boys sat watching from the sofa as the Groskaufs turned and left leaving their mother standing by the door with the baby.

Josephine walked over to the sofa and laid baby Renate across Ralph's lap, showing him how to hold the baby's head. Alex sat staring at this new little creature in his brother's arms. Baby Renate stretched and pushed her tiny arms outside of the blanket opening her eyes. Alex looked surprised at the movement of the baby and pointed at the baby's head and said, "Mommy's baby?" Josephine bent down and kissed Alex on the forehead and said, "Yes, Alex this is our baby."

Josephine gently un-wrapped the blanket away from the baby to expose her little legs, feet and toes. Alex moved closer to examine the baby when Renate yawed and stretched her arms over her head again this time she touched Alex's hand. Alex pulled his hand back and giggled and said, "Baby!" Renate began to fuss and cry, she wanted to be fed. Josephine scooped the baby out of Ralph's arms and said, "You can hold her again, but right now she is hungry." Ralph jumped up off the sofa and walked back over to the blocks. Alex looked at his mother and then slid off the sofa and followed his brother over to the blocks; he was content now knowing his mommy was home.

Karl had just gotten back to the base from a three-day inspection trip and a telegram was waiting for him from Mr. Groskauf. He tore open the telegram and read; "Josephine had baby girl today." Karl had to read the telegram twice before he realized he had a baby daughter. As he stared down at the telegram tears watered his eyes and there was a mixture of emotion that flooded him. His emotions went from happiness to having a baby daughter and then to disappointment that he was not there for her birth. A single tear dropped down on the telegram before he folded it up and put it in his pocket.

Karl immediately walked over to his commander's office to show him the telegram and ask for some time off. He stood outside the commander's office door for a moment before knocking. After a couple of minutes, he heard his commander say, "Enter." Karl stood at attention waiting for the commander to speak first. Then he handed the commander the telegram.

The commander was looking down at the telegram when Karl cleared his throat and asked, "Sir, may I have a few days off to be with my wife and children." The commander looked up and handed the telegram back to Karl and then said "Let me think about it. You are excused." Karl turned and headed out the door disappointed that he did not have the answer. Two days passed and still no word from his commander.

Karl was praying on the way back to base from work, he wanted some kind of sign from God that he had heard his prayers. When he got back into the barracks he saw a note lying on his bunk pillow. He flipped opened the note and read, "Karl you are released from duty to see your family, you have four days, beginning tomorrow." He decided that he did not have time to write and let Josephine know of his plans; he would just go home and surprise her. He knew how much Josephine loved surprises; he had already bought her anniversary gift the last time he was in town. A beautiful set of hair combs with a single row of emeralds on them, when he saw them in the store window he had to get them for her. He knew that the green in her eyes would stand out when she wore the combs in her hair.

At three the next morning Karl began his drive toward Berlin to see his family. It was dark and pouring rain as he drove, but not even the rain could dampen his spirit of excitement that was stirring inside him. It has been a week since Renate was born; he still regretted not being there. Karl was looking forward to seeing his beautiful wife, his sons and meeting his new baby daughter. The five-hour drive went by quicker than he thought and the rain never let up. Karl pulled his car up next to the curb by the apartment building. Turning off the car he pulled up his collar around his neck as he got out of the car before grabbing his bag out of the back seat and running up the steps to the apartment building. He wished he would have remembered his umbrella.

The pounding rain sounded hard against the window as Josephine sat on the edge of the bed feeding Renate. She looked down at her sweet baby girl and thought, "Renate is filling out nicely and her cheeks are rosy with color, I wish Karl could see her." Renate stopped eating and fell asleep in Josephine's arms. Josephine got up and laid her baby into the cradle. The boys were quietly playing in the living room with cars as she walked in and said, "Would you like egg pancakes or hot cereal this morning?" Both boys hollered without looking up from their play, "Egg pancakes."

Josephine walked into the kitchen to prepare the egg pancake mixture, she turned on the stove to warm, then she called from the kitchen, "Boys it's time to wash up and come to the kitchen table." Sitting at the kitchen table waiting to eat Alex asked, "Where is baby Renate?" Josephine replied, "She has already eaten and is sleeping."

The pan was hot and Josephine was about to pour the first pancake batter into the skillet when she heard the front door shut. Josephine caught her breath and froze for a moment, and then she quickly took the pan off the stove and turned off the burner before walking out of the kitchen. Both Ralph and Alex got out of their chairs and follow close behind. Karl set down his bag down and headed towards the kitchen. Just as he reached the kitchen door Josephine came bursting through the door and almost ran into him. Karl caught her in his arms as the boys bumped into Josephine legs.

Josephine's face lit up with excitement as she exclaimed, "Karl, what a wonderful surprise!" Both boys were so excited to see their father that they yelled in unison, "Papa!" After kissing Josephine Karl bent down and gave Ralph a hug before picking up Alex to hug him. Josephine said, "Karl, I was just fixing breakfast are you hungry?"

Karl carried Alex as he followed Josephine and Ralph into the kitchen. He sat Alex into his chair and then he walked over and gave her another kiss and said, "Josephine it is so good to be home." She smiled up at him and then pushed him slightly saying, "I'm glad you are home too, now go sit down so I can get our sons fed."

Breakfast was wonderful with Karl home; the family was whole again. The boys couldn't get enough of asking their papa questions. Josephine got up to clear the table just as Renate began to cry. Josephine said, "I guess the little one is hungry too." She left the kitchen to take care of the baby. Karl got up and cleared the table. Alex pointed towards the door as he heard the fussing baby and said, "My Baby." Karl smiled at Alex and said, "Baby Renate." He told the boys stories about the country side he has seen in his travels as he did the dishes; the boys hung on his every word.

Just as Karl finished the dishes and hung the towel to dry, Josephine walked back into the kitchen holding Renate. She walked straight over to him and handed him his daughter. Cradling his little girl in his arms, he looked down at his daughter for the first time. He was captivated by her beautiful little face, a love and emotion stirred deep within him that he had not known before. Tears pooled in Karl's eyes as he lightly kissed his daughter on the nose. Without looking up, his voice cracked with emotion as he said, "Josephine, thank you for being an amazing mother." Renate opened her eyes and looked up into Karl's face for a long moment as he stared down at her. Renate began to cry and Karl quickly handed her back to Josephine.

Karl looked forward all day to the time when he could get Josephine all to himself. Karl had the anniversary gift stuffed deep inside his pocket, even though it wasn't their anniversary yet. He wanted to give it to her now, since he did not know when he would see her again. The boys were bathed and Karl read them a story while Josephine fed the baby. The plan was to meet in the living room when they were done.

Karl arrived into the living room first. He reached his hand into his pocket and felt the tissue paper that the combs were wrapped in, thinking about how happy Josephine would be when she saw them. Josephine walked up behind him and put her arms around his waist laying her head against his back and said, "I have waited all day to have you all to myself."

Karl turned, took her into his arms and gave her a passionate kiss. Then he reached into his pocket and pulled out the gift. Josephine stepped back and said, "What's this?" He held it out to her and said, "It is an early anniversary gift." Josephine took the gift and slowly un-wrapped the tissue paper. She gasped when she saw the beautiful combs, the emeralds reflecting in the soft lamp light.

Josephine looked up at Karl and said, "Karl these are so beautiful, thank you." He looked lovingly into her eyes and said, "Let me see how they look in your hair." She pulled her hair up and placed a comb on each side of her hair. Karl watched and smiled and said to himself, "The green emeralds make Josephine's eyes a deeper green." Taking her into his arms he kissed her.

The two days that Karl was home flew by. Both Karl and Josephine enjoyed their peaceful little world of being together as a family, without a thought for what the next days would hold. The children loved having their papa home. Josephine knew in her heart what it was like without Karl there, being a single mother while her husband was off doing his duty, but she did not want to think about it now. Karl did not want to think about being away from his family, he just wanted to enjoy every moment they were together.

The morning Karl had to leave was here and everyone was gathered at the front door to say goodbye. Karl stood at the door with his small bag by his feet. He looked down at his two sons and Josephine standing there holding their daughter. A pain pressed into his heart like a knife at the thought of leaving them. Alex ran over to his father and wrapped his arms around his leg and began to cry, "No papa, don't go." Emotion filled Karl as he bent down and picked Alex up into his arms. Tears glistened in both Karl and Josephine's eyes and their hearts were overwhelmed with sadness as they looked at their two-year old son clinging to his father's neck. They both knew they had no choice and perhaps one day their son would understand.

Karl pulled Alex closer and held him for a long moment until he began to calm down his crying. Then Karl moved Alex away and said, "Alex, you are a big boy now, I need you to stay here and be brave and help your mother take care of baby Renate." Alex sniffed and wiped his eyes with his sleeve as tried to be as brave as a two-year old could be shaking his little head 'yes.'

Karl kissed Alex's chubby cheek and set him down next to Ralph. Karl bent down giving Ralph a hug and said, "I am proud of you son. Make sure you watch out for your little brother." Ralph did not answer instead wrapped his arms around his father's neck. Karl kissed his cheek and then stood up to say goodbye to his wife and baby daughter. He stepped over to her and kissed his little daughter on the cheek. After giving Josephine a long goodbye kiss, Karl turned, picked up his bag and went out the door.

Silence fell on the room as the three of them stood staring at the closed door. It was Renate's hunger cry that caused them to move away from the door and begin their day without Karl. Josephine said, "I need to feed Renate, when I am done would you boys like me to read you a story?" Both Ralph and Alex shook their heads 'yes' at the same time. Josephine carried Renate out of the room to feed her. Ralph took Alex by the hand and led him over to the small box of cars. He took the box of cars down off the book shelf and they quietly played with the cars until Josephine returned.

Chapter 10 Hard Times 1943

The winter was bitter cold with below zero temperatures. The wind blew the snow into high snow drifts around the buildings. Not only did the weather make Berlin cold but the increasing presence of the SS Elite soldiers filled the air with anxiety and fear. It had been over two months since a letter had arrived from Karl. Josephine checked the mail every day and found no letter from him, but today there was a letter from her parents begging her to come home. After reading her parents letter she laid it on her lap and thought about going home and being with her family. Then she thought about Karl, what if he needed to come home, she would be too far away for him. Sadness filled Josephine's heart as she struggled with this dilemma.

Each day that Josephine opened her mailbox she had an expectant heart that a letter from Karl would be there, only to be disappointed. With each passing day, she worried about her husband's safety. One of the young mothers in the upstairs apartment got word last week that her husband was found dead behind the barracks where he was stationed with no explanation. Karl had told Josephine when he was home what happens to any soldiers who questioned the SS Elite. Without word from him and not knowing if he was safe, a deep fear built up in her heart. This fear left a chill that penetrated to the depth of her soul. Only a word from her husband could warm her.

Josephine had not gone out much this winter due to weather and because the SS Elite soldiers had stopped and questioned her about Karl the last time she was out to get food. Josephine gave the soldiers very little information because Renate was crying the whole time they were talking. The shorter SS Elite soldier looked at Josephine with compassion and said, "Let her go and get her children out of this cold." Josephine thanked him and quickly walked home. After that experience, she asked Mr. Groskauf to pick up food or have Mrs. Groskauf watch the children while she went out shopping with Mr. Groskauf.

Last month when Josephine was out shopping with Mr. Groskauf she purchased some fabric and thread to make the children their Christmas gifts. Standing at the counter of the Taylor shop ready to purchase some fabric two SS Elite soldiers rushed into the store and went directly over to the owner. One soldier arrested him and the other one pointed his gun at the customers and told them to leave the store immediately. Mr. Groskauf took Josephine by the arm and led her quickly out of the store and straight home. She couldn't believe that the SS Elite would walk right in and arrest someone for no apparent reason. Anger and a deep-seated fear arose in her, she wanted to speak her mind about it on the way home, but chose to keep these thoughts to herself not wanting them to be overheard and put her children at risk.

With only three weeks left until Christmas Eve, Josephine sewed the gifts for the children every night after they were in bed. She was making each child a pillowcase and a handkerchief. She had no sewing machine so everything was hand stitched. Josephine worried she would not get the gifts done in time, so she sewed late into the night, even though she was exhausted when she laid her head on her pillow each night. But when she looked at the gifts she was making she thought it was all worth it. She set her alarm clock each night so she could prepare for her day before the children woke in the morning.

Christmas Eve morning, the snow had fallen hard overnight and everything was covered in white. Josephine stood looked out the window wishing Karl was there; she turned away from the window as she heard the laughter of her children. She watched the boys play with their one-year-old sister and a smile spread across her face. Her thoughts went to Karl and all he had missed since he was last home. Karl missed last Christmas and his daughter's first birthday. An aching came to her heart as she longed for him. She left the children playing and walked to the kitchen; tears filled her eyes as she washed the dishes and her tears spilled into the dish water.

Josephine had just finished the dishes and wiped her hands before wiping away her tears. Renate toddled into the kitchen holding Alex's hand. She had just learned how to say mama and as soon as she saw Josephine she reached her free arm toward her mother and said, "Mama." Josephine walked over and picked up her baby girl and thanked Alex for helping her into the kitchen. Alex looked up longingly at his mother and said, "Can I have a hug too." Josephine knelt on the floor with Renate in her arms and pulled Alex into a group hug.

It had been so long since Karl had been home. Josephine and the children never stopped missing him. The children would ask almost every day "When is papa coming home?" Late afternoon on Christmas Eve, Mr. Groskauf had stopped by with a very small Christmas tree. Alex was so excited to see the tree he hurried over to help Mr. Groskauf set the tree by the window. "Alex, you are getting to be such a big boy," Mr. Groskauf remarked as he adjusted the tree in front of the window. Ralph stepped over to the closet and took out the small box of Christmas ornaments; he carried them over to the tree. Ralph held the box of ornaments and waited while Josephine walked Mr. Groskauf to the front door and said, "Thank you, Mr. Groskauf for all your kindness and Merry Christmas."

Josephine closed the door and turned toward the children when she heard Alex say, "No, Renate we have to wait for mommy." Josephine walked over to the small tree and they began to decorate it with the twelve ornaments. Ralph asked if he could put the star on the top the tree. Alex looked in the box and said, "Mommy where are the candles?" Josephine picks up Renate who was trying to take the ornaments back off the tree and said, "Alex, we don't have any candles this year, but we can move the lamp by the tree and it will give the tree light."

That satisfied Alex as he watched Ralph turn and walk over to the lamp. Ralph put his hand on the lamp and asked, "Can I move the lamp by the tree?" Josephine walked over and helped him move the lamp next to the tree. The tree was small enough that the floor lamp stood above it and shone down filling the whole tree with light.

Josephine had prepared a light supper for the children and while they were eating, she left the kitchen and placed the wrapped gifts under the tree. Josephine came back into the kitchen just as the children were finishing eating. Both Ralph and Alex were excited and looked up at their mother; Ralph asked, "When will the Christ Child come?" Josephine took a clean cloth and wiped the children's hands and said, "Shall we go and see if the Christ Child has come and left any gifts?"

Alex was the first one out of his chair; he tiptoed out of the kitchen with Ralph following close behind. By the time Josephine took Renate out of the high chair, both Ralph and Alex ran back into the kitchen yelling, "We got presents!" Josephine carried Renate and let the boys lead the way back into the living room. She quietly said, "Sit down next to the tree and I will read you the Christmas story first and then we will open our gifts." The boys sat down by the tree as close to the gifts as they could get, but Renate wanted to sit on Josephine's lap as she read the story.

After the Christmas story Josephine sat down the book and asked Ralph to hand out the gifts. She watched as each one of her children faces filled with delight as they opened their gifts. She knew in her heart that the gifts would not satisfy their longing for their father. Once all the gifts were open, Ralph looked at her and said, "Where are yours and papa's gifts?"

Josephine looked at her eldest son and said, "We didn't want a gift this year." Alex looked up at her with expectancy in his eyes and asked, "Will papa come home tonight?" Josephine sat baby Renate next to Ralph and took Alex into her lap, pulling him into a hug, then she quietly whispered, "Son, I don't think he is coming tonight." Tears filled Alex's eyes and he began to cry, then Renate began to cry in unison. Josephine sat Alex on one knee and Renate on the other as she gently rocked her two youngest children. Ralph snuggled up next to Josephine and tears were running down his cheeks but he did not make a sound.

Josephine sat there holding and rocking her children trying to blink away the tears that threatened to fall. Alex stopped crying and reached up his little hand to touched Josephine's face. She smiled down at her three-year old and gently kissed him on the cheek. She moved Alex off her lap and sat him next to her because Renate continued to fuss. Josephine held her baby girl up to her shoulder and bounced her slightly up and down when out came a big burp, both boys giggled.

Renate finally stopped fussing and laid her head down on mother's shoulder and was still. They all sat there in the quiet starring at the small Christmas tree each in their own thoughts. Josephine began to sing the Christmas carol Silent Night. A sense of peace filled all of them; Alex laid his head upon Josephine's lap and Ralph leaned on her shoulder. When the song was done, Renate was fast asleep.

New Year's 1943 came with lots more snow and a cold wind became harder, winter looked like it was here to stay. There still was no word from Karl not even a letter. Josephine was very worried about him and nervous at the same time. The same sense of dread that filled all the hearts of the people in Germany gripped at Josephine heart. Her thoughts continuously were, "Wherever Karl is, I pray God is keeping him safe." She knew she had to be strong for her three small children and her number one priority was to provide for them and make sure they were safe.

Josephine did not want her children to worry about their father so she would tell them stories from the Bible, about brave men who fought lions and did many other mighty feats. At the end of every story she would add, "Your papa is a very brave man like these men in the Bible and he needs to be away right now to help other people." Ralph would always smile and say, "I want to be brave just like papa." The thought that their father was a brave hero gave the boys a sense of peace.

During 1943, the times were very hard on the German people, not only because the winter was bitter cold, but a depression had set in and it became harder and harder for people to find work. Day and night there were raids on people's homes and businesses from the SS Elite and gripping fear set deep into the hearts of all the German people. Heaviness hung over the city of Berlin and in Josephine heart like a dark curtain.

The monthly allotment money from the army had stopped coming a month ago. Josephine was thankful for the sewing skill she had from her childhood. She began to take in sewing project for neighbors that she would barter in exchange for food and supplies. It was not safe to go outside since the streets were flooded with the SS Elite. It seemed like an eternity since she had gotten a letter from Karl, she prayed she would hear something, anything, soon. Late at night after the children were in bed she would read Karl's old letters over again to help her fall asleep. His letters gave her the strength to carry on alone in this crazy world.

A few months ago, Josephine met a wonderful neighbor lady named Helga. She lived downstairs and seemed like she was an angel sent to watch over her and the children. Helga was always there to give a helping hand with the children. The boys loved Helga and they called her Auntie. When the boys were filled with too much energy, they begged to go out and play in the snow, but they were unable to go outside and became restless.

When Josephine needed to work on a sewing project she would say, "Ralph and Alex would you like to go and visit Auntie Helga?" Both boys began to jump up and down and shake their heads yes. Josephine instructed Ralph to watch Alex and Renate while she ran downstairs to see if Helga could watch the children for a couple of hours. Helga was unable to bear her own children and loved the children as if they were her own. Having them in her home filled her with joy. The boys were excited to go see Auntie; she always gave them something to eat and played games with them.

Josephine went out the door to go downstairs. Ralph sat on the sofa with Renate on his lap and Alex sat next to him as they watched the door and waited for their mother's return. The door opened and Alex jumped off the sofa and ran over to Josephine and said, "Play with Auntie?" She replied, "Yes, Auntie is home and wants you to come and play." Alex would be so excited to go downstairs he started down the stairs ahead of the rest of them. Alex loved his Auntie, she would read stories and play make believe games.

The children spending time with Helga not only gave Josephine time to sew but gave the children a different environment to play in. The moment Alex got to Auntie's apartment, he gave her a big hug and said, "I come and play today." Helga lifted Alex up and gave him a big hug before taking Renate from Josephine's arms. Being with Auntie made Alex feel special and happy, it was a place where he could forget about missing his papa.

It was the end of March and the snow had finally stopped falling. The air had warmed up just enough to begin to melt the snow and the sun on the snow made everything brighter. Josephine stood looking out the window, she was thankful that winter was over. It had been so long since Karl had been home that the children did not ask about their father very often. By the middle of April, the snow had disappeared from the ground and the ground had begun to show hints of spring colors. Spring always seemed to mean new beginnings and Josephine hoped that this spring would bring a new beginning and bring Karl home.

Josephine continued to check the mail box every day in hopes of finding a letter from Karl. The mail box was down at the bottom of the apartment building stairs. Before going downstairs to check the mail Josephine sat the children on the sofa and told them to stay there until she got back. Ralph sat holding Renate on his lap and Alex sat next to him as they watched their mother go out the door. It was hard for Alex to sit still and wait for his mother to come back, but he knew if he got up before his mother returned he would not be able to play and be sent to sit on his bed for a while instead.

Josephine took a deep breath as she slowly opened the mailbox door. There among all the propaganda from the government was a letter from Karl. She tossed the propaganda in the trash bin that sat next to the door and hurried back up the stairs. Alex jumped up from the sofa when he saw his mother enter the apartment and looked at her wondering why she was pressing a letter to her chest. Alex was not happy when she picked him up and sat him back down on the sofa next to Ralph. Alex began to protest, but when he saw the look in his mother's eyes he stopped. Renate had fallen asleep in Ralph's arms; Josephine sat down next to Alex and looked over at her sleeping baby. Ralph looked up at his mother and said, "Mommy is that a letter from papa?" Josephine shook her head yes; she could not speak for she was too choked up with emotion.

Josephine took in a long deep breath and then slowly opened the letter. She read the letter to herself first; while the children waited patiently looking up at their mother hoping to hear that their papa was coming home. Once Josephine finished reading the letter she pressed it to her heart and tears filled eyes as she softly said to Ralph and Alex, "Papa is okay, but he cannot come home right now." Alex folded his arms across his chest and began to cry as he shouted, "No, I want my papa to come home now." Alex's cries woke up Renate and she also began to cry. Josephine pulled him into a hug and held him until he stopped crying. Then she reached over and ran her finger along the side Ralph's cheek and said, "Ralph, I know you want your papa to come home and I am sorry, I also want your papa to come home."

Alex found so much comfort when he was wrapped in his mother's embrace. Josephine took Renate from Ralph and said, "I need to change and feed her." Ralph reached over and took Alex by the hand and said, "Alex would you like me to read you a story?" Josephine thought to herself how brave her oldest child was. After changing Renate, she sat on the edge of the bed to breastfeed her baby girl. Each time Josephine would hold her baby daughter in her arms her thoughts would wonder and a longing came over her for Karl, the thoughts of her beloved husband. She would worry if he was safe, and wishing he was home. A faraway look came into her eyes as she remembered the happy times.

A single tear ran down her cheek as she looked down at her sweet daughter and she thought, "This little one doesn't even know her papa.'" More tears began to sting her eyes, but she quickly blinked to make the tears go away. Josephine needed to be strong for she did not want her sons to see just how sad she was, they had enough sadness with their papa being gone. After burping Renate, she carried her sweet baby back out into the living room to check on the boys. Ralph was reading softly to Alex who had his head laid on Ralph shoulder and was fast asleep.

Since the last letter from Karl there had been no word, it was already late June and nothing. Worry filled Josephine's heart with each passing day that she did not hear from Karl. Each night after putting the children to bed Josephine would re-read Karl's love letters. After reading the letters Josephine would pray for her husband and many nights she would cry herself to sleep.

Ralph and Alex were young enough that they did not understand where their papa was or why he was not coming home. In order help her young children remember their father; Josephine would take Karl's picture down off the shelf and call the children to what she called, "Papa story time." Josephine sat on the sofa holding Renate on her lap with the boys gathered around her. She always began her story with a Bible hero and then talked about their papa and how much he loved them. Alex always was the one who wanted to hold his papa's picture during the story time; it was during these story times Alex felt the most comforted.

When Alex felt sad he would pull on his mother's dress and say, "Papa story time." Josephine always stopped what she was doing and took down Karl's picture. Then she would gather her children on the sofa and tell them stories of their papa. She always began the stories with, "Your papa is a very brave man and he must do his job until it is time for him to come home." She ended the story time with, "We need to be brave like papa and the men in the Bible story until papa comes home." While Josephine told the story Renate's small chubby hand patted her papa's picture.

After a while the papa stories did not comfort Alex. He was only a little over three but his big blue eyes were filled with sadness and he was angry and fought with his brother. Alex stopped asking for the papa story. One evening while Josephine was telling the papa story Alex pushed his papa's picture away and said in an angry voice mixed with emotion, "I want to see papa now not a picture!"

The words of her son pierced Josephine's heart and caused tears to sting her eyes. Josephine put down the picture and sat Renate on Ralph's lap before picking up Alex and pulling into a firm hug. She began singing hymns to the children. Ralph laid his head on his mother's shoulder and Renate sucked her thumb while she laid her little head on Ralph. Alex loved it when his mommy sang; she had a beautiful voice that filled his heart with peace. Alex pressed his head into Josephine's chest as he too listened to his mommy's heart beat and the melody of her voice. Josephine could feel Alex relax in her arms and she was thankful that she could calm her children with singing.

Chapter 11 Great Fear 1944

Fall of 1943, fear covered the people of Germany like a heavy blanket suffocating them; no one felt safe. More and more people were being arrested, women, children and even the elderly. The SS Elite soldiers put the people in a big truck. The truck sat in the street as the SS Elite went door to door and dragging people to the truck, once the truck was full of people they got in and drove away. As the truck pulled away the sound of women screaming and children crying could be heard and continued as the truck moved down the street. Alex ran to his mother and said, "Mommy, the noise hurts my ears." Renate always begin to cry. Josephine knew her children were frightened, so she would pull them close to her on the sofa and she would begin to sing, they listened to their mothers sweet voice singing out hymns until peace came back into their home.

The SS Elite pounded on doors any time day or night, they wanted to catch people by surprise. If the door did not open as quickly as they thought, they would break down the door, entering the home with their guns pulled. The people cowered and trembled as the SS Elite soldiers demanded their papers and searched their homes. Nobody knew exactly what they were looking for.

The first time the SS Elite soldiers began pounding on Josephine's door the children all began to cry at the same time. She quickly opened the door wide for them. She picked up Renate as she handed a SS Elite soldier her papers. They walked throughout her home looking through things. After examining her papers, they handed them back to her before leaving without a word. It took her over an hour to comfort and calm her crying children.

After that Josephine devised a plan to soften the fear her children felt during an SS Elite raid. She explained her plan to Alex and Ralph saying, "We are going to play a game of hide-and-seek the next time we hear pounding on the door okay?" Alex loved new games and shook his head in agreement. Ralph had a puzzled look on his face as he looked up at his mother. The game went like this, every time they heard a pounding on the front door Ralph would take Alex and Renate into the closet to hide while Josephine answered the door. After the soldiers left she would come and get them. Josephine practiced with the children until she knew they fully understood her plan.

Josephine also had a strict rule that no one was to pull back the drapes and look out the window. One day Ralph was so curious about the noise outside while Josephine was in the kitchen preparing dinner He looked around and then walked slowly over to the window. He split the drapes and put his head through so he could see outside. His eyes widened as he saw the SS Elite dragging people and putting them into the big truck; he quickly shut the drapes.

He bumped into Alex who was standing behind him as he turned from the window. Alex asked, "Ralph can I see?" Ralph sternly said, "NO!" Alex turned towards the kitchen and said to his big brother, I am going to ask mommy if I can look out the window. Ralph sighed grabbing his brother by the arm and said, "We can't tell mommy, here take a quick peep. He pulled back the drapes so Alex could look out the window for a moment, then he pulled him back and shut the drapes.

Alex looked up at his brother and said, "Do you think those men will take us away too?" Ralph drew him into a hug; Alex closed his eyes as his big brother held him and comforted him. Then Ralph let him go and said, "Come on I will read you a story and then we will play." He took Alex by the hand and led him to the sofa. He began to read Alex's favorite book to him in hopes that he would forget about the window.

A couple of days later while Alex and Ralph were playing cars and Renate sat next to them playing with the blocks, someone began pounding on the front door. They had practiced the drill so many times that Ralph knew what to do, he quickly picked up Renate and with Alex following close behind he led the way to the closet to hide. Ralph sat with Renate on his lap who began to suck her thumb and Alex was leaning into his side as they sat there in the dark. Alex blinked his eyes as he tried to adjust them to the darkness in the closet.

Josephine looked to make sure the children were in the closet before she opened the door. Two SS Elite soldiers stood with their guns drawn as they peered down at her, she said, "Can I help you?" A gruff voice answered, "Move aside, we need to search your home." They pushed into the house before Josephine could step aside. She said, "No problem come in, my children are frightened and are in the closet." The older heavier SS Elite soldier said, "Your papers." Josephine took the papers off the small table that stood next to the door and handed them to him.

Ralph and Alex could hear things being turned over and spilled out onto the floor as they sat in the closet trying to be very still. The younger SS soldier after throwing things around the room walked over and opened the closet door. He stared down at the three wide eyed children looking up at him; suddenly Renate began to cry. He quickly turned and shut the closet door. Once the closet door closed Renate stopped crying and she began to suck her thumb again. He walked back over to the older SS soldier who was still looking through Josephine's papers. The younger one said, "Nothing here, let's go." Handing Josephine back her papers and slamming the door behind them as they went out. The loud slamming of the door caused Renate to begin to cry again. Josephine let out a big sigh as she walked over to the closet to let her children know it was safe for them to come out.

Josephine slowly opens the closet door and says, "It is safe now, you may come out." She took Renate from Ralph's arms and held her close trying to comfort her. Alex and Ralph crawled slowly out of the closet; they looked around the room with big sad eyes at the mess that was all over the room. Fear struck them both as they thought the SS Elite might come back.

As small children Alex and Ralph did not understand what was happening. All they knew was fear each time they saw or heard the SS Elite soldier. Alex looked up at his mother and said, "Mommy, the bad men made baby Renate cry." Josephine reached down and took his little hand and then they all sat down in the middle of the mess that was left behind. Josephine heart was still beating fast from the encounter with the SS Elite, but she knew she could not allow her fear to show.

Josephine wished she could remove the fear in her children hearts; the only way she knew to calm her precious children was to sing to them. Singings always seem to comfort and quiet her children's fears. With Renate on her lap, one arm around Alex and the other around Ralph she pulled them to her side and gently rocked back and forth holding her children close. Josephine closed her eyes and began to sing; as she sang a sense of peace began to fill the room and encircle their hearts. Once Josephine knew all was well with her children, she told Alex to play with Renate while Ralph helped her clean up the mess.

Both Alex and Renate had nightmares that night. Many nights Alex would wake to the sound of his mother crying. His little heart filled with sadness at the sound and he became afraid. He did not understand why his mother would cry. He reached over and shook Ralph to wake him. Once Ralph was awake he asked, "Why is Mommy crying?" Ralph just wrapped his arm around Alex and pull him close before answering, "It's going to be alright, mommy will be all better in the morning." Alex felt safe in his big brother's arm and he fell back to sleep.

Ralph was a great big brother who always watched out for his little brother and sister. He thought since his father was not there, he had to protect his younger siblings and help his mother; it was his duty. Ralph was only four years older than Alex and at seven years-old he felt more like an adult than a child. Alex always looked up to his big brother. He thought Ralph was so smart because he knew how to read. He thought to himself, "I want to be brave like Ralph and papa when I grow up." Alex followed Ralph everywhere he went and Ralph did not mind being with his little brother.

When Ralph wanted to visit his friend Frank, who lived in an apartment upstairs, Josephine allowed Alex to tag along. Renate wanted to go too, but since she was only a year-and-a-half old she could not go. Her three-and-a-half-year-old brother Alex pointed his finger at her and said, "No Renate, you are too little." As the boys headed for the door, Renate began to cry and tried to follow them. Josephine reached down and picked up her baby, holding her close as she said, "It's okay baby girl we can go and visit Auntie." The promise to visit Auntie always stopped Renate's flow of tears.

While Ralph and Alex visited Frank upstairs they played hide-and-seek. Alex didn't know how to count correctly yet, so when it was his turn to count Ralph instructed him to keep his face in the corner until they yelled for him to come and find them. Alex had a hard time waiting in the corner facing the wall so he would look turn his head and look around the room. While he waited, he bent down and sat on the floor. One time he found a spider and played with it until he heard his brother's voice yell, "Ready!" Alex wandered around the apartment looking everywhere for Ralph and Frank, but he couldn't find them.

When Alex looked for awhile and couldn't find Ralph and Frank he got afraid and became mad. Alex thought maybe Ralph had left him like papa and he began to cry. Once Ralph heard Alex crying he came out of hiding to find him. Frank stood looking at him cry and then he bent over laughing at Alex and calling him a baby. Ralph gave Frank a disapproving look that made Frank stop laughing. Then Ralph wrapped his arms around Alex giving him a hug of comfort and said, "Alex don't be afraid, we are just playing a game, like the closet game." Then Ralph grabbed Alex by the hand and said, "It's Frank's turn, come on let's go and hide."

It was a hot summer afternoon; Ralph, Frank and Alex were playing with toys at Frank's apartment. Frank's mother and grandfather were sitting in the living room reading. Frank's grandfather had just fallen asleep with his book laying on his lap and snoring slightly. The peacefulness of the afternoon was ripped away by a loud pounding on the front door. The book fell from Frank's grandfather's lap as he jumped awake. Everyone froze at the sound and fear cut through their hearts like a knife.

Franks mother told the boys to go and hide. Ralph grabbed Alex by the hand and began to run for the back of the house as he said, "Alex we are going to play hide-and-seek now." Alex followed his brother as Ralph pulled him to the back bedroom to hide. Frank stood and stared at his mother before leaving the living room. Then the pounding got louder and a man's voice shouting on the other side of the door, "If you don't let us in now, we will break down the door!"

Frank's grandfather immediately opened the door as the SS Elite pushed in. When the door opened, they rushed into the room with a loud noise and began shouting at Frank's mother and grandfather. Ralph and Alex hid up in a closet cupboard that overlooked the bedroom, but there was no room for Frank to hide with them. Frank looked around the room and chose to hide behind the bedroom door. Ralph and Alex could see Frank through the crack in the curtains that hung over the closet cupboard where they were quietly hiding.

They could hear Frank's mother screaming and crying, "No, please leave us alone." Tension rose in all the boys as they heard footsteps coming closer to the bedroom where they were hiding. Frank's mother cried even harder and she screamed, "No, please leave us alone." An SS soldier slapped her and said, "Shut up women." Two SS soldiers entered the bedroom to search and make sure no one else was in the house. Ralph and Alex's eyes grew big as they watched the soldiers look under the bed and then they turned to walk over to the closet. One of them stopped, he had spotted Frank hiding behind the door. He pointed towards the door and said, "There's the child." Ralph put his hand over Alex's month so that he would be quiet. Alex wanted to cry out but Ralph pressed tighter on his mouth and he did not make a sound.

Alex and Ralph watched as one of the SS soldiers pick up Frank and threw him over his shoulder like a sack of grain. Frank was kicking and crying as the SS soldiers carried him out of the bedroom. Then Frank screamed, "No, leave my mother alone!" Frank's mother cried, "Please don't hurt my son." There was another sound of someone being hit and then the only sound was the soft whimpering of Frank as they forced Frank and his family from the apartment. Ralph continued to hold his hand firmly over his little brother's mouth as fear pressed in on them. Alex looked over at his big brother and saw fear in Ralph's eyes, Alex resolved to not move. As they lay hiding in the closet, the fear was overwhelming for both boys. Tears filled both their eyes and ran down their cheeks. A big part of their child innocence was robbed from them that day.

Ralph continued to hold his hand over Alex's mouth as they remained quiet in the closet up on the closet shelf. The tears were gone now only fear remained as they waited silently in their hiding place; the only sound was the fast beating of their hearts. Ralph thought that the soldiers would come back for them at any moment. It was quiet in Frank's apartment for a long time before Ralph finally took his hand from Alex's mouth and at the same time he held his finger to his lips to signal that Alex still needed to be quiet. The fear had caused Alex to wet himself and he didn't want Ralph to know, but he was so close to his brother that his pant leg was wet also. Ralph looked at his little brother and just shook his head that he understood. Alex looked over at Ralph and saw tear streaks down his brother's cheeks. He reached over and took his brothers hand. Ralph smiled at him in a silent thank you. They continued to wait in the stillness Ralph wanted to make sure it was safe before they left the closet.

Then Ralph remembered that their mother always prayed and sang when they were afraid. Ralph whispered a prayer, "Lord, keep mommy and Renate safe." Alex leaned his head on Ralph's shoulder as his brother hummed softly one of their mother's favorite hymns. Once he finished the hymn he looked over at Alex and whispered, "I think it is safe now, we need to go home." Ralph helped Alex down from the closet shelf and slowly led the way to the front door. Alex looked around and noticed that the house was a mess with things turned upside down and thrown everywhere. The front door was left wide open. As they stepped out of the apartment into the hall there was a strange eerie quietness that filled the apartment building. Both boys held the rail as they walked very slowly and quietly down the stairs to their apartment.

Josephine heard all the noise of the SS Elite banging on doors and quickly picked Renate up and held her close. Panic began to rise in Josephine's heart as she paced the floor with Renate and praying out loud for her sons. She stopped praying and froze at the sound of a loud commotion that was filled with screams and cries in the apartment building halls. Then a deafening silence as the SS truck pulled away. Tears began to roll down Josephine's face at the thought of her sons being taken away. Fear gripped her heart so strong she could barely breathe and it brought her to her knees. Renate began to cry as Josephine knelt there praying. To calm Renate's cries she began rocking her baby and singing softly in her ear to comfort her. Soon Renate fell asleep on her mother's shoulder. The only sound now was the clock on the mantle ticking, each tick sounded like loud gongs in her ears.

Josephine knelt there quietly praying and rocking her sleeping baby, she stopped and held her breathe to listen; she thought she heard a noise. There it was again, a light tapping on the stairs as someone was coming down the apartment hall stairwell. Then there was a very quiet sound at the apartment door. Josephine starred at the door as she heard the key move in the lock. Then the door knob turned and the door slowly opened to reveal her two sons standing there looking at her. Tears welled up in Josephine's eyes at the sight of her two sons. She got up and laid Renate down on the sofa before she ran to Alex and Ralph and quickly closed and locked the door before pulled her sons to her. They all clung together and cried releasing the built-up anxiety.

Alex in a soft hick-up said, "Mommy those bad man took Frank away and hurt his mommy." Josephine pulled her sons closer as Ralph told her how Frank's mother told them to hide. They saw the SS soldiers with guns come into the bedroom where they were hiding and take Frank away. New tears brimmed in Ralph's eyes, he tried to be brave; he told how he prayed as they hid in the closet waiting. Josephine wrapped her arms even tighter around her sons and fresh tears fell down her face as she whispered, "You both were so brave and now you are safe."

Alex had nightmares almost every night after that day. He dreamt that the SS soldiers came and threw him over their shoulders carrying him away. Alex would cry out in his sleep, Ralph would wrap his arm around his little brother to help comfort him. Alex would not be comforted or go back to sleep until they got up and walked to their mother's room to make sure their baby and mommy was safe. Ralph got out of bed and took Alex by the hand as they peeked in to make sure Renate and mommy were still there. As soon as they entered the room Josephine would get up out of bed and pick up Alex and say, "Everyone is okay, you are safe. Go back to bed." Alex looked around the room to make sure no SS soldiers were there before he looked at his mother and shook his head in agreement. Josephine carried Alex back to bed and sat on the edge of the bed until he fell back asleep.

Josephine went back to her room and checked on Renate before lying on her bed exhausted and thinking about Karl. She wished Karl would come home and that her children did not have to see the evil of this world. "Lord," she prayed, "Keep my children's hearts and minds safe from the terror that the SS Elite are causing. Please be with Karl and bring him safely home." Josephine drifted off to sleep as she continued to pray.

Chapter 12 Bombs 1944

Summer quickly turned into fall and the trees began to turn colors. The beauty of fall colors was over shadowed by the presence of the SS Elite soldiers. The SS Elite made a new law, which stated that anyone who was a Jew had to wear an arm bands with a star on it to identify them as Jews. Josephine's elderly friend Mr. Schawk stopped by wearing one of these arm bands.

Mr. Schawk warned Josephine to be careful and if she needed anything please let him know. Josephine looked at Mr. Schawk's arm band and asked, "What does all this mean?" Mr. Schawk did not answer; he just gave her a hug and then turned with his cane and walked out the door. Josephine stared at the closed door and wondered why this was happening, none of it made any sense. Renate began to cry and Josephine turned her attention back to her children.

Fall seemed short as another cold winter came in early November. Winter had set in with a heavy snow fall that blanketed the city of Berlin. The cold wind blew against the window and froze the window panes. Josephine turned up the heat to help keep the apartment warm but the winter seemed to come through the walls. She continued to check the mail every day, but there was still no word from Karl.

It had been over six months without a letter. Josephine tried not to worry, but worry pressed on her heart until sometimes she felt she couldn't breathe. The days seemed long and she tried to be cheerful for her children's sake, but at night she felt so alone with no one to comfort her fears. She often cried herself to sleep.

Josephine prayed that Karl would be able to come home this Christmas; it would make the children happy. There was no money for gifts this year. She wished she could give her children something to distract them from missing their papa and the fear of the SS Elite raids. She spent an evening the first of December sorting and looking through the leftover fabric she had from the sewing projects she had done for others. "There!" Josephine said to herself as she looked at the fabric she pulled out of the scraps, "Just enough material to make each one of the children a special teddy bear for Christmas." The thought of making a teddy bear for each of her children warmed her heart.

Each night after the children were in bed, she would hand sew the teddy bears. As Josephine sewed she would pray for her beloved husband, asking God to bring him home for Christmas. Josephine looked at the teddy bear she was sewing and thought that the greatest gift for her children would be to have their papa home for Christmas.

With just a couple of days till Christmas Josephine let out a sigh as she was trying to finish up the last teddy bear. She sat close to the lamp in the bedroom and sewed until her hands hurt. She heard the wind blowing so hard that she thought it would break the windows. Josephine looked over at the clock and it was well past midnight, she set down her sewing and rubbed her sore hand. As Josephine prepared for bed she could hear the wind whistling through the trees and the windows rattled again.

The next morning the sun shone bright through the window; the snow was covered with tree branches from the wind storm. Josephine had an idea about a Christmas tree, but unsure how she was going to do it. After lunch, she went down to check the mail and she saw the neighbor from across the hall. Josephine said, "Hello Mr. Schawk, looks like you are going out." The old man shook his head 'yes.' Josephine asked, "Would you bring me a couple of tree branches that are lying around. Mr. Schawk looked at her with a puzzled look and said, "Sure thing my dear."

Later that afternoon Mr. Schawk knocked on the door; he had found two nice evergreen tree branches for Josephine. Mr. Schawk was excited to show them to her. Josephine slowly opened the door just enough to see Mr. Schawk through the crack. Ralph, Alex and Renate were already heading for the closet. Josephine turned towards the children and said, "It's okay it is Mr. Schawk."

The children walked back over towards their mother. Josephine opened the door wide to let in Mr. Schawk; he had a big smile on his face as he held up the two evergreen branches. Josephine led the way to the window so Mr. Schawk could put the branches on the floor by the window. Alex stood in deep thought staring at the branches and trying to figure out what the branches were for. Josephine gave Mr. Schawk a quick hug before handing him his cane. Mr. Schawk took his cane and winked at Josephine as he walked out the door.

As soon as the door closed Alex asked, "Why did Mr. Schawk bring us trees?" Ralph said, "These are not trees they are branches from a tree!" Josephine chuckled to herself and then said, "These tree branches are going to be our Christmas tree." The children watched as Josephine moved the small round table that was sitting by the door over to the window and then went into the kitchen and brought back a small table cloth. "Okay Ralph, you and Alex can each place the tree branches on the table." Renate sat sucking her thumb and watching as her big brothers lifted and placed the evergreen branches unto the table.

Once the evergreen branches were arranged on the table, Josephine went to the closet and took down a small gold colored box from the top shelve. Alex wanted to help carry the box but Josephine said, "Not this time Alex." She sat the box on the floor and the children watched wide eyed to see what was in the box.

Josephine took off the lid and inside the box wrapped in red tissue paper were a small gold star and two red candles. Ralph said, "Pretty mommy." The gold star and red candles were the only decorations for their evergreen branch Christmas tree this year. The children watched in wonderment as Josephine placed the gold star in the middle of the branches and two candles on each side. Josephine stood back with the children and looked at their makeshift Christmas tree; Renate clapped her little hands in delight.

It was very early Christmas Eve morning well before the children were awake and Josephine sewed on the teddy bear button eyes, she arranged them in a row on her bed. Looking at the three little teddy bears made her smiled to herself. She hoped that Karl would somehow be home, but in her heart, she felt a disappointment that he would probably not be there.

Karl might not be there to see the joy these teddy bears would bring their children. Josephine wrapped the gifts and put them in the closet before going to see if the children were awake. Alex was already up playing with blocks when she came into the room; he had dressed himself but his socks didn't match, one was yellow and the other one blue. Josephine smiled to herself that her little boy was growing up so fast. Ralph stretched his arms over his head as he lay in bed and said, "Alex woke up too early and I wanted to sleep." Josephine smiled and asked, "Alex how would you like to help me make breakfast while Ralph gets ready?"

There was excitement in the air all day as Alex, Ralph and Renate played. Renate wanted to play with the star and every time she walked towards the Christmas branches, Alex would grab her hand and lead her back to the blocks. Josephine was filled with anticipation to be able to give her gifts to the children. She called the children into the kitchen to have a light supper.

While the children ate their sandwiches, Josephine said, "I need to go to the bathroom, stay here until I come back." Josephine went into her bedroom and pulled the three wrapped gifts from the closet and placed them under the small table that held the evergreen branches. Josephine returned to the kitchen. Ralph and Alex had finished eating and Renate sat playing with her food. Josephine moved the dishes to the counter and wiped the children hands and then she said, "Let's go and see if the Christ Child has come yet." Alex was the first one out of his chair and into the living room, he shouted, "Yes, mommy yes, come and see."

Josephine carried Renate as she walked over to the table and said, "Come sit here on the floor with me, then I will read you the Christmas story." Alex said, "Can't we open our gifts first?" Josephine just smiled as she shook her head 'no.' She sat down in front of the small table with Renate on her lap, the boys sat down on each side of her. After the story was read Ralph looked up at his mother and asked, "Is papa coming home for Christmas?" Josephine felt a stab in her heart as she heard the pleading in his voice, she sighed and said, "I don't know son, but I know he is thinking about us right now."

Josephine looked at her children's sad faces and decided it was time to open their gifts. Josephine stood up and sat Renate on the floor. Then she handed each child their gift. Renate clapped her hands as she waited for her gift. As each child opened their teddy bear their eyes shone with happiness and joy was on their faces. Each one smiled up at their mother. She had made each teddy bear a little different; Alex's teddy bear was brown with a white face and black buttons for the eyes. The sight of the joy on her children's faces made tears glisten in her eyes.

Josephine lit the candles on each side of the gold star that sat in middles of the evergreen branches. She walked over and turned off the lights, then returned and sat back down on the floor. The flickering candles reflected off the gold star and made the room glow. Josephine began singing some Christmas Carols. She had a beautiful voice and when she sang, the melody of her voice washed over the children.

Each child held onto their teddy bear, Renate playing with her bear's eyes while Ralph and Alex both holding their teddy bears and looking up at the gold star. Karl was not home to fulfill their longing for him, but it felt like a magical moment that filled their hearts with joy, peace and contentment. Josephine continued to sing and the children held their special gift close. Renate fell asleep in Josephine's arms. She knew it was time to put her children to bed, but she did not want to spoil the moment.

Alex loved his new teddy bear and took it everywhere with him. He named his teddy bear "Teddy" and Teddy became his best friend. Alex could not go to sleep without Teddy under one arm. He made up pretend games with his bear and even sat the teddy bear on his lap when he ate. One morning Alex woke up and looked at Teddy and discovered one of his eyes was missing. The sight of Teddy with one eye gone caused Alex to jump out of bed and run to his mother crying, "Mommy somebody hurt Teddy, look at his eye!" Josephine bent down to look at the bear, then pulling Alex into a hug she said, "I know just how to help fix your Teddy I will give him a new eye." He stopped crying and a smile came across his little face showing his big dimples as he handed his teddy bear over to his mother.

Alex watched his mother sew a brown button on Teddy because she had run out of black buttons. Josephine explained that Teddy would be a very special teddy bear now, since he will have a brown eye and a black eye. When she finished sewing the new button eye on the teddy bear she handed him back to Alex. It did not matter that Teddy had two different color eyes, Alex was happy. He took his bear and gave it a hug, before he wrapped his arms around his mother's neck, giving her a hug and whispered in her ear, "Thank you mommy."

Spring of 1944 should have had a promise of a new beginning with the warming of the sun and the blooming flowers, but not this spring. There were fewer jobs as the SS Elite took over more business and most of the cities were under the SS Elite's control. The beauty of nature around Germany should have filled hearts with joy; instead fear ran rapid among the people of Germany. No one was safe from the SS Elite; they continued to bust through people's doors at any time day or night.

The German people had compassion on their Jewish neighbors who were also German people; they had live among them for years. The SS Elite began to arrest anyone who was of Jewish decent or if someone was hiding any Jews from them. During an SS Elite raid on a home if they found any Jews hiding in that home, they were arrested along with everyone in the home, even the children and babies. No one knew where they were taking the Jews or those who tried to help them. Darkness shrouded the cities as grief and fear lay heavy on the hearts of all the German people.

One morning just as the sun was rising, there was a thunderous sound in the sky and then warning sirens sounded. The people knew by instinct that they needed to run to shelters as quickly as they could. Then a shrieking sound filled the air as the bombs began to fall. This was the first of bombings that poured out of the skies over Germany, the American planes by day, and the English planes by night. The night skies would light up brightly like fireworks when the bombs fell from the sky and explored into fire on the ground.

The SS Elite raids had slowed down giving the people some relief, but a new fear struck the elderly, the women, and the children who lived within the cities that were being bombed. Sirens could blare at any given moment sending out a short warning of the coming bombs. When a siren sounded, it would send everyone into sheer panic as they ran to find a cellar where they could find shelter and safety from the bombs.

The moment a siren sounded great panic set into the people. Fear caused the people to flow out into the streets like a wave in the ocean moving towards the nearest shelter. The stronger people pushed and shoved trying to get ahead of the weak and those with young children. Mothers pulled their children close to them, hoping the crowd would not drag their children away.

Many times, the crowd was so thick that a child would be pulled away from the mother and moved forward with the crowd or the child would fall and be stepped on by the crowd. The people had to move fast to get to the closest shelter before the shelter became full; once full the door would be closed and locked. The people outside the shelter would have to run to find another shelter as the bombs fell from the planes, hitting the ground and bursting into flames.

Josephine had to think of a wise plan to get her three small children to the shelter. Her utmost concern was the safety of her children. Josephine no longer allowed the children to go visiting the neighbors, not even to see Auntie. Josephine needed to know that when the siren blew all her children would be together and she could get them safety to a shelter.

The plan Josephine devised included a way to call her children to a spot by the front door where a small suitcase stood that held critical papers, the children's teddy bears and some food. Josephine created a special whistle of three short sounds to call the children when the siren sounded. Josephine explained and instructed Alex and Ralph that when they heard the whistle with the three short sounds they must go immediately to the front door where she and Renate would be waiting for them. Alex looked up and asked, "Mommy is it our new game?" She pulled Alex close and replied, "Yes, Alex but it is very important that you always go to the front door when you hear my whistle."

Josephine practiced the whistle signal with Alex and Ralph by playing hide-and-seek, and then she goes to the front door. Ralph was eight and Alex almost four-years old now. Josephine and Renate counted and the boys went to hide, after a few minutes Josephine stood by the front door and whistle three short sounds. She waited with Renate by the front door for Alex and Ralph. She practiced the game until she was certain that when she whistled the boys would immediately go to the front door.

Once she was confident that they understood, she needed to explain what was next. "Boys it is very important that you are at the front door quickly and then we will hold hands and go to a shelter, do you understand?" Both boys shook their heads 'yes.' Alex thought it was a fun game and did not realize or understand the danger that was involved in this game of life and death.

Josephine had just finished up the supper dishes when the siren blew; she quickly whistled the three short sounds and picked up Renate before she headed to the front door. Alex and Ralph jumped at the sound of the siren and then they heard the whistle. Ralph grabbed Alex's hand as they scurried towards the front door to meet their mother.

Josephine stood there with a very serious look on her face she said, "This is for real and you both must stay close to me at all times! Do you understand?" Both boys shook their heads 'yes' in unison. They walked down the two flights of stairs, Josephine holding Renate in one arm and the small suitcase in the other hand.

Going down the stairs, Josephine reminded Ralph to hold Alex's hand tightly. They stepped out of the house and Ralph grabbed his mother's coat as they stepped into a crowd of people who were pushing and shoving as they moved toward the shelter. The shelter was only a block away, but the fear that drove the people was like a river current pushing everyone forward faster and faster.

Mothers with their small children looked like a shepherd herding their children to keep them close. Babies and young children were crying as they were led to the closest shelter. There were loud whistling sounds of bombs as they fell from the sky with many people still outside the shelter. Fear caused people to do things they would never have thought of doing before. At the sound of bombs beginning to fall people ran and pushed to get to the shelters; if someone fell to the ground, they would not help them but try to step over them and keep moving toward the shelter in fear for their lives.

The pushing of the crowd was like a wave on the sea in a storm, moving so fast it will take everything in its path. What could not move at the same speed was pulled under the wave and the crowd moved over the top. Ralph held Alex's hand tight and with his other hand he held on to the suitcase as Josephine had instructed him to do. Josephine moved along the outside edge of the pushing crowd so the boys would not be hurt. It took longer to reach the shelter, but all of them arrived safely. At each shelter entrance an elderly man was assigned to keep count of the people that wanted to enter and close the door once the shelter was full.

The elderly man stood at the entrance of the shelter counting the people as they entered. The people behind Josephine pushed and pressed forward against Josephine and the children as they moved to the entrance. The elderly man held up his hand with his other hand holding firmly to the door he said, "I only have room for six more people." Josephine looked at the man with pleading eyes as she said, "I am with three small children."

The man waved them in, at the same time there was a large woman screaming and pushing her way through the people behind Josephine. This woman did not pause at the shelter door but pushed her way passed the elderly man and passed Josephine and the children almost pulling Alex with her. The large women did not stop but she pushed everyone in her way and kept screaming and crying as she moved to the back of the shelter. Josephine heard a bomb hit shaking the ground as she looked over at the elderly man and then down at a young mother with a small child standing before the entrance.

The old man looked at the women with the child who stood before him at the entrance and said, "We only have room for one." The women pushed her child in to the shelter and said to the old man, "Watch over her, I will find another shelter and return." She was weeping as she ran to find another shelter and the old man pushed the shelter door shut. The three-year old little girl began to cry out for her mother and the old man picked her up to try and comfort her, but she would not be comforted. After about an hour there was the all clear siren and then it became quiet except for a few crying children.

The elderly man opened the door to smoke filled air; the people were not in a rush to leave the shelter or to see what was left of their homes and their city. The three-year old little girl was screaming at the top of her lungs, "I want my mommy." The old man held her tight as he waited at the entrance for the return of her mother. Alex reached over and pulled Josephine's skirt and asked, "Mommy will the little girls mommy come back?" Josephine looked down at her son and said, "I hope so." In Josephine prayed in her heart that the mother found another shelter in time and would return soon.

After each bombing the city would be filled with more rubble and less standing buildings; there were small fires burning everywhere and a choking smoke filled the air. Josephine stood outside of her apartment building staring at her home it was on fire as were most of the buildings in the city. Ralph said, "Mommy it looks strange with only a few buildings standing among all the rubble." With most housing in the city gone now people began to migrate to the next city or town hoping the bombing would stop and they would be able to find safety. Josephine was tired but she knew she had to be strong for her children as she walked and saw that the church a few blocks away was still standing. She guided her children there for refuge.

Josephine was thankful that she always kept the suitcase packed with important papers, a few pictures some food and the teddy bears. The teddy bears eased the children fears and helped to comfort them, until the next bombing raid. There were lots of people in the church and Josephine found a corner to rest. Alex looked at his mother and said, "Mommy can I have my teddy bear." Renate began to cry and Josephine tried to comfort her. Soon the children had fallen asleep, but Josephine kept alert not wanting anyone to harm her or the children. Then the sound of another siren blaring out the warning of coming bombs, Josephine gathered the children and hurried into the basement shelter of the church just before it became full and the door was closed.

Hopelessness and despair filled the people's hearts like a heavy weight when they looked around at the devastation that the bombs had caused in their city. After a bombing raid, most of the city was in ruins along with all the people's possessions. The people would slowly leave the town with whatever they had with them in the shelter. Josephine gathered up the children to leave the shelter and then she would walk to the train station to hopefully find another town that was not bombed out. The only possessions that Josephine had were her three precious children and the small suitcase that she always took with her. Nothing mattered more than they were all safe and not hurt.

After weeks of moving from town to town with little food, Josephine felt exhausted, but she knew that she needed to keep her strength up to care for her children and keep them safe. She still had not heard from Karl and now how would he ever find her. A fear pulled at Josephine's heart, not knowing where Karl was and if he was safe. So many people have been lost in the war or gone missing, and worst of all, they had been killed. The things Ralph, Alex and Renate had to hear and see in the aftermath of a bombing caused Josephine great pain and grieved her spirit. Both Alex and Renate would have nightmares and wake up screaming and crying. At night, she looked to heaven and cried out, "Why God? Why?" But it seemed that the heavens were silent to her cries.

Each time the train pulled into a new town Alex filled with hope that this would be the last town and they would not have to leave so they could start over again and their papa would find them. Josephine and the children longed and prayed for the day when the day and night bombing would end. Alex asked each time they found a new home in their new town, "Mommy will the planes find us here?" Josephine sighed and pulled Alex into a hug, all they wanted was a place to feel safe. Since the bombing began the stores in most cities were either totally gone; or if they could find a store open, there were very little supplies left on the store shelves. The need for food was increasing among the people in Germany; many fights would break out in the stores to see who could keep the food.

In each new town after Josephine found a place to stay, she would look for work where she could help provide for the children. Most of the businesses were gone, destroyed by bombs. Josephine used her sewing skills from her youth to barter for food. Josephine always did her work from home so she could care for the safety of her children. Alex watched his mother and the way she would sit and furrow her brows together in worry and tried to understand why his mother never smiled or sang a joyful song. This made Alex's heart sad for he could not understand the burden on his mother's heart or that she had to always be alert and find ways to provide and protect her children.

The nights were the hardest for Josephine as she lied awake after the children were in bed. Tears stained her pillow as she would pray for protection of her beloved husband and that she would be given the strength to protect her children and for provision to feed them. There were many days when there was only a slice of bread to eat for the whole day. Josephine would pray over the bread and break it into small pieces to be shared between the four of them. Each had several small pieces of bread. For Alex and Renate, it looked like they had more to eat than just one piece of bread. When Josephine could see that the food was running low she would not eat her pieces of bread but split it among her children.

Little Alex was always hungry and did not seem to be filled with the small amount of bread and he would cry, "Mommy more bread, I am hungry." There were nights when the bread was gone and everyone had to go to bed hungry. As the children cried themselves to sleep, Josephine would try to comfort them with arms and with her soothing voice singing softly to her sweet children. The pain Josephine felt in her heart was almost unbearable as she sang and comforted her children for the lack of food. By the time the children had cried themselves to sleep. Josephine heart felt as if it would break into pieces. As she prepared for bed she said to herself, "What is a mother to do?"

Chapter 13 Lost 1944

The train pulled to a stop in another city, the sky was hazy with smoke as Josephine and the children got off the train. Alex complained, "Mommy, my eyes hurt." Josephine said, "I know son." Most of the city was bombed out as people migrated into this new town. Most family members lived together, the old and young, or two to three families would move in together to help each other. Josephine followed the crowd in hopes that she would be able to get into a building soon, her feet hurt and Renate was crying.

The living conditions were depressing, there was no electricity or running water due to the bombing and rats ran through the rubble. It was in these conditions that people were trying to find shelter. There were mainly women, children and the elderly; many were sick or wounded and needed to be cared for. The crowd was dwindling down as the people entered churches, building and apartments that had survived the bombs.

Josephine looked ahead and saw a very large house that was still standing. One family went in and then turned back to the door and said, "There are four bedrooms, looks like 6 families could live here." Josephine was the last family to enter and thankful that once she climbed to the top of the stairs there was a large bedroom that she and the children could live in. Ralph shut the door behind them as they entered the room. Josephine sat her fussy little girl on the bed and Alex climbed up and tried to comfort her as Josephine looked around the room.

The room had a large window with dark drapes and just down from the window, along the same wall, was a door that lead out to a balcony. There was one large bed, a dresser with matching closet and a table with a washbasin on it. The room looked like someone left and did not return because there were other people's belongings in the room. A sad thought crossed Josephine's mind, "What if they were one of those who did not make it back after the bombing." Josephine looked over at her children and thanked God for all His protection and bringing them safely to this place. Renate had fallen asleep and both Ralph and Alex watched their mother as she walked around the room. Alex looked at Josephine with a proud look on his face and said, "Look mommy I helped Renate fall asleep."

The older children from other families would wander throughout the house looking for other children to play with. There was a soft knock on the door, Josephine walked over and answered the door. Looking down she saw a young boy about nine years old with big brown eyes looking up at her. The boy reached out his hand and said, "Hello, my name is Peter can your boys play?" Both Ralph and Alex jumped off the bed and said in unison, "Mommy, please." It made Josephine happy to see her sons happy, so she said, "Yes, but be listening in case I whistle." Alex and Ralph shook their heads 'yes' as they followed their new friend Peter down the stairs. Josephine left the door open to make sure the boys could hear her whistle.

By living together with other families, they all became close and it helped the children to have other children to play with. When the children were playing, it helped keep their minds off the lack of food and all the devastation their eyes had witnessed. As a small child during the war Alex did not understand what was happening that made the planes bring the bombs. He thought to himself, "Why he could not see his friends again, why there was not enough food and why people had to bleed and die? The children who lived during a war sees things which no child should ever have to witness and what they see is forever etched on their minds.

Josephine had not heard from Karl in over a year, she had no idea what may have become of him and feared the worst. She lived in constant fear for her children's lives, whether they were safe, where to get food to feed them, and how to keep a two, four and eight-year old close enough to her just in case another air raid of bombs fell or the SS Elite came bursting into the house. Josephine prayed and cried every night. She asked for wisdom to keep her children safe in this war-torn country. Even when the bombs were not coming down, Josephine had to be alert all the time with three children to care for and protect. Even as a small child Alex could sense the fear and sadness in his mother's heart. He began to have nightmares again from what he witnessed during and after each bombing raid.

They lived in Haldenstein for almost two weeks and it was quiet except for a few SS Elite watching and pushing into people's homes. There were still a few stores standing but there was little food on the shelves. The families who lived together pooled any money they had or bartered their skill to be able to share what food they could get with the families in the house where they lived.

The people began to feel safe again even though there were still SS Elite raids because there was no bombing. Josephine would still not let Ralph and Alex play outside and she would practice the game of hide-and-seek every day to make sure Ralph and Alex would come at her whistle in the new house. As a four-year old little boy, Alex was a very curious child who always wanted to see how things worked and would try to fix it if it was broken. Alex found broken toys and fixed them and then shared the toys with other children.

The clear blue sky and the flowers brightened up the city, and hope filled the people's hearts as they ventured out into the city. It had been three days since the last SS Elite soldiers had left town and a strange sense of peace came over the people and they thought the war was over. The people went to bed with peace in their hearts and hope for a better tomorrow, but in the middle of the night there was the blaring sound of the siren. Josephine gathered up the children and headed for the shelter. She would have to try and keep her children safe in yet another bombing raid. The bombing had begun all over again and it dawned on the people that there was no safe place where they could find safety from the bombs.

After a few days of bombing, those who survived came out from the shelter to find their homes were demolished. They would again have to move on to another town in hopes that the bombs would someday stop. Josephine's heart sunk as she walked back toward the house they were staying in. She saw it was also demolished and now a pile of rubble that spread into the street. She moved through the rubble with her tired children walking towards the train station. Alex was hungry and abruptly stopped, crossed his arms and whined, "I don't want to ride the train anymore!"

Josephine stopped and knelt on one knee to wrap her free arm around Alex and pulled him close. Renate stopped crying and looked at her brother as Josephine said, "I know son, but we don't have a choice." Josephine stood up and said, "Ralph hold Alex's hand okay?" They continued to walk towards the train station.

A train was just coming to a stop in the station, no one departed from the train and people were beginning to board the train. The train was full of tired people with crying children and Josephine prayed to find a seat. Ralph pointed and said "Mommy there is a seat" The train began to pull out of the station just as Josephine and the children sat down.

They were on the train again moving to a new town. Renate was still crying and both boys were hungry. Alex began to cry, "Mommy my stomach hurts." There was no food, so Josephine pulled Alex close and whispered, "Alex you are tired, go to sleep now." Josephine tried to comfort her children by humming the song Amazing Grace. Then she began to sing out loud, "Amazing Grace how sweet the sound," and a hush came over the whole train as the sound of Josephine's voice flowed through the train.

The train pulled into another town where there were some buildings still standing; the people exited the train just as the sun was just peeked over the horizon. Josephine and the children walked into an old building next to a church she prayed for food to feed her children. Renate was crying; it seemed like her little two-year old girl cried most of the time, from fear and hunger. Alex also was crying and saying between his sniffles, "Mommy, I am hungry." Ralph was such a wonderful big brother so brave always trying to comfort his younger brother and sister. Josephine wished her eight-year old son didn't have to grow up so fast.

Josephine looked around the new room where they would live for now, it was much smaller than the last place; the bed was also smaller, but there was a stuffed chair in the corner next to the balcony doors. The best thing about the room was the balcony that had a small table and chair on it which made the small room seem larger. There was a light tap on the door. Josephine turned and walked over to the door and opened the door only a crack to peek out and see who was there. The children stopped crying and looked wide eyed towards the door, wondering if they should hide.

An elderly woman stood outside the door with a soft smile on her face. Josephine opened the door wider and said, "Please come in." The woman entered and extended her hand as she said, "Hello, my name is Mrs. Schmidt, I heard your little boy crying with hunger, so I want to share my food with you." Josephine's eyes teared up as she shook Mrs. Schmidt's hand and her voice shook with emotion as she said, "Thank you so very much." Mrs. Schmidt reached her hand into the bag she had in her other hand and pulled out a large slice of bread and two slices of cheese, she handed them to Josephine. Then Mrs. Schmidt excused herself to leave. Josephine wrapped her arm around Mrs. Schmidt neck and said, "Thank you for being an answer to my prayers." Mrs. Schmidt smiled and was on her way. Josephine slowly closed the door and looked at her children, so relieved she could feed them.

The second day after they had moved into their new family house with the others from the train, the siren sounded so loud that it was hard to hear anything else. Josephine gathered the children together and began to move them towards the shelter, yelling at Ralph, "Stay close and don't let go of Alex's hand." Josephine always managed to keep them all together as they rushed along in the sea of fast moving people towards the shelter. There was something different about this time, the planes' noise was louder than the siren and she could see them in the distant sky moving quickly towards them. Josephine feared the bombs would fall before they got to the shelter, she prayed out loud as she felt the crowd of people pushing harder as they pressed and shoved forward against her, "Lord, keep us safe."

There was so much noise between the loud siren and the planes, small children were crying and people were screaming. Alex tried to cover his ears with his hands, but Ralph held tighter to Alex's hand as he tried to pull it away to cover his ear. Ralph yelled, "Stop pulling away!" Alex yelled back "My ears hurt." Then there was a very loud boom sound as the first bomb hit the ground, the bomb shook the ground and people swayed in the movement but kept moving forward at an even faster pace. The shaking caused Ralph and Alex's hands to slip apart. Alex put his hands on his ears and looked back to where the noise was coming from. Someone picked up Alex and sat him outside the crowd next to a building. Alex looked but he could not see Ralph or his mother in the moving crowd. Fear caused Alex to cry and he did not know what to do as stood there staring into the crowd and crying, "Mommy, mommy."

Alex's heart was beating fast with fear and he did not know where to go. He looked back and could see their house; he decided to go back into the house and climbed the stairs to the third-floor balcony and look for mother from up there. Alex climbed up the bottom rail of the railing that circled the balcony to see better. Terror filled Alex's eyes as they opened wider, he saw the bombs falling from the sky and hitting the ground bursting into flames.

The bombs were phosphate bombs so there was fire everywhere. People were on fire; they were burning and screaming as they ran. Alex put his hands over his ears and began to scream from the sheer sight of the horror. Those images would forever be tattooed on his mind. Alex was so full of fear that he did not feel that a small piece of shrapnel had pierced into the skin above his knee and blood began to trickle down his leg. The smoke and burning flesh smell caused Alex to begin to cough and gag; tears were streaking down his face as he stood there frozen. He began to scream at the top of his lungs, "Mommy!"

In the meantime, Josephine had arrived at the shelter and turned to pull Ralph and Alex close. Surprised to see only Ralph, fear gripped at her heart when she did not see Alex with his brother. With panic in her eyes and a loud voice she screamed at Ralph, "Where is Alex?" Ralph began to cry as he told his mother, "The ground shook and Alex's hand slipped away, I don't know where he went but when I looked I could not see him. I looked for you and could barely see you ahead. I had to run and push people to catch up with you. I am so sorry mommy." Ralph's tears ripped into his mother's heart as she was trying to think what she should do, they entered the shelter. Josephine and her two children were safe, but her four-year-old son Alex was missing. She was beside herself with fear for Alex.

Josephine turned to the woman standing next to her in the shelter and asked if she would watch over her two-year and eight-year old children while she went to look for her middle child. The women saw the fear in Josephine's eyes and smiled at her as Josephine handed Renate to her. Renate was crying and Ralph stood wide eyed next to the women watching his mother walk away. Josephine moved through people to the shelter door and said to the person in charge of the door, "I need to go and find my son, let me out." The older man looked at her as if she was crazy, but opens the door to allow her to squeeze out.

Josephine saw the fear on people's faces as she pushed hard against the crowd trying to find Alex. The air was thick with smoke making it hard to see as Josephine kept shouting above the noise, "Alex, Alex!" Pushing through the rushing of people moving in the opposite direction slowed her down. BOOM! Another bomb dropped even closer. Steading herself from the shaking ground, she moved forward. Josephine began to pray for protection and thanking God that the shelter was only five houses down the street. Tears were streaking down Josephine's face and the smoke from the fires burnt her eyes, as she screamed out a prayer, "God where is my son?"

The last couple of blocks she didn't have to push through people, the crowd had thinned to only a few people running and screaming. Josephine saw her house still standing and began to think that Alex must have gone back home. She heard people screaming in pain not too far ahead of her; the air smelled awful with the smell of burnt flesh. Josephine held her nose with her fingers as she ran up the stairs of the house, searching floor by floor. Josephine could hear more bombs falling as she kept yelling out, "Alex, where are you?" Alex was so fixed on the terror that played out in front of him that he could not hear his mother yelling or whistling. The whole building shook as Alex watched another plane drop more phosphorus bombs just down the street from the house. Alex's eyes burnt from the thick smoke and he could still see and hear the burning people. He sat down on the balcony and put his hands over his ears to muffle their screams.

Alex felt his mother's arms wrap around him and pick him up, she said, "Alex, thank God." Josephine moved down the stairs into the street towards the shelter as fast as she could. Alex's arms were wrapped tightly around his mother's neck and his face pressed into her shoulder. Just as Josephine arrived at the shelter door another bomb hit the earth and shook the ground so hard that Josephine fell against the shelter door almost dropping Alex.

Josephine began kicking the shelter door and screaming at the top of her lungs, "Please let me in, my children are in there." After a few minutes the door slowly opened and an arm reached out pulling them into the shelter and quickly closing the door behind her. The shelter was over full and people were stuffed into it like sardines. Josephine had to step over people as she moved towards the back of the shelter looking at faces for the lady she left her children with.

Josephine let out a sigh of relief when she saw the woman with Ralph and Renate. Renate had cried herself to sleep and Ralph jumped up when he saw his mother and gave her a hug. Josephine sat Alex down next to Ralph and thanked the woman for caring for her children as she took Renate from her. Josephine stood there for a moment pulling her children close to her as tears of relief ran down her face. BOOM, another bomb shook the shelter so hard Josephine thought it might collapse and Renate woke up screaming in fear. The shelter shook but stayed intact. The rumble of the planes overhead sounded louder than normal. Josephine was exhausted as she slid down the wall onto the floor with her children.

Renate stopped crying and pointed at Alex's leg; Josephine looked down at his leg and saw that it was bleeding from the top of his knee. She handed Renate to Ralph to take a closer look. There was a cut about a half inch wide above his knee. Josephine tore off the bottom part of her dress and wrapped it tightly around Alex's wound. She did not know that a piece of flying shrapnel had entered just above his knee, nor did Alex. He was in such a state of shock with what he witnessed when he was on the balcony that it caused him not to feel any pain from the injury.

Josephine pulled her children close to her and began thanking God out loud for getting her and Alex back in to the safety of the shelter where her other two children were. Some of the people looked at her strangely, but she did not care. As Josephine continued to pray everything outside the shelter became quiet, the bombing had stopped. There was a cheer inside the shelter as they waited for the all clear siren.

Then the all clear siren blew and at the same time there was a loud crashing sound as the building next to the shelter crashed to the ground. The man by the door waiting until it got quiet again before opening the door. He slowly opened the door and then yelled back into the shelter, "It is all clear, but be careful." The people began filing out the open door unto the street and smoke came into and filled the shelter. People began coughing and gaging as they moved out of the shelter onto the street.

Josephine just sat there still with her eyes closed, holding her precious children close as the people moved out of the shelter. The last person was gone, only darkness, smoke and that horrible smell remained. She looked down at her exhausted children that slept in her arms and leaning against her, wishing the war was over and that this was just a terrible dream. Josephine moved Renate to her shoulder hoping she would continue to sleep as she shook Ralph and Alex gently and quietly saying, "Wake up boys, it is time to go." Alex kept his eyes closed and said, "Mommy my eyes hurt." Josephine stood up and said, "I know son, but we must go now." Alex opened his eyes blinking them and got up, but held his nose closed.

Ralph picks up and carries the suitcase. Josephine takes Alex by the hand and Renate was still asleep with her head cradled on Josephine's shoulder. Josephine prayed for wisdom on what to do next as they slowly walked out of the shelter into the street. Josephine gasped as she stopped and just stood there for a moment taking in the horror all around. Everywhere Josephine looked the city was in ruins.

Ralph and Alex looked wide-eyed as their eyes drained, there was devastation everywhere. This was the worse bombing so far; it looked like the whole town lay in a pile of rubble. Josephine wished her boys did not have to see all the devastation that was before them. She kept praying as they slowly walked toward where they lived. Their temporary home also lay in heap of rubble with burning flames shooting up out of the rubble.

Everything above ground was burnt down and still smoking. They could hear the cries of people and the smell was so bad that all of them coughed. Alex thought it felt like he could not breathe as he kept coughing and gaging. Tears were running down all their faces as the smoke burned their eyes. Josephine was thankful that even though Renate was coughing, she was still asleep on her shoulder. Alex held onto his mother's hand ever so tightly, as he did not want to lose his mommy again. They had to walk slowly as they went around the rubble and Josephine tried her hardest to direct their walk away from the dead people who lay among the rubble.

The air smelled of the burning flesh and the smoke burned their throats. Ralph looked up at his mother with his eyes tearing and running from the smoke and asked, "Mommy, my eyes and throat hurt, can we go someplace else?" A lump caught in Josephine's throat as she gently answered, "I am so sorry son, but there is no place else to go and we have to walk this way so just hold your nose shut with your fingers."

The further they moved away from their house was when they saw more people in the streets covered in rubble or still burning. Josephine walked passed where the church had once stood, but now was just a pile of burning rubble. Josephine looked up towards the heavens and said out loud, "God help us!" The sights that were all around them were so horrible that Josephine kept telling the boys, "Look straight ahead, and don't look down." She was trying to keep her children's innocent eyes from the devastating effects of this war. Alex and Ralph tried not to look down or around them but it was too late they had already seen too much from the war to remove what they had seen.

Josephine was so exhausted from the lack of sleep and food that she wanted to give up, but that was not an option and she forced herself to press on knowing she needed to do whatever it took to get her children to a safe place. Her mind was filled with jumbled thoughts and fear pressed in, she did not know where to go next; and then she remembered the letter that came from her parents a few weeks ago. The letter said that in the little town in the woods where her parents lived the bombing had stopped and the American's had come to keep them all safe, the letter ended pleading for Josephine to come home.

At the time the letter had arrived there was no bombing and Josephine did not want to make such a long journey with her three small children. But now there was no other choice; the decision was made that night that needed to go back home and stay with her parents. Josephine was worried about the transportation on how to get back home since there were fewer and fewer trains that were still moving through Germany since many of the train tracks had been bombed. Josephine was jolted from her thoughts to the here-and-now as Alex began to cough so hard he vomited and then began to cry. Renate woke up coughing crying also. Stopping for a just a moment to check on Alex before she said, "Children I know this is hard but we have to keep walking."

Josephine and the children walked for what seemed like forever and there was less burning rubble as they walked towards the train station. Renate was still crying, Alex's littles legs were hurting and he stop and try to sit down many times as he felt he could not walk any longer, but Josephine always tugged him back onto his feet and said, "I know you are tired son and want to rest too, but we cannot stop yet; we need to keep moving."

There was great disappointment when they looked at the train station, it was nothing but rubble, Josephine felt as if she could not continue so she shouted a prayer into the air, "Lord, please help us to find a way, you see how tired the children are and we just need to find a place to rest a short while. She looked to her left to adjust Renate in her arm and she saw that the train station restroom was still standing. She looked up and said, "Thank you!"

Josephine lead the way over to the restroom being careful not to trip over the rubble that was all around it, she slowly opened the restroom door hoping it would be empty and thanked God that it was. It took a minute for their eyes to adjust to the dark restroom. Once the door was closed, Josephine with a sigh of relief told the children to use the toilet and then come and sit next to the wall by the sink. There was no running water or electricity, but they all felt save for the moment. Ralph and Alex sat there in the dark and Josephine put Renate on Ralph's lap. Renate continued to fuss and cry; her little face was stained with tears that ran down over her cheeks making streaks in the smoke residue that was on all their faces. She tried to comfort Renate with her words, "Hush baby, it's okay."

Josephine opened the suitcase to see if there was any food left in it, to her surprise and with a thankful heart she found a half slice of bread. She divided the bread between her three children. Josephine broke the bread into six pieces, so each child had two pieces of bread. Alex ate his up very quickly and then looked up at his mother and said, "Can I please have another piece of bread." Josephine eyes filled with tears as she looked tenderly on her hungry children and hated to have to say, "Sorry the bread is all gone." Renate and Alex both stared to cry, Ralph was the only brave one and he looked at his mother with more wisdom than an eight-year old should have and said, "That's okay mommy." Josephine took Renate from Ralph and sat down next to Alex and wrapped her arm around him as she gently rocked Renate trying to comfort her hungry children.

In the darkness, the children all soon fell asleep; even though Josephine was exhausted she could not rest for fear and worry of what to do next. A few hours passed when the children woke to a loud knock on the restroom door. A man stuck his head inside the door and shouted, "You take those children and get out of here now! It is not safe to be in here. Josephine looked at the man with a puzzled look for a moment, but obeyed his command and with urgency in her voice she said, "Come children get up we need to go now!" The children knew when Josephine had that tone in her voice that they had better listen right away, so they jumped to their feet followed her out of the restroom.

The man pointed to a large hole at the foundation of the restroom that looked like it would fall over any moment. The man kicks on the wall and the whole restroom crashed to the ground. They stood there in awe with a surprised look on their faces as the small building collapse to the ground. Josephine thanked the man as he walked away; she thought that the man must have been an angel who was sent to warn her of the danger.

Josephine carried Renate while Ralph carried the small suitcase and held Alex's hand as they began to walk again. The smoke was lighter and the smell was not as strong as they walked through and over the rubble towards the next train station. Renate was tired and continued to fuss, but Ralph and Alex were both quiet as they walked. Fear consumed all their hearts as they slowly walked on, for they did not know what would happen next or if planes would come again and bring more bombs. The further they moved away from the train station the rubble became less, this gave Josephine hope. She was exhausted, but she knew if she stopped moving she would not want to move on. Her legs felt like they had weights on them and her arm and shoulder ached from carrying Renate. She pushed on with her two brave sons following her closely.

The sun rose high in the sky, the haze of the left-over smoke filtered out its brightness, but the air smelled fresher. Josephine heard a train in the distance. Hearing the train made Josephine smile as she pointed in the direction of the train station. They were almost there and it sounded like trains were running. When they reached the train station it surprised Josephine as she looked around, because this station seemed to be undamaged and trains were still running on time. Josephine reached into her pocket and pulled out the all the money she had left to purchase the train tickets for the four of them to go to her parents' house. The man gave Josephine the tickets and said "The train will depart in fifteen minutes."

The train arrived on time. They boarded the train and Josephine found a compartment with a door that closed off from the aisle. The compartment was large enough to seat four adults. "Good," Josephine thought to herself as they entered the compartment, "I can keep the door closed and then Renate can move around." Ralph and Alex went in first and each one got on their knees on the seats and pressed their noses against the window to look out.

The train began to move before Josephine and Renate could sit down. As the train pulled away from the station, sadness filled both Alex and Ralph's hearts as they saw more rubble piles. Young children should not have to experience war, but the only thing the young children in Germany knew was war. They did not know what the world was like without war and always having to move from place to place to find safety with fear ever present in their hearts.

Josephine sat Renate on the seat and lifted the suitcase to put in the storage rack above the seats. As she reached up and placed the suitcase on the rack above Alex, looked out the window and saw what her little ones were looking at and why they were letting out a soft moan. Josephine gently grasped each of her sons by the arm as she helped them to sit down and said, "You need to sit down now."

They both sat down, Alex folded his little arms in protest with a pout on his face as he looked up at his mother. Alex did not understand why he couldn't look out of the window. Josephine face was sad as she looked at her two sons and wondered why her children at such young ages had to see the ugly side of life. A memory of her happy carefree childhood filled her mind and she wished in her heart that she could protect her children from the war and all the effects of it, but knowing all the while that it was impossible when her home had become a war zone.

The trip home took over twelve hours with three train changes. At first, the boys were excited to be on the train, since the train always seemed to move them to a better place where they could feel safe again. But this trip was long and each time they had to board another train the children became more tired and restless. Josephine tried to keep her children quiet by telling them stories until they fell asleep, but she had to keep awake and alert. The SS Elite soldiers checked everyone getting off trains asking for their papers and once the people had boarded the train they would walk through the train checking people's papers again. Once the SS Elite were done they gave a signal to the train conductor that he could move on to the next station. The atmosphere on the train was strained and filled with fear until the SS Elite soldiers left the train and it began to move.

Josephine forced herself to be alert as the train began to pull to a stop in the city of Hammel. This was the last stop and train change before they reached Magdenburg. She woke up the children as she snapped out instructions to the boys. She took down the suitcase and handed it to Ralph. With Renate in one arm and taking Alex by the hand she said to Ralph, "Come now, follow me, make sure you stay close we need to get off this train and get onto another train and we do not have much time. Do you understand?" Ralph shook his head 'yes' as he followed close to Josephine heels.

Alex was hungry and vocalized his hunger by continually saying as they walked to the next train. "Mommy, I am hungry." Josephine had no food or money for food, she did not answer as tears brimmed up in her eyes at her son's request and her desire was to satisfy her children with food. Then Renate started to cry, it sent a sharp pain into Josephine's heart to hear her children crying with hunger. Josephine began to pray loud, "Lord, help my children, give me strength and protect us as we travel."

They entered the new train and Josephine said softly, "Keep close so we can find our seats on the new train." Renate continued to cry and Alex was still complaining that he was hungry, as Josephine led her children down the aisle of the train to find seats. She was tired, when she stopped walking, Ralph bumped into her as she turned to Alex and said, "Please son be still now, and we will get something to eat when we get to your grandparents' house okay?" Alex looked up at his mother with his eyes that filled with sadness. He obeyed her request but tears brimmed in his eyes. The tone in Josephine's voice also made Renate stop crying. Josephine found a seat next to a window and sat between Ralph and Alex just as the train began to move away from the train station.

Renate began continued to cry and Josephine began rocking her. Alex still wanted something to eat and looked up at his mother and asked, "Mommy, don't you have one more piece of bread in the suitcase?" Josephine looked down at Alex with the saddest eyes she had ever seen and her voice cracked as she replied, "No, son, let's all close our eyes and I will sing you a song and perhaps you can rest awhile. Before you know it we should be at your grandparent's house." Josephine did all she knew to comfort her children and so wanted to give them food to fill their empty stomachs. Josephine quietly began to sing another one of her favorite hymns to her hungry children, "Great is Thy Faithfulness."

Josephine sat staring out the window, Renate in her arms became quiet and Ralph and Alex relaxed, one on each side of her leaning their heads on her arms. The train was quiet except for a few fussy babies. The clacking of the wheels on the train track created a rhythm that lulled the children to sleep, for which Josephine was thankful. She sat and watched the trees go by the train window in a blur as the train swayed on the tracks. Tears began to stream down Josephine's face as she thought about Karl. Fear again gripped at her heart telling her that Karl was dead, but a hope rose in her heart telling her to pray for him to be safe and the he would come back home to his family. As she continued to look out the train window, she yearned for the days when she had first married to Karl; there were so many happy memories.

Without warning the train came to an abrupt stop. Alex and Ralph woke up and looked around wide eyed and then they looked at their mother, Renate began to cry. Josephine put her finger to her mouth praying her children would be quiet as she gently rocked Renate. Alex and Ralph sensed something was not right so they obeyed and kept quiet as their eyes filled with fear. Josephine wiped the tears from her face with her sleeve as they heard men's loud voices approaching them.

Two SS Elite soldiers walked through the train with their guns pointed towards the people as they approached. The SS Elite slowly walked down the train aisle looking at every person carefully and looking through their belongings as they asked to see their papers. Children's cries began to fill the train. Josephine whispered a prayer, "God please protect us and get us safely home to my parent's house." Just as Josephine finished her prayer the two SS soldiers stopped and pointed their guns at Josephine and the children.

One of the SS Elite soldiers took down the suitcase and looked through it, as the other one said to Josephine, "Your papers!" Then they looked at Josephine and her three small children with fear-filled faces. The SS soldier handed Josephine back her papers and walked on to the man and woman in front of them. Josephine breathed out a sigh of relief and pulled her children closer to let them knowing they were safe as she breathed a quick pray of thanks.

Renate began to cry again as she heard the SS Elite soldiers shouting to the man and women who sat in the seat in front of them, "Your papers!" There was a big crash as the SS soldier went through their suit case. Then the woman began to cry as she screamed out, "No, we are not Jews." But the SS Elite soldiers did not care as one of the SS Elite soldiers pulled them off the train and handed them over to more soldiers who was standing on the train platform. Then SS Elite moved onto the next seat until they had finished searching the train.

Before long the train began to move along the tracks again, only Renate fell back to sleep. Alex sat there with his arms crossed and thought, 'I am going to punch those bad men if they come back again.' Alex looked over at Ralph who also sat with his arms crossed. Alex relaxed his arms and laid them at his side, Ralph reached across Josephine's lap and took Alex's hand and gave it a slight squeeze. Alex felt safe for the moment with his mother close and his big brother holding his hand. The only noise now was the clanging of the train wheels on the track and a few crying babies. Josephine began to hum one of her hymns in hopes that the boys would fall back asleep. It worked.

Josephine let out a sigh of relief when her children were asleep, for she knew how very tired her boys were. She hoped this rest would keep her little ones content for a while where they could forget about their hungry stomach and the fear in their hearts, even if it was for just a short time. It was dark out as Josephine looked out the train window, all she could see was her reflection in the window pane looking back at her. Her eyes had dark circles under them and her face looked strained. Josephine closed her eyes and began to pray for her husband again.

Chapter 14 Home 1944

Just after midnight the train pulled into Magdeburg train station, it was dark; the streets were quiet and deserted. This was the last train to pull into the station that night and very few people were getting on the departing train. Exhaustion and the strain of the day were set on Josephine's face like an iron pressed shirt. She was not sure she could keep going as all she wanted to do was sleep, but she forced herself to push on.

The stopping of the train woke Renate and Alex who both began to cry. Ralph was exhausted and did not awake. Josephine shook Ralph and said, "Ralph get up." Ralph did not wake up, so Josephine shook him again and she raised her voice, "Ralph get up now!" Alex stopped crying and looked at his mother. Alex could not understand why his mother was speaking so loudly and sharply to Ralph. Alex thought his mother was mad at him and his brother and sister, so he tried to quiet Renate by saying, "It's okay Renate."

Josephine was tired and frustrated; she knew they needed to get off the train as Ralph rubbed his eyes and was slow in getting up. A well-dressed elderly man stepped up to Josephine and asked, "Can I help you depart the train?" Josephine jumped at the sound of his voice and then turned her head around to see the nice man standing there with a smile on his face, she quickly responded, "Yes please, that would be very kind of you." Josephine willed her exhausted body to pick up Renate and gather her suitcase to depart the train.

The elderly man took the suitcase from Josephine and led the way with Ralph and Alex walking behind him. Josephine was the last to step off the train and thanked the man as he hurried back to board the train just in time for the doors close behind him. Josephine and the children stood watching the train pull out of the station and move down the tracks. Taking a deep breath Josephine looked around surveying the area to see if there might be a taxi or a city bus, but none were there this late at night. Renate began to cry again and Alex pulled at her coat saying, "Mommy, I am hungry."

The long train trip to Josephine's parents' home had created anxiety for all them, but now they were almost there. Josephine's eyes now had some peace in them even though her face was drawn with tiredness. This was the first time since she left home that she was glad to come back home. Josephine thought to herself, "No matter how old you are it always feels safer when you are with your parents." Her parents lived in the small town of Suderode which was about twenty-five kilometers away from Magdeburg (about 15.5 miles).

Once the train pulled away from the station Alex looked around as they stood there watching the lights of the train move away and become distant. The streets were dark around them with the only light that filled the night came from the full moon. Josephine looked up at the moon and let out a sigh before looking down at her children and saying, "Listen we need to walk for a while to get to your grandparent's home, it is dark and I need you to do what I tell you to do, okay?" By the tone in her voice Alex knew he better listen. Both boys shook their heads to say 'yes'; even two-year old Renate was quiet when Josephine spoke.

Josephine asked Ralph to carry the suitcase, while she carried Renate and held tight to Alex's hand for fear that he might wonder off somewhere in the dark and she would not be able to find him. They walked away from the train station and followed the road south to Suderode. After a short time, Renate began to cry and Alex's legs were tired so Josephine had to pull him forward. A couple of times Alex wanted to sit down, his legs hurt and he did not want to walk any longer. Alex began to cry out, "Mommy I don't want to walk anymore, my feet hurt." Alex tried to sit down, but Josephine would gently yank on his hand to get him to his feet and tenderly say, "Alex not yet, just a little further."

Ralph never complained. Josephine had to force one foot in front of the other to keep herself going. Josephine let out a sigh and said a silent prayer. Within five minutes a large truck that carried the name of her father's business pulled up beside them. They were a sight to see, a woman walking in the dark carrying one small child and holding the hand of another while an older boy trailed behind her carrying a small suitcase.

The truck driver was in his late fifties, with salt and pepper hair that was slicked back. He leaned out the window and looked at Josephine and her three small children who were looking up at him. Sympathy filled his heart and he asked, "Frau, where are you going this time a night?" Josephine let out a sigh of relief as she answered, "We are going to my parents' home in Suderode." The truck driver threw back his head and let out a loud laugh before he replied, "That is strange, I am heading that way since I also live in Suderode. I am late in getting back from one of the last delivery trips I had in town today, so to make up some time I decided to take a shortcut past the train station. I usually leave town much earlier and go another route, someone must be watching out for you."

The truck driver smiled and his eyes twinkled as he said, "I would love to give you a ride to your parents' house if you would like me to." Josephine looked up into the truck driver's kind eyes with her tired eyes. Their eyes met and Josephine just stared up at the truck driver for a long minute while she prayed thanks to God, for she knew in her heart that this was the answer to her prayers.

The truck driver waited in silence for her answer. Josephine smiled and said, "Yes, thank you, that is wonderful of you." The truck driver got out of the truck and walked around the truck to introduced himself, "My name is Mr. Fritz, where do you need to go?" Josephine gave him the address to her parents' home. The truck driver's voice sounded surprised as he said, "Oh, I know the place well, my boss lives there." Josephine smiled at Mr. Fritz and said, "Thank you for the ride." Mr. Fritz helped Josephine and the children into the truck.

They were all able to squeeze into the front seat of the big truck. Alex was the first one in and he sat right next to the driver. All tiredness left Alex and he became alert. This is the first-time he had been in a truck and he was fascinated with all the instruments. Alex's mind raced as he looked at the instruments, he wanted to know everything about the lights and buttons. He wanted to touch everything he could see as the man drove, but he knew to keep his hands to himself.

Alex began to ask Mr. Fitz questions, "How does this button work? What are those lights for?" Josephine tried to hush Alex, but Mr. Fritz said, "It's okay." Mr. Fritz did not seem to mind any of Alex's questions and once he let Alex push one of the buttons for him. Alex was so happy sitting next to Mr. Fritz that he forgot all about being tired and hunger during the trip. With the movement of the truck both Ralph and Renate fell asleep. Alex was non-stop talking asking questions until they arrived at their grandparents' home.

During the trip Josephine found out that Mr. Fitz was one of her parent's neighbors. He was the man who oversaw Josephine's father's transportation business. Currently the American soldiers were using the transportation business to move food and supplies to other cities. Josephine stared out the window looking out into the darkness and listening to Alex talk, she knew in her heart that Mr. Fritz was truly a Godsend and was thankful for all the times her prayers were answered during this journey home. The truck ride was over before Alex was finished asking all sorts questions. The truck began to slow down and make a right turn at the next street.

The truck pulled to a stop in front Alex's grandparents' home and Mr. Fritz honked the horn. Both Ralph and Renate woke up and Mr. Fritz turned off the truck. The children's grandfather (opa) came running out of the house with a puzzled look on his face wondering why one of his trucks would stop by his home in the middle of the night. Opa hoped it was good news and not trouble.

When he saw the logo number on the truck he knew it was Mr. Fritz, but he could not imagine why he was there. Before opa could get to the truck Mr. Fritz was out of the truck and opening the passenger side door. He helped Josephine, who held Renate get out of the truck first, then Ralph and Alex. Opa stopped when he saw his daughter and her three children staring at him. They all just stood there watching as he turned around and ran back to the house. He opened the front door and hollered for the children's grandmother (oma) to get up and come quickly.

At the sound of her husband's voice oma jumped out of bed and hurried down the stairs. She came running out of the house in her night gown to see what opa was hollering about. Once oma saw her daughter and three small grandchildren, a huge smile spread across her face. Opa shook Mr. Fritz hand and said, "Thank you," before he quickly turned to his daughter and took Renate from her arms. As he took his granddaughter she started to cry, he then gave Renate to her grandmother. Looking at his daughter's face and seeing how strained and exhausted she was, he bent down and picked Josephine up into his arms carrying her into the house. Josephine laid her head against her father's chest and took a deep breath. Alex heard his opa say to his oma, "Josephine needs rest and I will take her up and lay her in bed."

Renate cried harder the moment her mother disappeared into the house with opa, Ralph and Alex looked at each other with fear in their eyes as they watched their mother disappear into the house. Alex wondered why opa had taken his mommy away. Oma tried to comfort Renate as she looked down at Ralph and Alex and saw fear on their faces. She continued to rock Renate in her arms as she spoke gently to the boys, "Don't worry, I am your oma; your mother will be alright, but she is so tired and she needs to get some rest. I will take care of all of you until she wakes up." Renate was crying so hard she began to choke and gasp for air, oma's words did not comfort her or Alex, he was afraid that he would not see his mommy again. Big tears began to run down his cheeks. Ralph was brave and did not say anything he just stared up at oma with apprehension.

The children's grandparents were strangers to them. Alex thought that opa was taking his mommy away just like the men had come and taken his friend Frank away. Oma began walking towards the house with both Renate and Alex crying and Ralph trailing behind caring the suitcase. In between cries Alex kept asking, "Why did opa take mommy away?" Oma stopped just inside the front door; Ralph sat down the suit case and took Alex by the hand. Ralph looked at Alex's tear stained face and said, "It is going to be okay Alex; mommy would not have brought us here if it wasn't safe or if oma and opa would hurt us." Ralph always watched out for his little brother and sister and he tried to comfort them. Alex stopped crying and looked up at his oma's face, oma smiled down at Alex, this made him feel better and he wiped away the tears from his face with his sleeve.

Oma immediately took the children up the stairs and into the bedroom where opa had laid their mother on the bed. Oma wanted to show Alex where his mother was and that she was okay. They walked into the large bedroom, Renate stopped crying and Alex looked at his mother lying very still on the bed with her eyes closed in a deep sleep with opa sitting on the edge of the bed next to her. Alex had seen dead people before and most of them had their eyes closed. Tears welled up in Alex's eyes and fear in his shaky voice as he asked, "Why are mommy's eyes closed, is she dead?"

Opa stood up and looked down at Alex's with sadness in his eyes as he told him, "Your mother was so exhausted and tired that as soon as her head hit the pillow she fell fast asleep." Oma handed Renate to opa and then knelt down next to Alex and gave him a hug as she said, "You know your mother will feel much better once she gets rest. When she wakes up you can talk to her, okay?" These words comforted the fear in Alex's heart and for some reason he knew that he could trust his oma and opa.

Oma took Renate back from opa and guided the children back down stairs and led them into the kitchen. Alex was wide eyed as he looked around the large kitchen that had a large table in the center of the room and a large window draped with lace curtains. Renate was sucking her thumb and watching her brothers every move. Oma said, "Boys why don't you climb up in one of the chairs."

Renate was now clinging to oma and did not want to sit in a chair, so she held her and said, "Let me wash your hands and face before I get you a little something to eat." She took a clean wet cloth and washed Renate's face and then she gave the cloth to Ralph and said, "Please wash yours and Alex's face and hands." She walked over to the kitchen cabinets. While she balanced Renate on one hip, she reached up and took out some bread and butter to give to her grandchildren. She buttered the slices of bread and gave the children each one full slice of bread.

Alex's eyes got big and he exclaimed, "Do I get to eat this whole big piece of bread by myself?" Oma smiled and replied, "Yes, dear." She sat down in a chair with Renate on her lap and broke the slice of bread into four pieces making it easier for Renate's small hands to pick up the bread. Opa walked into the kitchen and stood watching the boys eating the bread as fast as they could. He looked over at his wife sitting there with their granddaughter on her lap and smiled. Alex and Ralph were hungry; it had been more than a day since they had anything to eat.

Opa took a chair next to Alex and watched the children as they devoured the food that was set before them. He got up and walked over to the counter to butter another slice of bread for each of the children. After the long journey and with food in their tummy's Alex's eyes grew heavy and he laid his head down on the table. Oma rose from the table and said, "I think it is time that the three of you went to bed." Alex's grandparents' hearts went out with an abundance of love toward their grandchildren and hoped that these little ones would never have to feel hunger like this again and perhaps someday forget the horrible things they saw during war.

Alex looked up and asked for another slice of bread. Oma softly replied, "Not now Alex, in the morning you can have another slice. Alex slid down off the chair and began to look around to see if his papa was there. During the trip to his grandparents' house Alex keep thinking that when he got there his papa would be waiting for him. After walking throughout the kitchen, he turned to his oma with confusion in his eyes as he asked, "Where is my papa?"

His grandparents looked at each other with sadness in their eyes as they tried to assure Alex's little heart that all was going to be okay, but his papa was not here yet. Opa bent down to Alex level and said, "Alex, your papa is not here now, but hopefully he will be one day soon." This did not bring comfort to Alex; he crossed his arms across his chest and frowned as he looked at his opa. Since what he saw on the balcony during the bombing just few days before, he was not so sure in his heart if anything was ever going to be okay. Opa pulled him into a hug and said, "I think it is time to get you ready for bed."

Opa and oma took the children upstairs to the bathroom and oma ran warm water in the tub adding soap to give them a warm bubble bath. She needed to wash away the dirt and smoke that covered them from head to toe. The bath water felt so good and warm that when it was Alex's turn to get out of the tub he did not want to leave the water. Ralph persuaded Alex to get out so he could take his bath. Opa had laid out three of his tee-shirts on the bed for the children to sleep in; they did know if the children had a change of clothes. Oma wrapped each child up in a big towel and brought them one by one into a large bedroom that had a very big bed in the middle of the room. Opa was waiting there and helped each child get into a tee-shirt.

Ralph put on his tee-shirt and oma pulled back the covers for all of them to get into the large bed. Renate was put in the middle of the bed while Ralph and Alex were to sleep on each side of her. Renate was asleep before Ralph and Alex was tucked into the bed. Oma hushed Alex by putting her finger to her lips so he would not wake Renate. She finished tucking in each side of the bed and said, "Now it is time for you boys to go to sleep." Alex stared up at his oma as fear gripped his little heart, he was afraid if he went to sleep he would not see his mommy again.

Oma saw this is his eyes so she decided to sit there on the edge of the bed and sing to the children softly until both boys were fast asleep. Alex fought going to sleep with the thoughts of his mother singing to him, his eyes became heavy and sleep enveloped him. Now that the children were asleep oma went back to the bathroom to clean up. She gathers up the dirty clothes to wash them. She looked at the clock and thinks to herself as she leaves the bathroom, "It was almost four am, so there is no sense in going to bed." She washes the children's clothes and hangs them to dry before going back to the kitchen to clean up. Opa joined her there and made some coffee.

Chapter 15 New Adventure 1944

The sun had already risen over the hillside and moved up in the sky making everything bright. A stream of sunlight flowed into the bedroom where the children were sleeping. The sunlight spread across the bed, Alex opened his eyes and stretched his arms over his head. He blinked his eyes a few times looking around. At first he became afraid and his heart began to pound. Nothing looked familiar and he did not know where he was. Then he looked over and saw his sister and brother sleeping next to him.

Alex let out a quiet sigh, he remembered he was at his grandparents' house and knew he was safe. The house was very quiet except for the ticking of the clock. He laid there looking at the sunlight come through the window. Alex tried to lie still not wanting to wake his brother or sister. But after a few minutes his curiosity kicked in. He slid out from under the covers and crawled quietly out of bed, an excitement stirring in him as he looked forward to a new adventure in this new place.

The floor was cold on his bare feet as they touched the hardwood floor and opa's tee shirt hung down to his feet. He wanted to see everything, but first he had to check out the sunshine that came through the crack in the drapes. He tiptoed over to the window and climbed up on the window seat slowly pushing back the drapes and sticking his head through the hole to see what was outside the window. The sunlight was so bright he could not see anything, so he pulled his head back and pushed the drapes together.

Alex climbed down off the window seat and his imagination soared as he wanted to investigate everything; perhaps he would find a treasure. Opa and oma's house was much larger than any of the other houses where he had lived. The rooms were large and had lots of furniture in them. Alex only remembers living with other families and each family having to live in one bedroom and share the bathroom and kitchen. His grandparents' home seemed like a castle full of great adventures.

Alex recalled an adventure he had at one of the apartments. He had gotten out of bed early and went to explore the kitchen by himself. He found a pillowcase on a top shelf filled with white crystals. He put his hand in, some crystals stuck to his finger and he tasted them. It tasted so good and was so sweet that he closed his eyes and put his whole face into the bag eating it by the mouthfuls. He did not know that he had found sugar; he just knew it was the most wonderful treasure he had ever discovered. His mother found him covered in sugar and was not happy because the sugar belonged to another family. She exclaimed, "Alex, did you eat the sugar?" He shook his head 'no,' with 'crystals' sprinkling down off his face. He wasn't lying; he just didn't know what sugar was. She cleaned him off, gave him a scolding and put him back to bed.

As Alex thought about the sugar adventure, he now wondered if there were more adventures at his grandparents' house. He tiptoed as quietly as his little feed could walk out of the bedroom. He stepped into the hallway and saw three more doors. He slowly opened the first door and peeked into the bedroom in hopes to find another great treasure. The bedroom looked like it belonged to his grandparents; the room was large filled with big furniture and a wash basin table stood next to the large window. The window curtains were pulled back and the window was open, a cool breeze was blowing into the room. The bedding covers were pulled back and the bed was empty. He took one step into the room to look for treasures, but the room was cold from the air blowing through the window.

Alex stepped back and slowly closed the door and looked towards the next door that was open just a crack. He walked towards the door and slowly pushes it open. He saw his mommy sleeping in the bed. A smile came across his face when he saw that she was still there. He decided not to go into the room and wake her, so he slowly closed the door. He looked to his right and saw the stairs that lead down to the kitchen. He was hungry again and remembered the bread he had the night before. He moves towards the stairs and reaches his hand to take the stair rail when he suddenly stops he heard a noise coming from the bathroom.

He turned and tip-toed towards the bathroom; a happy thought filled his mind, it must be papa. But just two steps passed the top of the stairs; he smelled a wonderful aroma coming up the stairs. His tummy grumbled. The need to eat was stronger than the need to see if his papa was in the bathroom. Alex turned and slowly walked down the stairs to see if he could find out where the wonderful smell was coming from. He thought to himself, "Perhaps this treasure would be an even better treasure than the sugar he had found at that other house."

Alex followed the smell that led him straight to the kitchen. He stood outside the kitchen listening, he could hear noises in the kitchen. He wondered if his papa was in the kitchen. Alex slowly pushed open the kitchen door just enough to peek in. There was oma standing in front of the stove stirring something. He looked around the kitchen in hopes of seeing his papa, his heart sunk, papa was not there. He pushed the door all the way open and slowly walked over to see what oma was cooking, inhaling deeply and said, "I am hungry, can I have some of that stuff that smells so good?" Oma turned around with a surprised look on her face to see Alex up and standing right behind her. She looked down at him with a pleasant smile. He looked up as her with his sky-blue eyes filled with a yearning to have something to eat.

Oma's smile widened as she looked down at her grandson and said, "Child, I am sorry, but the food isn't ready to eat yet. I know you are hungry, why don't you go over and sit at the table and I will bring you a little something while we wait for the others to get up and come down to eat." Excitement filled Alex's heart; he turned and hurried over to the table as he thought to himself, "I have the nicest oma." He sat in the chair and watched his oma open the cupboard to make him a little something to eat. She walked over to the table and gave Alex a small piece of bread that she had spread with marmalade. She leaned down and gave him a quick hug before she went back to the stove. He sat quietly at the table, swinging his feet back and forth as he ate his bread and enjoying the sweet taste of the marmalade. Oma turned off the stove and said, "Alex I need you to stay seated at the kitchen table while I go upstairs to see if opa is ready to eat."

Alex finished his slice of bread and was just beginning to think about getting down from the kitchen table to look at the food that was cooking on the stove. The food smelled so good and he was still hungry, he just wanted one taste. While Alex was still in his thought process he heard his oma's voice as she came into the kitchen, "Good boy Alex, we will eat soon." He was disappointed as he looked up at his oma and crossed his arms. Then he heard a noise by the kitchen door, he turned and looked at the door. It opened and his mother walked into the kitchen. His heart leaped for joy at the sight of his mother. He was so excited to see her that he jumped off the chair and ran over and wrapped his arms around her. Alex looked up at his mother with a beaming smile as his mother looked down at him still with tired eyes. She bends down and wraps her arms around Alex pulling him close in a big hug. She picks him up and looks at the marmalade smeared around his mouth and smiles. She walks over to the kitchen table sat Alex in a chair. Alex didn't care if she sat him in the chair he just was glad to see his mommy. He looked up at her and asked, "Mommy will sit next to me?" She replied, "Yes Alex, but I need to get a cloth and wipe you and the table first."

Alex studied his mommy's face as she sat down next to him. She looked relaxed as she watched oma by the stove; it was like someone had wiped all the worry off her face. She asked her mother, "Whatever happened to our cook Helga?" She turned towards Josephine and replied, "Since the war began people wanted to go back to their families. I had to learn many things since then and one of them was how to cook." A grin filled both of their faces as their eyes locked for a few seconds. Then Josephine looked down at Alex and gently said, "Alex, I will be right back, I need to go and get your brother and sister up so they can eat." Her face changed into a stern look as she continued, "You stay here with oma, sit in your chair and behave yourself do you understand?"

Alex looked up at her and said, "Okay mommy." She stood up and gave Alex a quick kiss on the cheek and walked toward the kitchen door. Opa came into the kitchen at the same time, giving Josephine a hug on her way out the kitchen door. He walked over to Alex and gave him a pat on the head and said, "Good morning little man." Then he walked over and gave oma a hug and he looked at the food in the pan and took in a deep breath before saying, "That smells wonderful."

Opa walked over to the kitchen window and stood looking out with his hand clasped behind his back. Alex observed his opa's every move since he came into the kitchen; he was staring at his opa when his mother came back into the kitchen carrying Renate with a sleepy-eyed Ralph walking by her side. Renate leaned her head against Josephine's shoulder, and Ralph walked over and sat down on a chair next to Alex.

Josephine took the chair on the other side of Alex holding Renate on her lap. Opa turned away from the window and walked over to set the table while oma pulled out some hot pads for the pan. Alex was so excited to see what was in the pan that he got up on his knees in the chair. Opa took the hot pan off the stove and sat it in the middle of the table and oma said, "Here is our late breakfast." The breakfast was fried potatoes with scrambled eggs on top. Alex could hardly contain himself as he watched oma put a spoon of the meal on each plate.

Alex thought to himself after taking his first bite, "Yep, this treasure is almost as good as the sugar." He quickly ate his food in anticipation of getting on with his adventure for the day. This is the first-time Alex could remember his tummy being full; he sat down in his chair with a satisfied look on his face as he rubbed his full tummy. Opa looked at Alex and said, "It looks like your done eating would you like to get down." Alex shook his head 'yes' as he climbed down out of his chair, because he wanted to look to see if he could find any other hidden treasures in the kitchen. Alex began to walk around the kitchen with his hands clasped behind his back the way he had seen his opa do.

As Alex walked around the large kitchen taking in everything in sight, he also remembered what his mother had taught him about not touching other people's things. After walking a circle around the kitchen, he decided there wasn't any treasure in the kitchen. He looked over at the window where opa stood earlier and thought there must be a treasure out there. In their other house, he was not allowed to look out the window so he asked, "Mommy may I look out the window?" She said, "Yes you may." Alex was so excited to see what was out the window, he ran towards the window and thought to himself, "I know there must be a great adventure waiting for me out there." Oma looked over at him and said, "No running in the house child." He slowed down to a fast walk to the window as anticipation built.

Alex climbed up onto the window seat and with both of his hands he moved the curtain over so he could see if there were any hidden treasures out the window. He pressed his little face against the window in excitement. The back yard was very large and well kept, there were fruit trees and back in the corner of the yard was a huge oak tree. He imaged himself climbing to the top of the tree and looking for faraway lands.

Then Alex noticed a little house near the oak tree, but was not sure what it could be, perhaps it held a hidden treasure. He was lost in his imagination when he heard the clatter of dishes as oma began clearing the table. He turned to look at opa and with anticipation in his voice asked loudly, "What is the little house doing out in the backyard?" He did not wait for an answer before turning and pressing his little face back against the window to continue to look out. He was so excited and yearned to venture outside and look at everything. Opa still had not replied to his question. With Alex's face pressed hard on the window pane he hollered the question again, "Mommy, what is in the little house way out there by the fence?"

Just as Alex finished hollering opa had slipped up on the window seat next to him. He was so focused on looking outside that he did not notice him at first. Opa pressed his face next to Alex face and wrapped his large arm around Alex's shoulder. They both looked out the window together. His thoughts went to his papa and how he wished his papa there with him. He longed every day that his papa would come back home. Ralph came over and sat on the other side of opa.

The warmth of opa's arm around Alex shoulder cause him to relax and his thoughts went back to the back yard and the little house. He pointed out the window and inquired again about the little house in the back yard. Opa's voice was soft and gentle as he responded, "The little house is called a shelter and inside of the shelter are cages where some pigeons and rabbits live." Ralph got up and walked over to look out the window with them. Opa told them the story of how the little house came to be a shelter.

Opa sat on the window seat with his grandsons, his arms wrapped around each of them as he spoke, "After the war had begun our town had one bombing raid that destroyed about half of the town. The next day the American soldiers came to town and they took over my transportation business so they could move supplies and food. They kept a few of my employees, like Mr. Fritz, to drive trucks locally for them but most of the trucks were military trucks that moved supplies and food across the country."

He continued, "With a lack of income, I built the little house and purchased pigeons and rabbits to raise them for our family." Alex looked at his opa with a puzzled look on his face as his opa continue to explain more, "The pigeons are used to send messages to people." Alex interrupted, "Opa why do people need messages from pigeons?" Opa chuckled as he answered, "Pigeons are faster than the mail and during the war people pay me to send their messages for them." This satisfied Alex for the moment. "The rabbits are raised to sell for food and for us to eat. I am so happy that the American soldiers are here because it is much safer now and there have been no more bombs."

Alex was done listening and turned to look up at his opa who was already looking down at him. Opa smiled when Alex stated, "I want to go outside." He frowned as opa smile went away as quickly as it came, and then opa chuckled and said, "I have to go out to the little house every day to take care of the pigeons and rabbits. I must feed them and make sure that their cages are clean. Would you like to go out with me and look at the rabbits and pigeons?" Alex's face beamed with excitement. Ralph touched his opa shoulder and said, "I want to go too!" Opa turned and smiled at Ralph and said, "Of course you can come." Alex's heart was filled with joy of his new adventure and he jumped down off the window seat and ran towards the kitchen door that led out to the backyard. Ralph did not run but followed close behind. Alex heard oma's voice, "Alex, we don't run in the house." Alex wanted to obey but his little legs kept running towards the door.

By the time Alex reached the door and touched the door knob, opa grabbed him around the waist and picked him up with one arm. Then opa took Ralph's hand and walked both boys back to the kitchen table. Opa set Alex in his chair and said to Ralph, "Go and sit in your chair." Both Ralph and Alex were disappointed; they sat with sad eyes as they looked up at him. Opa stood next to their mother and asked, "Josephine what do you think about the boys helping me with the rabbits and pigeons?" Both boys looked over at their mother she looked pleased and smiled as she said, "Father that is a great idea."

Josephine rose from the table with Renate in her arms, then she looked over at her sons' happy faces, she said, "Ralph and Alex, you cannot go outside the way you are dressed, you will need to wash up and get dressed in your clothes before you can go outside with opa." Alex had a big grin on his face as he jumped out of his chair to follow his mother out of the kitchen; Ralph turned toward opa before leaving the kitchen and said, "Thank you opa." Alex thought to himself and he climbed the stairs, "This is going to be the greatest adventure ever."

Josephine led the boys into the bathroom and said, "Wash up and come into the bedroom when you are done." By the time Alex and Ralph entered the bedroom their mother has laid out the fresh clothes she always kept in the suitcase. She was dressing Renate as Alex jumped up on the bed. Before long each child had on their only change of clean clothing, Josephine was glad she always had extra clothes for each one of them. She said out loud to herself as they were finishing up getting dressed, "I do hope I can get the smoke smell out of your other clothes once they are washed." She did not know that her mother had already washed them last night.

Once they finished dressing they stood before their mother for inspection, she had just finished dressing Renate and then she looked Alex and Ralph up and down. She sat Renate on the floor and said, "Alex your shirt is not button correctly, let me help you." She unbuttoned and button Alex's shirt and then stood up and looked at them again before saying, "Okay you are ready." Alex shouted, "Yeah!" as he followed his brother down the stairs to find their opa. Ralph pushed open the kitchen door for them to enter and they saw opa standing in front of the kitchen window with his hands grasped behind his back deep in thought. Opa turned when he heard the kitchen door shut and saw his two young grandsons looking up at him. With a smile on his face and excitement in his voice he said, "Are you boys ready to go and see the shelter in the backyard and see the cages that are inside?" They both began jumping up and down and said in unison, "Yes opa, yes, we are!"

Opa lead the way out of the kitchen door, down the steps and walked through the grass towards the shelter. Alex and Ralph followed behind. Alex talked about what he thought he might do once inside the shelter. He stopped talking and looked down at his shoes; they were wet from yesterday's rain on the grass; then he looked up to hear birds chirp from the top of the large oak tree in the corner of the yard. The air smelled fresh and cleans from the rainfall. Both boys loved being outside and today was special for them, because since the war began they were not allowed to play outside.

Ralph and Alex had to walk fast to keep up with opa's long stride. Then Ralph shouted, "Do you want to race and see who can beat opa to the shelter?" Of course, Alex wanted to race; he would never turn down a challenge. Ralph hollered again, "On your mark, get set, go!" Ralph bolted off before he finished saying go and ran right passed opa. Alex was close behind but his four-year old legs could not compete with his brother's eight-year old legs. Both boys started laughing with the joy and excitement of being a child with no worries. Opa smiled as he watched his grandsons laughing and having fun. Opa stopped to pick up a large limb he would cut later for firewood.

Alex and Ralph stopped laughing and looked around for opa but did not see him. They were both very curious to see the cages that were inside the shelter; Ralph looked down at Alex and said, "I think opa went inside already, let's look." Ralph slowly opened the door of the shelter and they peeked their heads inside the door not knowing what to expect. It was dark in the shelter except for the light that came through the doorway; the floor was made of dirt. Alex was afraid and stepped back away from the door; he did not want to go in. Ralph held the door open and looked at his brother. Ralph saw a big rock right next to his foot, he pointed and said, "Alex you hold the door open and I will roll the rock over to hold the door open."

Alex looked down and saw the rock and then immediately obeyed. He held the door while he watched his big brother roll the rock over to the door. Once the rock was in place Ralph took Alex by the hand and they slowly walked into the dark shelter. Alex called out, "Opa where are you?" Opa stood watching the boys from the large oak tree where he had taken the branch he had found in the yard. He heard Alex call his name and chuckled to himself as he walked towards the shelter.

Opa walked into the little house to find the boys, he saw them staring in amazement at what they saw in the cages. Opa walked over and pulled the string on the light that hung in the center of the shelter. The light was bright and lit it up allowing the boys to clearly see what was in the cages. Then he walked to the other side of the shelter to open the shutters and let in some daylight. Alex and Ralph had never seen live rabbits or pigeons before, only in picture books.

Opa stepped between Alex and Ralph, kneeling on one knee to get closer to their height; he wrapped an arm around each of their small shoulders and began to explain that this shelter is here to keep the animals' safe. He explained just how important it is to take very good care of these small creatures. Alex asked, "Can I hold one?" Opa turned to look at him and said, "No, not now, but I will teach you how to take care of them." That satisfied Alex and he was eager to learn how to care for the animals.

Opa stood up and took both boys by the hand; he walked them over to show them where the food and cleaning supplies were stored. Alex's eyes took in every detail; there was a big pile of paper, a pail, a small shovel, two rakes and a small broom in the corner across from the cages. Opa said as he pointed at the items, "These are the cleaning supplies for the rabbits and the pigeon's cages." Leaning up against the wall near the cleaning supplies were two large bags of food.

One bag of food had a picture of a rabbit and the other a picture of a pigeon. Opa instructed both Alex and Ralph to look at the picture on the bag before filling the scoop with food, he explained, "You want to make sure you are giving each animal the correct food, do you understand?" They both answered, "Yes opa." Alex was listening intently to everything his opa had to say. Opa's idea was to teach the boys how to feed and care for the rabbits and pigeons, not so much to help him, but to teach them responsibility and help them to feel that this was their home too.

Opa gave Alex some papers and the small broom, he gave Ralph the pail and small shovel and told them to go back over to the cages and set down their cleaning supplies. He followed them bringing with him the two rakes which he leaned on the wall between the rabbit and pigeon cages. There were six large cages, two filled with pigeons and the other four cages were filled with rabbits. Before opa allowed the boys to do anything he needed to show them first how to clean out a cage.

Alex watched closely as opa explained each step on how to clean out the rabbit cage. First he pulled out the tray under the rabbit cage and took the dirty paper out and put it into the pail and said, "We will use this later to fertilize the garden." Next he took the small broom and swept everything to the corner of the cage and then he took the small shovel and scooped up the droppings putting them into the pail. Finally, opa took one on the clean papers and put it on the tray before putting the tray back in the cage. Alex watched patiently taking in each step. After opa put the tray back into the cage he stood up and Alex immediately said, "My turn." Opa, looked down at him and said, "Not yet, I will clean one more rabbit cage and then you and Ralph can each clean the two other." Alex's lip dropped in disappointment and he crossed his arms, but said, "Okay opa."

After cleaning the second rabbit cage opa turned to Ralph and said, "Okay Ralph, I want you to do the next cage, Ralph looked at him in surprise as he said, "Wow opa, I really get to help." Alex with his arms still crossed looked up at opa and said, "I want to help too!" Opa bent down to look at Alex in the eyes and said, "Alex you will clean the next cage." He just shook his head in agreement. He allowed the boys each to clean one of the pigeon cages as he watched them closely so none of the birds got out.

Alex did not know that cleaning out cages was work; he just thought he was having fun helping his opa. Once all the cages were clean opa stood back with his hands on his hips and looked at the cages. Alex copied him and stood back with his hands on his hips also. He looked down and saw Alex standing next to him and a smile spread across his face before he said, "Well done boys, you did an excellent job, now let's go and get some food for the rabbits and pigeons." Opa led the way back over to the food and reminded the boys to make sure and look at the picture on each bag before taking a scoop of food out to feed the animals. Alex looked at the bags and pointed at each bag saying, "Rabbit, pigeon." Opa said, "That's right Alex."

Opa reached into the pigeon food bag and pulled out a scoop full of food, he walked over to the pigeon cages. Alex was curious on how to get the food into the cage as he and Ralph followed their opa back to the cages. The food bowls were inside of the cages right next to the door. Opa explained as he moved the scoop towards the cage door, "You will need to open the door with one hand and at the same time move your other hand with the food into the open door and pour it into the bowl. As soon as you are done pull your hand out and immediately and close the cage door. You must be very careful to not let any of the animals out of their cages."

Both boys said, "Yes, opa," as they watched closely as he put the pigeon food into the cage. The pigeons flapped around the cage as he put his hand into the cage with the food, he decided that it would be better if he took care of the pigeons and let the boys feed the rabbits since one of the pigeons could fly out while they fed them. Opa turned towards Alex and Ralph and said, "I will take care giving food to the pigeons and you boys will feed and water the rabbits. Stay here while I get another scoop of food for the other pigeons." Alex was a little disappointed to not be able to feed the pigeons and Ralph noticed and said, "It is okay Alex we will feed the rabbits." Opa returned and finished feeding the pigeons. He looked down at his grandsons and said, "Feeding the pigeons will be my job and your jobs will be to feed the rabbits, never open the pigeon's cages."

He turned to walk back over to the food bags and said, "Okay boys it is your turn to feed the rabbits." Alex was so excited that he could help feed the rabbits and in his excitement, he asked, "Opa can I feed the rabbits first?" Opa smiled and squatted down next to Alex and said, "Alex, which bag holds the rabbit food?" Alex had a big smile on his face as he pointed to the bag with the picture of the rabbit on it. Then opa took Alex little hand as he reached into the bag placing the scoop in Alex hand and said, "Okay Alex scoop out some food." Ralph was disappointed, he thought since he was the oldest he should go first, a frown ran crossed Ralph's forehead as he watched Alex scoop out the food, but he did not say a word. He watched and waited patiently for his turn.

Alex pulled the scooper full of food out of the bag with a proud look on his face and said, "Look opa." Opa stood up and walked next to Alex as they walked together over to the rabbit cages. Some of the rabbit food pallets began to fall out of the scoop onto the ground as Alex hand began to tilt to one side. Opa reached down taking Alex hand so he could show him how to take his other hand to help balance the scoop, helping the food in the scoop so it won't fall out. Alex looked up at his opa who had a smile on his face, he smiled back. Opa said, "Alex you are doing a great job." Seeing opa smile made him feel happy. They stopped in front of the first rabbit cage and he looked up at his opa. Ralph was already standing by the cages waiting for them. Alex said, "Look Ralph," as he held up the scoop full of food. When opa smiled at Ralph, it made his frown disappeared. Opa looked over at Alex and said, "After we are done feeding the rabbits you should pick up the food that dropped on the floor, so we can use it next time."

Opa repeated the feeding instructions again to Alex, "Now, see if you can open the cage with one hand while holding the scoop in the other." Alex carefully held the scoop with his right hand and opened the rabbit's cage door with his left hand. He paused at the door, he was a little afraid to put his hand in the cage with the rabbit; He heard his opa softly say, "They won't hurt you." Opa's words gave Alex courage and he stretched his arm into the cage and poured the food into the bowl. Opa knelt down on one knee next to Alex as he watched him fill the food bowl, he smiled at him and said, "Make sure you close the door and latch it or the rabbits will get out and run away. He looked over at his opa as he closed the door and latched it and then asked, "Opa like this?" Opa stood up and gently patted him on the top of his head and said, "Good job Alex."

As soon as Alex closed and latched the cage door Ralph began bouncing up and down in the same spot. Opa reached and took Ralph's hand and led him back over to the food sacks. Alex stood by the cage and watched the rabbits eating the food that he had just put into their cage. He poked his finger through the wire and touched one of the rabbit's soft fur then he quickly pulled his finger back out and giggled with delight. Ralph and opa returned and went to the next cage with the food. Opa gave Ralph a quick review of the instructions, Alex stood next to the cage and watched as his brother opened the cage door and slowly reach in and put the food into the feeding bowl.

Ralph quickly pulled out his arm and closed and latched the cage door. Opa smiled and rustled Ralph's hair, then clapped his hand and said, "I am so proud of both of you boys, now take turns feeding the rabbits in the other two cages." Ralph handed Alex the scoop, he took the scoop and pick up the fallen rabbit pallets that had fallen on the ground when he brought it over to the cage the first time, then he walked back to the food bags. When Ralph had fed the rabbits in the last cage and put the scoop back into the rabbit food bag he looked up at opa waiting for his approval. Opa had a big smile on his face as he said, "We are not done yet, the animals still need water."

Opa pointed to the long round tubes that were attached to the outside of each cage and said, "See these lids on top of the tubes, you will need to take them off before you go and get the water." He walked over and picked up the large water pitcher from behind the door and walked out the door, Alex and Ralph followed him to see where he was going. In the backyard, next to the house there was water spout. Opa sat the water pitcher down under the water spout and slowly turned the handle of the water spout and water trickled down into the pitcher.

Alex walked over to get closer to the pitcher so he could watch the water flow down into the water bucket. He felt a true sense of happiness as he watched the clear water fill the pitcher and said, "Look opa water." Both boys were excited and filled with anticipation as they closely watched their opa's every move. Once the water pitcher was about half full, opa turned off the water and asked Alex if he wanted to pick up the pitcher and carry it to the shelter. Alex bent down and with all his four-year old strength; he let out a loud grunt as he barely picked the pitcher up off the ground.

The weight of the water pitcher was too heavy for Alex and he dropped it to the ground. The water splashed out of the pitcher and water ran over the tops of Alex's shoes. He began to cry when the water pitcher slipped out of his hands, he thought that his opa would be mad at him. Opa bent down and wrapped his arm around Alex and said, "Alex you did a good job." Alex looked up into his opa's soft green eyes and knew it would be okay. Opa then picked up the water pitcher and began to fill it up again. Once it was half full he turned and asked Ralph, "Would you like to try to pick up the water pitcher?" Ralph who was eight-years old had no problem picking up the water pitcher and carried the water pitcher back towards the shelter.

Alex's shoes sloshed with water as they walked back to the shelter. When they entered the shelter opa looked down at Alex and said, "I am sorry Alex, but Ralph will be the one who will give the water to the rabbits." Alex got a sad look on his face as he looked up at his him. Opa patted Alex on the head and said, "Don't worry, when you get bigger you will be able to carry the pitcher too. For now, you can turn on and off the water spout for your brother." Alex brow furrowed as he thought about it for a minute and then smiled up at his opa and said, "Okay." Alex stood next to each cage as he watched Ralph fill up the water tube and replace the lids.

After the rabbits and pigeons were feed and watered, opa had Alex and Ralph wait outside the door while he took the rake and pulled anything that was left on the dirt ground towards the door to smooth out the dirt floor. They continue to observe their opa as he put the rake back in the shelter and turn off the light. Opa came out of the shelter and closed the door. He looked down at his two grandsons and said, "Thank you boys for your help today, would you like to help me every day?" Alex jump up and down and said, "Yes," and then Ralph chimed in. Both boys liked helping their opa and whenever they were outside and saw opa they would run up to him and say, "Opa, do you need us to help you?" Opa was delighted with their eagerness to help. Most of the time he said, "Not now boys, you go and play there will be more work later." Excitement filled the boys as they ran off to play tag.

Chapter 16 Army Tanks 1944-1945

Every morning after breakfast Alex and Ralph fed and watered the rabbits. Once they were done is when the fun began. First the boys play tag and then Alex would say, "Ralph, do you want to help me look for a hidden treasure?" Ralph agreed and Alex picked up a stick and used it as a hiking stick as he led the way around the yard. Behind the shelter were a couple of thick bushes, today when Alex walked by the bushes he poked the stick into them and the stick hit something hard. Alex turned to Ralph and said, "I think I found a treasure."

Both boys pushed the bushes back and sticking out of the ground was the top of a small metal box. Alex took his stick and dug around the box while Ralph held back the bushes. Once the small metal box was loose he pulled it out of the bushes and sat down on the ground with the box in front of him. Ralph sat down next to him and they both examined the small metal box, it was rusty and there was dirt on it but there was no lock on the small latch that kept the box closed. Ralph reached over and slowly opened the box. Inside was a black bag fill with something, Alex grabbed the bag out of the box and said, "I knew I would find a hidden treasure." He pulled the string on the bag to open it and began pouring the content into the small box. It made a loud plunking sound as a couple of dozen marbles rolled around the metal box.

Ralph stood up with the box and said, "Let's go and show opa what we have found." Alex followed Ralph as he yelled, "Opa where are you, we found a treasure." Opa came from around the side of the house with a puzzled look on his face and said, "Let me see." Ralph handed him the metal box and he laughed as he looked inside. Then he said, "These marbles must have belonged to the people who owned the property before we moved in. I don't think they will mind if you play with them.

Opa asked, "Do you know how to play marbles?" The boys looked at each other and shook their heads 'no' at the same time. Opa took the string and put it in a circle on the ground and then he poured the marbles in the center of the string. He took time to teach Alex and Ralph how to play marbles. Once he thought the boys knew how to play the game he got up to go back to his chores and let them play. As opa walked away he said, "You boys can store the box in the shelter next to the water pitcher. Alex was so excited, that when it was time to go inside for dinner all he could talk about was the metal box that held his new treasure called marbles.

It had been several years since Alex had seen his papa, sometimes he would sit and see if he could remember what his papa's face looked like. His father's face was always cloudy and out of focus but he remembered being held by his papa. He asked his mother to show him the picture of papa. The war brought with it many sorrows, but the greatest sorrow for Alex was not having his papa home. Being with his opa helped with his longing for his papa, even though papa was not there he felt safe living with his grandparents.

Josephine looked sad most of the time, the only time Alex saw his mother laugh is when she and his oma sat on the back step watching his little sister trying to keep up with her big brothers. The only time Alex can remember being happy was when his papa was home and now being at his grandparents' home they were creating new happy days to remember. They had been with opa and oma for about a month now and it seemed like opa and oma always had enough food to eat and they all had a safe place to sleep each night. A peace settled into Ralph, Renate and Alex's heart that they had never had before.

The sun was up and promising it would be a warm summer day. Alex sat at the kitchen table eating his breakfast and dreaming about another adventure. There was a loud knock on the front door which brought Alex back to reality. Renate began to cry; even though she was only a baby when the SS Elite soldiers raided their home, fear was in her heart. Alex and Ralph jumped off their kitchen chairs and began looking for a place to hide.

Josephine knew what was going on with her children as she picked up Renate and gently called to Ralph and Alex, "Come here sons, it will be okay, just stay close to me." They stopped in their tracks and walked over to their mother. Alex sat down on the floor by his mother's feet hugging her leg and Ralph wrapped his arms around her waist. There was another loud knock on the front door and opa and oma left the kitchen to answer, while they stood frozen in place. Alex's thoughts filled with the fear that the SS Elite soldiers had found them and were here to take them away. Renate continue to cry as Josephine tried to comfort her.

Opa slowly opened the front door with oma standing on her tip toes behind him peering over his shoulder. Both were surprised to see their daughter-in-law Liselotte with her two young children standing there, they all looked tattered and worn from traveling away from the bombing. Liselotte also needed to take refuge at her in-law's home. Oma pushed passed opa and gave her daughter-in-law a hug; opa took the children by the hand and led them into the house. Opa and oma did not know where their son Hans was, they had not heard from him since the war began.

Both oma and opa were glad to see their son's family. Opa lead the children to the sofa and Liselotte followed him into the house. Oma closed the door and excused herself as she walked back into the kitchen and said, "Josephine come quick, your sister in-law and children are here." Josephine handed Renate to her mother and quickly walked into the living room throwing her arms around her dear sister in-law neck, both women wept in each other's arms. Josephine pulled back and looked in her eyes and saw the look of war and what it takes to be a mother out in the middle of the war trying to protect her children. Oma carried Renate and led Ralph and Alex into the living room. The boys had puzzled looks on their faces as they looked at the strange woman and her two children in the living room.

Alex stood staring at his aunt standing there with her son and daughter, they look tired and dirty. He thought to himself, "I guess that is the way we looked when we first came to oma and opa's house." Alex's cousins Michael and Krista looked at Ralph and then Alex with a frown on their faces as if they were wondering why they looked so happy. Oma handed Renate back to Josephine and walked over taking Krista's hand and then led Liselotte and the children upstairs so they could clean up. Josephine said as they walked upstairs, "I know you must be hungry, I will make you some breakfast." Oma came back down shortly to help her fix breakfast for her son's family.

Alex has long forgotten about his adventure that he was dreaming about during breakfast and stood in the kitchen watching his mother prepare food. Oma looked over at Alex and said, "What fun it will be to have your cousins here." Ralph looked over at Alex but did not say a word, they both hoped it would be fun, but didn't know for sure. His aunt and cousins walked into the kitchen and sat down at the table to eat. Alex and Ralph sat at the window seat as they were told and watched their cousins devour their food and ask for more, just as they did when they first arrive. Oma cleared her throat and softly asked Liselotte, "Have you heard anything from Hans?" Liselotte looked over at her and with tears filling her eyes and a soft strained voice answered, "No, not for a long time now.

For Alex, it seemed as if the war had stopped since he came to live at his grandparents' house. There were no more sirens or bombs falling from the sky at oma and opa's house. Alex felt a new-found peace in his heart and a new hope that if his aunt and cousins have come home so would his papa come home.

Right after the chores opa left for his weekly trip into town to his transportation business to see the American officer who would give opa a small amount of money for his business. As opa walked through town he noticed a lot more military tanks and other vehicles than there was the week before. Once he arrived at his transportation business, the officer handed opa an envelope containing the money. Opa looked the officer in the eyes and asked, "What's going on?" The officer looked at opa's wrinkled face and tired eyes before responding. The officer closed the office door and said, "There has been more bombing and more cities have been destroyed, hence the army is coming here. Go home now and only come to town when you need to." An uneasiness filled his heart as he walked back home; and the full August sun caused him to squint thinking about what the officer had said.

The summer was warm and Alex's blond hair looked almost white with his sun kissed tan skin. Whenever opa was outside Alex followed him to see if he could help him. When opa got home he went into the backyard and Alex came running up to him. He turned to Alex and said, "Go and get you brother and cousins I need to talk to the four of you. Alex did not question but ran over to where the others were playing marbles and said, "Opa needs to talk to us." They all got up and followed Alex. Opa just finished putting some branches he had pruned from one of the fruit trees in a pile. Ralph who was wise for being nine-years old asked, "Opa are you okay?" A smile spread across opa's face as he answered, "I want you to never go around the house to the front yard, even when you are playing hide-and-seek. You may only go into the front of the house when an adult is with you."

The children did not understand why they could only stay in the backyard, but they listened and the four of them played together in the backyard without a care in the world. Playing hide-and-seek and climbing the big tree to look for far off lands. For the first time the children were genuinely happy. One day while Alex was sitting up in the big tree dreaming of new adventures he saw some very big cars or trucks coming down the street. He wondered what they were; he had never seen anything like them before.

Alex was so curious that he thought he would sneak around the house and go into the front yard to take a closer look at these strange vehicles. He slowly climbed down the tree, Ralph and his two cousins were playing marbles under the tree. He did not say a word to them just walked by and slowly walked towards the side of the house. He got to the edge of the house that leads to the front yard and peeked around the corner and saw the last huge vehicle drive past the house. A big smile came on his face as he turned and hurried back to the backyard wondering what it was.

Alex could hardly sleep that night and was up before the other children were awake. Oma and opa were in the kitchen talking when Alex pushed open the kitchen door. Oma said, "Alex, what are you doing up so early?" He rubbed his eyes and said, "I am not tired." Oma said, "Would you like to help me set the table for breakfast." He had a hard time keeping his secret, he wanted to blurt out what he had seen, but knew he had disobeyed and didn't want to get in trouble. He kept quiet as he helped set the table. Oma watched Alex and wondered why he was so quiet, he usually talked a lot. Opa and the rest of the family came into the kitchen for breakfast.

This was the first-time Alex did not look forward to feeding the rabbits, all he wanted to do was get done and head back to the front yard. Once the animals were fed, opa turned to the children and said, "Okay go and play. Alex followed Ralph towards the big tree remembering what he saw the last time he was up in the big tree. At the foot of the big tree Ralph decided to climb up the tree. Alex stood at the bottom of the tree and watched, instead of climbing up the tree after Ralph; then he turned and headed toward the side of the house. In Alex's excitement, he began to run around the corner of the house. Alex could hear his opa holler at him, "Alex, stop!"

Before opa got "stop" out of his mouth Alex was around the corner and looking at the front yard. He hesitated for only a moment and then he saw the big truck again and did not stop. Alex was mesmerized and walked into the front yard towards the small picket fence so he could get a closer look. Opa came around the corner of the house into the front yard; he let out a big sigh as he saw what Alex was looking at. Opa walked up to Alex and placed his hand on the top of his shoulder, Alex jumped at the touch of his opa's hand, then he pointed and asked him, "Opa, what is that?"

Just then Ralph, Michael and Krista came running up to the fence and stood next to Alex. The big vehicle had just passed the house and was moving down the street. They all pointed and with excitement in their voices they ask in unison, "What is it opa?" He squatted down next to his grandchildren as he answered their question, "That is an American Army tank." Alex's eyes grew big with wonderment and he needed to ask more questions, "What is an American Army tank and where do they come from?" Opa smiled down at Alex and answered, "The Americans are here to help keep us safe. Then opa explained what it would be like if the American soldiers were not here, "This town would be just like all the other cities that you have been in and the bombs would fall from the sky." Alex got a serious look on his face as he responded to his opa "Oh." Ralph said, "Opa I want the Americans to stay here."

Alex understood immediately what opa had meant, since he had seen the effects of the bombing in those cities and how he always had to leave everything behind to move to another new city in hopes the bombing would stop. He looked up into his opa's eyes and said, "Don't let the American Army tanks leave, because it is good that the American soldiers are here to keep us safe." Opa patted the top of Alex's head and smiled. But he still had more questions, "Will the American Army tanks stay here to keep us safe for a long time? Do you think they will come back by our house again?" Opa looked from one grandchild to the other and he could see that fear had returned to their eyes as they stared at him, this saddened his heart.

Opa bent down between his grandchildren and gathered them toward himself, wrapping them into his arms to comfort them as he softly replied, "I think the soldiers will be here for some time, but the Army tanks will not be back today, they don't come by every day. Perhaps tomorrow they will return." Then he said to all of his grandchildren, "You children must promise me this one thing that you will never come out to the front yard by yourselves. Instead you may look out the living room window and if you see the American Army tank you come and tell me, okay?" Opa kept his eyes fixed on Alex as one by one each child answered, "Yes, opa."

Alex's eyes shone with adventure and with excitement in his voice he said to his opa, "Opa, I can climb up into the big tree in back yard and watch out for the American Army tanks." Opa smiled at Alex's sense of adventure, but pressed again with his request, "Each of you need to promise me you will never come out to the front yard alone again." "Okay opa," they all answered again as they each looked up into his serious face. He pulled them into another hug and said, "Okay, I know you understand how important this is and that you obey." The warmth of opa's words encouraged them and the love in his voice as he spoke caused the fear to leave their hearts and it was replaced with peace. Opa could see the peace in his grandchildren's eyes. Ralph, Alex, Michael and Krista knew they could trust their opa.

Opa stood up and stretched before saying, "Now it is time to go in and have some lunch. The children all followed opa to the back of the house. There was an excitement that filled each of the children about the American Amy tanks they had seen. Ralph and Alex could hardly wait to tell their mother and oma what they had seen and what opa had told them about how the American tanks and how they were there to keep them safe. Michael and Kristin also ran into the house to look for their mother. Alex and Ralph had so much excitement that wanted to burst out of them by the time they entered the kitchen; both boys began to talk at the same time as loud and as fast as they could. Their mother and oma both looked over to opa and then looked at the excitement in the boys and smiled down at them.

Josephine had a smile on her face as she said, "Slow down, I can't understand what you are saying; I need one of you to talk at a time. Ralph began to tell the story as Alex listened to him; it was at this point that Alex's young mind began to understand what opa had told them about how important it is to have the Americans soldiers coming into the small town of Suderode. The soldiers would keep them save and no bombs would fall from the sky. When it was Alex's turn to talk, he turned and looked up into opa's eyes and asked, "Can the American soldiers stay forever?" Alex's mother bent down and pulled him into a hug as she softly said, "We don't know how long they will stay, but we pray they will continue to keep us safe."

The Roads in and out of Bad Suderode were cut off because of the bombing and very few supplies could get into town. There began to be a food shortage. Alex sense that the adults were worried and sometimes his mother and aunt would sit at the kitchen table talking softly with sad looks on their faces. If Alex came into the kitchen they would perk up and smile asking, "Alex is everything alright?" He smiled back and answered, "Yes, mommy everything is okay." But he knew in his heart that things were not alright and sometimes late at night he would hear his mother or aunt crying.

It was difficult for both women with the heaviness of worry and concern for their husbands and then daily trying to stay strong for their children. One night Alex got up out of bed to see why his mother was crying. He tip-toed into her bedroom and touched her on the cheek as he asked, "Mommy are you okay?" Josephine stopped crying and wiped her face with her handkerchief and then without saying a word she pulled Alex into bed with her. Alex wrapped his arms around his mother's neck and fell back to sleep. Once Alex was asleep, Josephine carried him back to his own bed.

Alex woke up the next morning wondering how he got back into his bed. He pushed back the covers, climbed down out of bed and headed down toward the kitchen. Alex slowly pushed open the kitchen door; he saw his opa sitting at the kitchen table sipping on a cup of hot coffee. Alex hurried over and tapped his opa on the knee; Opa looked down at him and sat his cup down on the table, taking Alex up into his lap and gave him a big hug. Alex looked up into opa's eyes and asked, "Can we go out into the front yard to see if there are any American Army tanks coming down the street again today?" Alex wanted to see the tanks again and maybe one of the American soldiers will come out of the tank. Opa had a sad look on his face as he shook his head 'no.' Alex's heart sunk and a feeling of sadness filled him as he slipped off his opa's lap and started walking toward the kitchen door. Opa raised his voice with a tone of fear in it and said, "Stop!" Alex stopped immediately and turned towards his opa.

Opa was afraid Alex would try to go out in the front yard by himself again, so he walked over to Alex and knelt on a knee next to him looking him in the eye as he began to explain again the importance of never going into the front yard without him. Then he sternly said, "Alex, do you understand what I am saying? If you disobey you will stay inside and not play outside for a long time." Alex's eyes brimmed with tears and a single tear ran down his cheek as he shook head and said, "Yes opa." Opa picked him up into his arms and wrapped him in a big hug. He laid his head on his shoulder and let out a deep sigh.

Opa held Alex until he felt his body relaxed in his arms and then opa whispered in Alex's ear, "You need to go back upstairs and wake your brother, sister and cousins up for breakfast. When we are done with our chores we can take a walk around to the front yard." A smile beamed across Alex's face as he gave opa a big hug and whispered back into his ear, "Thank you opa!" Oma came into the kitchen just as opa sat Alex down onto the floor. Alex was so excited to go back upstairs and tell his brother what opa said that he almost ran into oma on his way out the door.

At the bottom of the stairs Josephine turned toward the kitchen carrying Renate. Alex bumped into his mother and said, "Sorry mommy," without stopping as he hurried up the stairs. His mother said, "Alex slow down, next time you come downstairs make sure you are dressed for the day." Alex stopped and turned towards his mother and said, "I will mommy, I am going to see the American Army tanks today."

Alex got to the top of the stairs and bolted into the bedroom. Ralph was already up and getting dressed when he came bursting into the room. Alex ran over to him and was breathing fast with excitement as he told Ralph that after they did the chores opa was going to take them out into the front yard to see the American Army tanks today. Alex dressed himself as quick as possible and then the boys went to wake up their cousins. The boys waited at the top of the stairs for Michael and Krista to get dressed. Once their cousins met them at the top of the stairs, Alex told them, "After we finish the chores opa is going to take us to see the American Army tanks." They screamed, "Yeah," just as they heard oma yell at the bottom of the stairs, "Breakfast is ready, hurry up."

Alex chatters to the others about their adventure for the day as they enter the kitchen. Mother had just finished setting the table and said, "You children are excited today, but I need you to settle down and take your seat at the table." The children quietly and quickly went and sat in their chairs. The breakfast was only a piece of bread and a spoonful of scrambled eggs; the last of the butter was used yesterday.

The food shortage was getting worse, there were long lines at the store to get food and portion controls on how much food each family could buy. Alex looked down at his half slice of bread and said, "Where are the potatoes?" Oma and opa looked at each other, but his mother answered, "Today, we only have bread and eggs." At the sound of his mother's words Alex remembered the many times before when they had little to eat and was thankful for even the smallest morsel of bread. Alex said, "Okay mommy, thank you."

It did not take the children long to finish breakfast. Alex looked over at his opa and said, "Can we get our coats and wait for you by the back door so we can do our chores?" Opa looked at each one of his grandchildren's eager faces and then chuckled as he answered, "Yes, go and get your coats." By the time opa rose from the table and got his coat all four of the children were standing by the back door watching him. He walked over to the back door and said, "I've never seen children so excited about doing their chores." He opened the back door and walked down the steps, each one of the children followed him out the door in a line like little ducklings following a mama duck.

Alex always like feeding the rabbits, but today was different; he wanted to get done so he could go out into the front yard. Alex began to hurry and dropped the scoop full of rabbit food onto the ground. Opa had to remind all the children several times to slow down and how important it is to make sure to clean the cages and feed the rabbits without making a mess or spilling food and water on the dirt floor of the shelter. Alex looked up from picking up the rabbit pallets on the ground and said, "Okay, opa." He slowed down because he wanted opa to be proud of him.

Opa went outside to water the garden while the children finished taking care of the rabbits. Once they were done, Alex ran out to the garden and said, "Okay opa, we are done with all our chores, now we can go into the front yard to see the American Army tanks?" By the time opa turned to face Alex the others children were standing next to him. Opa looked down at the smiles on each one of his grandchildren's faces and couldn't help but smile. He turned off the water and put down the hose as the children stood there waiting patiently for him. He looked at his grandchildren and could see the anticipation on their faces, a feeling of love swelled in his heart for them.

Opa said, "Okay, first let me check to see if there are any messes made while you were doing your chores and if I find no messes then we can go out front yard." The children waited by the garden and soon opa walked back over and said, "I am proud of each of you for doing such a great job with your chores." He turned and walked towards the front of the house and the children followed him lined up in a row from youngest to the eldest. Opa suddenly stopped right before turning the corner to the front yard and the children all lightly bumped into each other. Opa turned and said, "We need to go to the back yard if we don't see any Army tanks today. I need your help to gather some small sticks from around the backyard and stack them by the shed for the winter. Eager to get into the front yard each child said, "Okay." He turned and they continued to follow him around to the front yard.

Once they turned the corner into the front yard, Alex made a bee line for the fence and the others children were right behind him. One by one each child climbed up and stood on the bottom rail of the fence, leaning out and looking up and down the street for the American Army tanks. Opa stood behind them and looked at his watch; he let his grandchildren talk among themselves as they turned their heads watching for one of the Army tanks for about fifteen minutes. There were no American Army tanks that drove by that day, he looked down at his grandchildren and said, "It is time to go and gather up the sticks for winter." Alex looked at his opa with a sad face that was filled with disappointment. None of the children argued with their opa to stay longer. They each jumped down from the fence and this time they did not run but slowly followed opa back into the back yard to help him gather the sticks.

Each morning after the chores were done Alex asked his opa if he could go into the front yard to see if there were any American Army tanks out there. Opa was glad that Alex got so excited about seeing the army tanks and most of the time he would agree. Right after the chores were done all the children raced to the side of the house and waited for opa.

Once out in the front yard it was a game to see who could get to the fence first. Opa enjoyed hearing the laughter of his grandchildren. It had been three days since the last American Army tank came up the street. Just as opa looked up from his watch to call the children to go the back yard, there was a loud noise of an army tank that had just turned the corner to head down their street.

The children got excited and waved as the army tank passed by; today one of the army soldiers was waving from the top of the tank. Alex thought to himself, "What a great adventure, maybe someday I will ride in one of those army tanks." The children watched the army tank until it drove out of sight. Opa clapped his hands and said, "Okay, time to go into the back yard. Alex jumped down off the fence rail and ran to the back yard; he ran straight to the large Oak tree and began to climb it. Opa said, "Alex, what are you doing?" Alex yelled back, "I am going to see the army tank from the top of the tree." Opa chucked to himself as he watched the other children began to climb up the tree behind Alex.

On one occasion two American Army tanks drove up the street as the children waiting on the fence rail. Alex yelled out as he pointed at the army tanks, "Opa, look there are two army tanks today." Out of each tank two soldiers looked down at the children and the tanks slowed down as they passed the house. The soldiers began to wave back at the children and yelled out, "Hello." Alex was very excited as he waved back more fervently and copied what the soldiers said, "Hello." Hearing Alex caused the soldiers to smile down at Alex.

Once the army tanks were out of site, Alex jumped down off the fence rail and pulled on his opa's pant leg as he said, "Opa, did you see the soldiers' wave at us?" Opa looked down at his youngest grandson with a smile on his face as he shook his head, 'yes.' Alex ran around the house and climbed up the large oak tree to see if he could still see the army tanks. As he sat on one of the top limbs and looked at the dust that was left from the army tanks, he dreamed about being an American soldier and driving one of those army tanks when he grew up.

October was warmer than normal in 1945; the fall leaves had begun to fill the ground around the large oak tree. Alex's birthday was just a few days away; he was excited to be turning five-years old. Today before Alex could go out to the front yard and look for army tanks he had to help his opa rake up the oak leaves. Opa whistled as he raked and Alex bent down and gathered up arms full of leaves to put them in a large basket. Alex stopped, he put his hands on his hips and said, "Opa do you hear that? The army tank noise." Opa stopped and listened as he looked down at Alex with a smile on his face. Then he put down his rake and said, "Alex, shall we go out front and finish the leaves after we see the army tank?" Alex jumped up and down and called out, "Ralph, we going to see the army tanks now." All the children stopped what they were doing and began to run towards the side of the house to wait for opa.

The American Army tanks were just beginning to drive by the house when the children ran up to the fence and began waving. There were two army tanks again today. One tank kept driving, but the second tank pulled to a stop right in front of the house. The two soldiers who were looking out the top of the army tank got out and climbed down from their tank, they walked over to where the children were leaning over the fence. Alex was excited as they came closer to the fence and the tall American soldier looked straight at Alex and smiled at him. All the children were excited and were startled by the tone in opa's voice as he commanded, "Children step back from the fence, they obeyed immediately and opa stepped in front of the children with uncertainty in his eyes and said to the soldiers in German, "Can I help you? "

The two soldiers did not say a word but kept walking forward toward the fence with smiles on their faces. Opa thought this was strange, but since the soldiers were smiling they must not mean them any harm so he allowed the children to climb back up on the fence rail. The soldiers stopped at the fence and both reached out their hands to shake opa's hand. Opa extended his hand to the soldiers giving them a firm hand shake. The tall soldier asked opa in German if they could give the children a chocolate bar. He was surprised at the soldiers' kindness as he his head and answered, "Yes, thank you." Alex and Ralph had never eaten a chocolate bar before and did not know what it was or how it tasted. Alex looked at his opa, he was having a hard time pronouncing the word chocolate so he asked, "Opa what is it?"

The soldier with the round face and red cheeks and the biggest smile held out a chocolate bar to one child at a time. Once Alex took the chocolate bar he stared into the kind eyes of the soldier and said in German, "Thank you, American soldier." The taller soldier patted Alex on the head and seemed happy as he smiled down at him. Both soldiers turned at the same time and climbed back up into their army tank. The children were so excited about seeing the soldiers up close but more excited today about receiving a chocolate bar. All of them waved and yelled goodbye as they watched the army tank drive down the street and out of sight.

Alex looked at his chocolate bar in his hand with wonderment observing the pretty paper and then he held it up to his nose and smelt it; he took a deep breath of the amazing sweet smell. Ralph had already ripped off the paper of his chocolate bar and took a big bit of the chocolate and said, "Mmm, this is so good." Alex looked over at his brother before he quickly tore the paper off his chocolate bar. He took his first bit; this is the best thing he had ever tasted, even better than the sugar treasure he found. With each bite, he thought to himself, "This chocolate bar is so good and like nothing I had ever eaten before, it is sweet and wonderful melting in my mouth with each bite." It did not take him long to devour the whole bar.

Opa stood watching all four children enjoying their special treat. After they had finished eating the chocolate bar opa looked down at each of their faces and hands which were marked with chocolate and said, "Don't touch anything," He lead the children around to the backyard and said, "Wait here at the bottom of the steps." He climbed the four steps and opened the back door hollering into the kitchen, "I need a wet cloth for the children's faces." Alex licked the chocolate off his fingers as they waited.

Before long the back door swung open and oma held a wet cloth in her hands, she looked at the children's faces and asked opa, "Where did all that dirt come from?" Opa laughed as he took the cloth and began wiping the children's faces and hands while he explained to her, "The American Army soldiers stopped, got out of their tank and gave each one of the children a chocolate bar."

By the time it was Alex's turn to get washed he was sucking on his fingers to get every last taste of the chocolate off them. Josephine was changing Renate when she heard the commotion, she finished and walked out the kitchen door and stood at the top of the stairs holding Renate's hand. She just shook her head as she looked down at Alex's face. When Alex saw his little sister, his first thought for just a moment was, that he should have saved some of the chocolate bar for her, but dismissed the thought at the memory of how good the chocolate bar tasted. Opa wiped Alex's face and handed the cloth back to oma, He then turned his attention to his grandchildren and said, "Now go and play until lunch is ready." Alex ran over to the big oak tree, he wanted to climb up and see if he could still see the army tanks.

After Alex had his first taste of chocolate he got a sweet tooth and always wanted to eat anything sweet and asked his oma for a chocolate bar. Oma answered him by saying, "There are no chocolate bars here and we have no money to buy any." Each morning after the chores opa took the children around to the front yard to look for army tanks, Alex loved this daily adventure. For over a week the army tanks did not come by and Alex's heart felt disappointed as they had to walk back around the house.

It was the last day of October and Alex delighted as one of the army tanks pulled to a stop in front of their house and two American Army soldiers crawled out of the tank and walked over to the fence, they greeted opa with a handshake. Alex was hoping for another chocolate bar, but this time they handed each child a banana and an orange. Alex had never seen or eaten a banana or orange so as he held them up to opa he asked, "Opa what are these?"

Both soldiers laughed among themselves as they walked back and climb up into the army tank. Opa looked down at Alex and said, "Alex those are fruit, called a banana and an orange." Then he said to all the children come let's go into the backyard and you can eat your fruit. You need to wait and I'll show you how to eat them first." Alex had a puzzled look on his face as he looked down at the bright yellow and orange fruit in his hand. The children followed opa back around the house where he had them each sit on the lower steps that lead up to the back door. Opa took Ralph's banana from him and showed the children how to peel it before they ate it. Alex peeled back the banana skin and tasted the firm white inside, he wrinkled up his nose at the taste he was expecting it to taste sweet. He was hungry, so he ate the banana.

Opa then gathered the oranges from the children and said, "We will share these oranges with everyone, later today." Alex frowned as he handed his orange to his opa. Food was scarce so opa wanted to use the oranges as one of the families' next meals. Alex looked at opa and said, "Can we go and play now?" Opa answered and pointed, "Yes but first put those yellow banana peels over in the compost pile. Alex ran ahead to the other children to the compost pile and then scurried up the big tree.

Chapter 17 Food Lines 1945

The bombing of the major roads in Germany caused a shortage of food and supplies into Suderode. Josephine, Liselotte, and opa went to town every day to see if any food had arrived. Oma always stayed home to care for the children. If any trucks hauling food could get into town people had to stand in line on a first come first serve basis to buy food. The rain had just begun to fall as opa stepped up to the front of the line, the store owner asked, "How many people in your household?" Opa answered, "There are nine of us." The store owner pulled out a loaf of bread, a dozen eggs and a jar of marmalade, he handed the items to opa and said "That will be ten bank notes."

Opa handed the owner the money and moved out of line, he walked over to where Josephine and Liselotte were standing waiting for him. Each time they went to town opa did not know if he would return with food, since once the store owner ran out of food they would close their shop doors. Many who had stood in line for hours were sent away empty handed and often, it was days in between before the store would have food to sell again. If you were one of the lucky ones who got food you would try to make it last for a week.

In the center of town there were American soldiers gathered with their tanks to guard the town. Over the past month there were very few army tanks which drove down the street by their house. Josephine and Liselotte were watching the soldiers and their army tanks when opa walked up and touched Josephine of the shoulder, she jumped and turned towards him as he said, "We got some food today. Let's take the boys to town with us tomorrow!" Josephine looked surprised that her father wanted to take the boys to town as she shook her head in agreement; she knew she could trust her father's decisions.

The rain was still falling as they hurried home; opa was excited to tell the children about his plan to go to town. Opa sat the wet bag of groceries on the table and headed for the back door. Opa looked around the yard and all he could see was Alex, they were playing hide-an- seek in the rain it was his turn to find the others. Opa looked around the yard and said, "Alex where is your brother and cousins?" Before Alex could answer opa yelled, "Ralph, Michael and Krista come here." Alex wondered what was going on with opa; he kept smiling down at him.

Ralph, Michael and Krista came out from their hiding places and ran over as quickly as they could to where Alex and opa stood. A big smile came across opa's face as he instructed the children that they needed to go inside and get cleaned up and go and sit on the sofa. The children looked at each other and then at their opa before heading into the house. They waited with anticipation as opa looked at each one of them, then he took a deep breath and said, "I want to take two of you to town with me tomorrow and the other two the next day, would you like that?"

All four of the children stood up and began to jump up and down and dancing in a circle as they yelled, "Yes! Yes! Yes!" Opa had to raise his voice so the children could hear him above their cheering, "Okay settle down, remember I said only two of you can go into town at a time. Sit back down I will be right back."

Opa came back and stood in front of them. He had his hand closed into a fist and there were four small twigs sticking out of the top. He stretched out his fist and held it in front of the children. The children looked up at the twigs with a puzzled look on their faces. Alex scratched his head as he was trying to figure out what the twigs were for.

Opa spoke softly to the children, "I want each of you to take one of these twigs and the two with the shortest twig will go to town with me tomorrow." Alex did not wait for opa to say another word; he reached over and tried to pull one of the small twigs out of opa's fist. Opa pulled back his hand and said, "Alex we will choose from the oldest to the youngest, Ralph you need to go first." Ralph reached out and pulled one of the twigs from opa's fist. Since Alex was the youngest he had to wait until all but one of the twigs was left in his opa's fist. Alex pulled the last twig and his opa said, "Now hold your twigs up in the air I will see who has the shortest twigs."

Alex held his twig up as high as he could for opa to examine. Then opa said, "Ralph and Alex, you go to town tomorrow and Michael and Krista will go the next day." Michael and Krista were disappointed as they looked up at their opa. Alex looked over at his cousins and said, "We won fair and square." Then he took Krista by the hand and pulled her to go out into the yard as he said, "Let's finish our game of hide-and-seek." Alex put his hands over his eyes and started counting as the others ran to hide. After the game was over Michael and Krista played marbles under the large tree while Alex and Ralph climbed to the top of the tree and talked about their big adventure to town in the morning.

That night both Alex and Ralph could not get to sleep; they were filled with anticipation about their adventure to town, they had never been to town before. The boys still slept in the large bed with their sister sleeping between them. They continued to talk and giggle about their adventure. Renate who was barely three-years old was not allowed to town and she did not understand why. Renate rubbed her eyes and said, "I am tired." Both boys ignored her and kept talking. Renate in her tiredness and frustration at her brothers cried out, "Mommy, Mommy," Alex and Ralph stopped talking and pulled the covers up and pretended to sleep as they heard their mother's footsteps in the hallway.

It was well past 10 p.m. as Josephine walks into the bedroom to see why Renate was crying. The boys had the blanket all the way up to their chins and Alex squeezed his eyes tight to keep them closed. Mothers know things and she knew they were not asleep, just pretending. She picked Renate up giving her a hug. Renate pointed at her brothers and said, "Alex and Ralph make too much noise." After wiping away Renate's tears and kissing her on the cheek, she laid Renate back in bed. As she pulled the blanket up over Renate she said in a soft but stern voice, "That is enough boys, if you are not to sleep in five minutes, you will not be going anywhere tomorrow!" Both boys knew their mother meant business and they had better get to sleep. Josephine sat on the edge of the bed and began to sing one of her hymns. When she sang, the melody always seemed to sooth her children. Alex relaxed and drifted off to sleep.

Early the next morning the sunlight streamed into the bedroom through the slit in the drapes, Alex opened his eyes and stretched his arms over his head before reaching over and shaking his brother to wake him. Ralph rubbed his eyes and looked at Alex wondering why he was already awake. Ralph began to say something, but Alex put his finger on his lips to let Ralph know they need to be quiet. They quietly climbed out of bed trying not to wake up their little sister. Alex whispered to Ralph, "Today we get to go into town." They put on the clothes that their mother had laid out the night before. Thoughts filled Alex's head with imaginary visions of what he thought he might see on his adventure to town.

Once they washed up in the bathroom they tiptoed towards the stairs. Josephine came out of her room and looked at both of her sons with surprise that they were up and already dressed. She said, "I was just coming to wake you both up." Alex pointed to his clothes and said, "Look mommy we are all dressed and ready to go to town with opa." She smiled and walked over to the bathroom. Ralph led the way down the stairs towards the kitchen, where their oma and opa were standing by the sink talking quietly.

When they heard the door open they stopped talking. Alex bolted into the kitchen, his face filled with excitement. Oma looked at her grandsons with amazement and said, "Wow! You are both dressed before breakfast today." They both smiled up at their oma as she continued, "Your mother should be down shortly, come here sit down at the table and I will make you each a slice of bread for breakfast."

Josephine came into the kitchen with Renate still in her pajamas following close behind. Renate still looked tired as she rubbed her eyes. Josephine smiled at her son's happy faces; it made her heart happy to see them filled with joy and expectation once again. She said, "After breakfast you will still need to help opa feed the animals before we can go to town." Alex's face dropped, he stuck out his lower lip into a pout, at the same time crossing his arms across his chest. He wanted to go to town now; being patience was hard for him. Josephine said, "Alex if that is the way you are going to act then maybe you should stay home." Alex dropped his arms immediately.

Liselotte and her children came into the kitchen and sat down at the table. The only thing they had for breakfast that day was a slice of bread each. Opa stood up out of his chair and walked over to the back door. Alex and Ralph jumped down out of their chairs and put on their coats before they followed him out the door and into the backyard. Michael and Krista still in their pajamas had to get dressed before they could go outside. Opa whistled while they worked together feeding and caring for the rabbits and pigeons, the time went fast and before Alex knew it they were done.

Alex skipped as he headed back to the house. Opa opened the back door and said as they entered the kitchen, "Go up and wash your hands, then we will be ready to go." Walking as fast as they could to get up the stairs and into the bathroom, they talked a mile a minute about their adventure, the soap slipped out of Alex and unto the floor. He picked the soap up and put it back on the sink before rinsing his hands. Then he grabbed the towel wrapping around his hands to dry them, he put the towel back as Ralph led the way down the stairs where their opa and mother were waiting.

The walk into town was about twenty-minutes, but today with two small boys it took an extra ten minutes before they arrived at the town square. Alex's eyes got big as they rounded the corner and the town square came into full view; he saw that four American tanks were parked right in the center of the square. American soldiers stood by their tanks and more soldiers were walking around town.

Alex pointed at the tanks and yelled with excitement, "Look mommy at all the army tanks there are in the town!" Josephine looked down at Alex with a stern look that he did not understand, she took Alex's hand and scolded, "We don't need to yell and point." By the time they had arrived into town there was already a long line for food. Josephine turned towards her father and said, "Why don't I go and get in line and wait while you take the boys on a walk past the army tanks." Both boys' faces lit up with delight and excitement. Opa looked down at his grandsons with a big smile and a twinkle in his eyes.

Opa took both Alex and Ralph's hands they walked slowly past the four army tanks that were in the center of the square. One of the soldiers recognized Alex and Ralph; he was the tall soldier who had given them the chocolate bars. The soldier walked over towards them and asked their opa in the German language, "Would it be alright if the boys look inside my tank?" Alex and Ralph looked up at their opa with excitement and enthusiasm as they waited for him to respond. He looked down at his grandson's faces and could not resist the look of expectation of their face. He looked back at the solider and said, "Yes, thank you, that is very kind of you, I know the boys would love to see inside one of your army tanks."

Opa held the boys' hands tight as they walked closer to the American Army tank. Alex's eyes grew big as he looked up at the huge vehicle that stood before him. He began to imagine what it must be like inside the big tank and maybe they would let him drive it. Opa interrupted Alex's thoughts as he pulled on his hand and said, "Do not touch anything and listen to what the soldier tells you."

The soldier looked down at Alex and Ralph as opa let loose of their hands. Then the soldier turned to Ralph first and lifted him up onto the rim at the bottom of the army tank. The soldier climbed up into the tank and reached down and took both of Ralph's hands and pulled him up to the top of the army tank. The soldier scoops him up by the waist and lowers him down into the tank where another soldier was waiting to guide him into the tank.

Once Ralph disappeared into the army tank Alex reached over and tugged on his opa's pant leg, the fear of people being taken away came back to Alex again; he thought that maybe Ralph would not come back out of the army tank. This fear rose every time someone Alex loved was taken away by someone. Alex's heart was always fearful that they would go away and not come back, just like Frank did when the men came and took him away. Tears came to Alex's eyes as he asked his opa, "Is Ralph going to come back?"

Opa could see the frown that had formed on Alex's face and the tears in his eyes, so he took Alex by the hand and patted it as he said, "Yes, it is okay, your brother will come back out soon and then you will have your turn to see what is in the big American Army tank." The ten minutes that Ralph was down in the tank seemed like forever to Alex as he kept looking up at the top of the tank

Ralph came up out of the army tank with a big smile on his face. The soldier sat him down on the ground, he turned around towards the soldier and exclaimed in German, "Boy that was fun, can I have another turn?" The soldier just smiled as he walked Ralph back over to his grandfather. Opa took Ralph's hand as he said, "Not today Ralph, it is your brother's turn."

It was Alex's turn and without reservations he reached out for the soldier's hand. The soldier lifted him and stood him on the ledge at the bottom of the army tank. Then he pulled him up and sat him on the opening rim of the tank. The soldier put his hand around Alex's waist and gently lowered him down into the army tank. The soldier inside the tank grabbed Alex's legs and set him down next to the soldier who sat at the driver's seat of the tank.

Alex had to adjust his eyes to the dim light in the army tank and as he looked around his eyes grew big with wonderment. There were so many lights, knobs and buttons in the army tank, more than were in the truck that brought them to his grandparents' house. The soldier who sat in the driver seat turned and looked down at the little blond haired boy sitting next to him, the glow of wonder on Alex's face, reminded the soldier of his own five-year old son back home. He asked Alex, "Would you like to sit on my lap, so you can get a better look at the controls?"

Alex looked up at soldier a little afraid at first, he did not know what controls were, but Alex wanted to get closer to the lights, buttons and knobs. Alex timidly shook his head 'yes', and he hoped in his heart that he could drive the tank. The soldier gently lifted him on to his lap. He allowed him to turn the steering sticks and touch some of the knobs. Alex was so amazed and filled with excitement at all he saw that he turned and look up into the soldier face and asked, "Can I drive now?" All the soldiers in the tank, who understood German, let out a loud laugh, and the one who held Alex said, "You need to be a lot bigger before you can drive a tank." Alex thought he was already big enough to drive the army tank but accepted his answer.

Alex's time in the tank was up, but he did not want to leave. The soldier said, "I know this is lots of fun, but I think your family is waiting for you and would miss you if I don't take you back to them." Alex looked up at the soldier and asked, "Can I come back into the army tank again and maybe drive it down my street?" They all looked at Alex and the soldier who helped him into the tank said, "Only soldiers can drive army tanks, but perhaps you will be able to come back again and sit at the controls."

The next thing Alex knew the soldiers lifted him back up out of the tank and set him down in front of his opa. One of the soldiers came out of the tank holding two bananas, he walked over and handed Ralph and Alex each one. Both boys both said at the same time, "Thank you." Alex turned to look up at his opa and said, "Someday I am going to drive an army tank." Opa and the soldiers looked down at Alex with smiles on their faces. The soldiers bid them goodbye with a warm smile and a wave as they walked back over to their army tank.

Josephine walked back towards her father and sons with a sad look on her face, by the time it was her turn in line to receive food, the store had run out of food. Opa looked at his daughter and saw the sadness in her eyes and he knew. She said, "Father, they ran out of food again today and the store keeper said it would be two days before they would have food again." Opa let out a heavy sigh and said, "We must come earlier next time."

Alex and Ralph looked up at their mother and lifted high the bananas they were holding and said, "Here mommy, you can have our bananas." Tears welled up in both mother and opa's eyes; she took the bananas and put them in the empty bag she was carrying. Opa's voice crackled with emotion as he said, "Okay, let's get these two boys home; I think they have had enough excitement for one day." Alex and Ralph both reached at the same time for their opa's hand. As they turned to leave town Alex looked back over his shoulder at the army tanks and thought, "One day I am going to drive an army tank."

Alex had many nights filled with nightmares about the bombs falling with bright flashes of lights, the sounds of sirens and screaming people, and the towns filled with rubble and foul smells. The sights Alex saw with his four-year old eyes during the World War II bombing raids, with all its many terrors and the sight of burning people was still haunting his mind. Alex, as all children that have grown up in a war zone, will have scars that people cannot see on the outside and these scars will remain with them for the rest of their lives. But for now, most nights the nightmares were replaced with dreams of American soldiers and Alex driving an American Army tank down the town streets with the soldiers. Alex could dream and take delight in the American soldiers and their army tanks and this gave him a great amount of peace and a feeling of safety. In these pleasant dreams, all the fear and pain of the war were invaded by hope.

Alex, Ralph and their cousins continued to follow opa around the backyard helping him with the chores. Alex's favor part was when the chores were over and they would play American soldiers who drove around in their pretend army tanks and helped people or Alex would climb up as high as he could in the tree and pretend to find a faraway land. It had been many months since Alex arrived at his grandparent's home. Alex began to feel a great sense of security and played care free for the first time. There was still always the feeling of hunger, since the food supply continued to become more and more scarce every day. Often there was no food and Alex was still hungry when he went to bed, but not living in fear somehow made being hungry feel okay.

The food shortage had gotten so bad that most of the time when opa and Josephine returned from the food lines they were empty handed. All the food had to be portioned out for a week or more and they began to only eat once a day. On Saturday nights after the children had gone to bed opa would kill one of the rabbits to eat for Sunday dinner, he never told the children what kind of meat they were eating.

The town people began to barter with the farmers for any food they could spare. For example, opa would take a few rabbits down to the famer and in exchange would bring home a chicken; and if the farmer had plenty of eggs he would bring home eggs also. The people in the small town of Suderode began to band together and were willing to share what they had with a stranger, even taking them in if the strangers had no place to stay when they came to town.

One day when Josephine and her father came home from town they brought a lady and her baby home with them. Alex stood and stared at them and wondered why they were there. The lady was young and had sad eyes; she and her baby's clothes were dirty. She had been living with her baby in an old abandoned building just outside of town. Most of the buildings just outside of town were bombed and lay in rubble. The lady and her baby had stood in the food line behind Josephine and her father. The baby fussed with hunger the whole time they were line. When those in line were told that the food had run out, Josephine turned to the young women her heart filled with compassion as she asked, "Excuse me, my name is Josephine and this is my father. Do you have any food for you and your baby?"

The young women stretched out her hand taking Josephine's extended hand in hers. Tears filled the women's eyes as she answered, "My name is Kathrine and this is Jacob, we have no food and my milk has dried up so I can't feed my baby." Josephine pulled Kathrine into a hug. Then she asked, "Would you like to come to our home and share lunch with us?" Kathrine began to weep as she told Josephine the story of being bombed out and her sister being killed. She had been moving from town to town trying to provide for her baby and keep him safe. Josephine and her father walked with Kathrine to where she had a few items hidden in the bushes. The baby finally cried himself to sleep as opa lead the way back home.

Kathrine stood by the front door and looked down at the four wide eyed children staring up at her and her baby. Josephine said, "Okay children go in the kitchen and see if oma needs any help." Ralph led the way into the kitchen and as soon as they entered Alex said, "Oma, a lady and her baby from the bombs are here." Oma looked at the children and said, "Sit down at the table we have soup for lunch today." Then she walked over to the pot on the stove and added more water to the soup to stretch it so there would be enough for everyone.

Josephine led Kathrine and her baby Jacob upstairs to the bathroom to clean up. While they were in the bathroom Josephine brought in one of her dresses and an old clothe that could be used as a diaper for Jacob. Tears of gratitude filled Kathrine's eyes as she accepted the gifts. The soup they ate was mainly liquid with a few vegetables in it. Kathrine and Jacob spent the night and shared Josephine's bedroom with her. The next morning there was only a half a slice of bread for everyone to eat. Right after breakfast Kathrine rose from the table and gave Josephine a hug, she thanked her for her kindness and began to explained that she could not stay, she needed to keep searching for her mother who was missing in the war.

Many people had lost loved ones in the war, not knowing if they were dead or alive. Josephine hugged Kathrine back and thought how very blessed they were to still be all together with only the men not accounted for, it sent a pain in her heart that they no idea if their men were dead or alive. Kathrine and Jacob left and Alex asked, "Mommy, will she come back again?" She smiled down at Alex and said, "I am not sure." Josephine said a quiet prayer for Kathrine and the baby to find her mother and for Karl and her brother that they would be found and come home safely.

It has been over two years since Josephine heard anything from Karl; Alex asked to look at his father's picture each time he missed his papa. After a while Alex stopped asking about his father, for every time he did his mother's face would smile but there was sadness in her eyes that caused Alex to be sad. He wanted to be brave for his mother like his big brother Ralph. Josephine tried not to worry even though she did not know where Karl was or even if he was alive.

During the war, many people were taken by the SS Elite soldiers or killed and missing during the bombing raids. Sometimes Alex would watch his mother sitting at the kitchen table staring into space with a sad faraway look on her face. She would be deep in thought about what to do if Karl never came home. The longer he was away the more pain filled her heart and she cried herself to sleep. Most days she was drained and exhausted. When Alex observed his mother looking sad, he would walk over to her, wrap his arms around her and say, "Mommy needs a hug." Josephine would close her eyes and hug Alex back as her little boy tried to comfort her.

A few men began to come home; Alex sat in the top of the tree and watched the men with their children walking down the street. Alex wiped a tear away from his cheek as he longed for his papa. He wondered if his papa would ever come back home. Alex sat up in the tree by himself for a long time remembering the times his papa played with him.

One of his best memories were the times when his papa would look at Alex pick him up and give him a hug and a kiss on the cheek before setting him back down. Alex's heart was filled with joy as he looked up into his papa's face smiling down at him. Alex felt better when he would think about those happy memories with his papa. He climbed back down from the tree; Ralph and Michael were playing marbles under the tree. Alex asked, "Can I play the next game with you?"

Renate did not have any memory of her papa since she was just a baby the last time he was home. Alex and Ralph would tell Renate stories of their papa before she went to sleep, these stories helped calm her down. Before going to sleep Alex would think about the American Army tanks and dream he was driving one of them. Alex loved being at his grandparents' house, he felt happy and content there. His grandparents' home was a haven where no bad men would come and take him away and no bombs would fall from the sky. Alex loved to play in the big backyard and climb up in the big tree and dream about great adventures he would have someday. Alex liked helping his opa take care of the pigeons and rabbits. All was well with Alex except for the lack of food.

Chapter 18 Russian Soldiers 1945-1946

World War II had been declared over and the American soldiers pull out of part of Germany with all their equipment. The day was warm when the American Army tanks came rolling down the street where Alex and his family lived. The soldiers were standing looking out of their tanks, waving their arms in the air while shouting in English "The war is over! We are going home." People came out of their houses to see what the commotion was all about. No one understood English and did not understand what they were saying. Opa and the other adults in town looked at the American soldiers trying to figure out what was happening.

The people in the small town of Suderode had no idea that the war was over and did not understand why the American soldiers were leaving. Just before the children's bedtime a military jeep pulled up in front of the house. An officer got out of the jeep; he walked up the front steps and began knocking on the door. Opa rose from the sofa to answer the door. The rest of the family moved back away from the door in fear not knowing why someone would come to the door this late at night.

Opa opened the door and he recognized the officer right away; it was the same officer who used his business as a transportation point for the Army. The officer smiled at opa and said in German, "Thank you for the use of your business while we were here, I have orders to leave. Here is a bag of food for you and your family." Opa graciously took the bag from the officer. The officer immediately turned and left. Opa closed the door and turned around to see his family wide eyed staring at him.

What the people in Suderode did not know is why the American soldiers had to leave or what agreement was decided by America and England regarding their country. At the end of the war other government leaders made the decision that Germany should no longer be a united country. At that point Germany was divided into two halves. One half of Germany was named West Germany and it would be built into a democratic state that would be overseen by America and their allies. The other half of Germany was named East Germany, which became a communist state and was in the control of the Russian government.

In the smaller towns, the people had no idea that the war was over and that Germany had been split into two sections. Within a week after all the American soldiers had left the town of Suderode, Russian troops came into town; these soldiers were from the Siberia region of Russia. A wall was being erected in Berlin and barbwire was strung along the countryside; watch towers were being built at each city boarder. With all the movement that was going on in Germany, there was very little communication being given to the people in East Germany. The people became confused and fear began to set into the hearts of the people again.

Alex still did not truly understand why the American soldiers and their army tanks did not come back down his street. He became sad when his opa would say to him, "Alex, the American soldiers are not coming back." Every morning Alex went over to the front window and looked outside in hopes that one of the army tanks might still come back down his street again. Opa had to call him to get him away from the window to help feed the rabbits.

Alex's mind wandered while doing his chores and he thought about being inside the American Army tank. Once the chores were done he climbed up to the highest limb in the large oak tree longing to see an American Army tank. He thought if he watched long enough they would come back again. While he sat up in the tree he licked his lips as he thought about the chocolate bar the American soldier had given him. At the memory of the sweet tasting chocolate bar his mouth water and his stomach growled with hunger.

Alex woke up early just as the sun was coming over the tree tops, the only noise he heard came from the kitchen. The kitchen noise made his stomach grumble as he remembered opa coming home from the farmer's house yesterday evening with potatoes and eggs. Ralph and Renate were still sleeping as he slipped out of bed on to the floor boards of his bedroom. As he did every morning he went down the stairs and over to the front window seat to look for Army tanks. He moved the curtain aside and climbed up onto the window seat. He sat there dreaming about the American Army soldiers and their tanks as the smell of his oma cooking breakfast the aroma filled his nostrils.

Alex sat on the window seat staring out the window dreaming of eating a chocolate bar and driving an army tank when he saw something coming up the street. He pressed his face against the window thinking it was an American army tank that had come back, excitement began to fill his heart. Then Alex notice they were not American army tanks at all that were coming up their street.

Opa walked into the living room and said, "Breakfast is ready." Alex turned towards his opa and asked, "Opa can we go outside and wave at the man on the little horse before breakfast." Opa quickly walked over to the window to see what man he was talking about. Once opa looked out the window, he grabbed Alex and pulled him away from the window and quickly closed the curtains. Alex did not know what to think as he looked up into his opa's stern eyes looking down at him as he said, "No!" He had never heard his opa speak in that tone of voice before and it frightened him.

Opa took Alex by the hand and led him to the kitchen table where his oma and mother were sitting talking about their day. Alex looked up with tear-filled eyes into his opa's stern eyes and didn't understand why opa was acting the way he was. He began to cry as he asked," What's the matter opa?" Opa looked away from Alex and did not say a word as he lifted Alex into the kitchen chair next to his mother. Both Josephine and oma immediately stopped talking and looked at the fear in opa's eyes.

Oma reached over and took opa's hand as he sat down in the chair next to hers. He looked at his wife and then over at Josephine before he commanded, "Josephine I need you to go and get the rest of the family down here now, I need to talk to the whole family." Josephine quickly rose out of her chair and left the kitchen. Alex sat at the table and fear began to eat away at his peace at he watched his opa and oma holding hands staring at each other. The five minutes it took for everyone to come into the kitchen seem like an eternity to Alex.

Josephine returned with everyone and they all took a seat around the kitchen table. Everyone turned their eyes towards opa waiting for him to talk. He cleared his throat as he began sharing his feelings of the men he saw coming up our street. Opa described his fear, "There are men coming up the street today and these men are not American soldiers, the look on their faces told them that they are not kind men. Some of the men are walking and some of the men are riding small horses. They are not dressed like soldiers; they are wearing animal furs and have rags wrapped around their feet instead of shoes. I think these men may be Russian soldiers. I don't know what to expect, but we will need to be careful and keep the children away from them until we know more about why they are here."

Then opa looked directly at Alex, making sure he was listening, as he spoke to all the children, "You may not go into the front yard at any time and you will not look out the front window, do you understand?" One by one each child answered, "Yes, opa." The new soldiers filled the town and began to take over business and control the stores. Since Alex was not allowed to go into the front yard or look at the front window, he would climb up as high as he could in the large oak tree and watch these men opa called Russians. He thought it looked funny with such big men riding around on small horses with their feet dragging the ground as they travel the streets of Suderode. These soldiers also had machine guns draped over their shoulders. The men moved up and down the streets every day observing every house carefully.

If these new soldiers saw anyone walking down the street or even standing in their front yards, they would shout out for them to get back in the house so loud that it could be heard inside the houses. They pulled their guns off their backs and would point them at the people and yell out commands to them, "Get back in your houses or you will be shot." Alex did not understand why they acted so mean. Memories of the SS Elite soldiers came back to him, including the memory of SS Elite taking away his friend Frank. Fear began to build in Alex as he watched from the tree top. He wished the American soldiers did not leave. He thought, "Why are the people afraid of these men who have no tanks to drive, but only ponies to ride on and wore no shoes, just rags on their feet?" These thoughts puzzled Alex, but when he heard them yell and saw their guns from the tree top, he was afraid.

One evening after supper opa gathered his family and told them what he had learned that day. "The war is over and these men are Russian soldiers and they are here to stay. Things will change and I am afraid some of those changes we will not like." Alex stared up at his opa for a long time before saying, "I don't like these soldiers they are mean." Opa looked at Alex and said, "I know, but this is who oversees where we live and we must obey their rules." Josephine stood up and said, "Okay children I think it is time to get you ready for bed." Alex sat there with his arms crossed in deep thought when his mother said sharply, "Alex that means you also." Alex got up and followed them up the stairs.

Alex did not understand why everyone was afraid these soldiers who had no tanks. He did not want to be afraid; he wanted to be brave like an American soldier. One afternoon, Alex turned and looked up at his opa and quietly asked, "Opa, why is everyone afraid of these Russian soldiers who ride on ponies? Is it because they shout and have those big guns hanging on their backs?" Opa pulled Alex to himself and said, "These soldiers are very angry men and they are not kind like the American soldiers were, they have a different belief than we do, so you must stay away from them and not speak to them."

Opa placed his hands on both of Alex's shoulders and looked straight into his eye to help him understand and know the importance of this warning, "Alex, in order to stay safe, we must always do what these Russian soldiers tell us to do without question, do you understand?" Alex got a puzzled look on his face and asked "Why?" Opa wanted to help Alex understand the danger as he began to explained, "I need you to listen carefully. Do you remember what it was like before you came here? With all the bombs and people being hurt?" Alex's eyes grew big and he slowly shook his head 'yes' as memories filled his mind. He understood the danger and tears welled up in his eyes as opa said, "That is why you need to listen." The same fear that Alex had before settle again into Alex's heart that day.

Since the war ended and the new Russian soldiers came to town, it was difficult for the children to understand the whys. Ralph was nine, Alex five, Renate three, Krista eight, and Michael was six years old. As young children in this new world they found themselves, there was no way that they could comprehend the depth of the sadness and suffering that would come upon the people of East Germany.

Soon more Russian soldiers dressed in uniforms began to come into the little town of Suderode. These soldiers brought with them a tyranny and rule that would oppress the residents who lived there. The whole town seemed to be veiled with a dark cloud, and a great fear pressed into the hearts of the people. This was a different kind of fear, because the people did not know what to expect living under the rule of their new communist government.

As Alex grew older and attended school he began to understand just what the cloud of darkness was that covered East Germany, the cloud of darkness was call Communism. This dark doom hung over the whole town like a heavy cloak, the people lived in fear of the Russian soldiers who always had their guns pointed at them. Most people stayed indoors and did not go out into the streets to town unless it was necessary to try and get some food. Food became even less available with the Russian soldiers in charge of the stores. Opa had to find people who would trade rabbits for food.

The Russian soldiers made many changes to East Germany. One of the major changes was to change the money to a new money system where everyone would be given the same amount. Opa had money put away in a box that he would use to purchase food in the food lines when the Americans were in their town. Russian soldiers started going from house to house demanding that people to give up all their German marks, which was German money before the war ended. The soldiers told the people that German marks were no longer worth anything and demanded that all German marks be given to them. It did not matter how much money you had in German marks the soldiers exchanged it for 300 vouchers or bank notes this now became their new money. Now when someone needed to purchase anything these vouchers would be used as their only money exchange.

As the soldiers went from house to house demanding the people give them all their German marks that they had to exchange for the 300 bank notes, people became fearful when the soldiers knocked on their door. As one soldier stood at the door taking the money, two other soldiers searched the house to make sure no one was hiding any German marks. If the soldiers found money in the house that was not given to them they would arrest the oldest male and take him out into the street and shoot him, so others could see what that they meant business.

The word quickly spread around town that all must obey and if anyone did not abide by their rules or try to resist or disagree with the Russian soldiers, they would be shot. The new communist government inflated the prices in the stores by twenty-five percent, which created another hardship on the people of East Germany.

The food store lines continued to grow longer at the government run stores that always ran out of food. Not everyone was able to get their food even if they stood in line for hours. When the food or supplies were gone the door at the store would be shut and the people in line were told to come back another day. If someone went to the store to purchase food with German marks instead of the bank notes, their money was confiscated and they were turned away with no food and then a soldier came and arrested the head of the house hold.

The store owners were required to turn the people into the government officials. The store keepers by law could only take the vouchers as the currency exchange and they very afraid of the government officials if they did not report offences. Hunger became widespread across East German as food became more and more scarce. There was a black market for food, certain people worked underground and would sell food for triple the rate of the government stores. Theft also became a big problem to the East German people. Hunger will make men do things they would not do in other times; no one wanted to see their child get sick or die of hunger.

The farmers were government owned, but many chose to secretly exchange food for other items they needed with the town's people. Opa exchanged rabbits and Josephine began to exchange her most cherished wedding gifts that she had left with her mother when she moved away. Josephine had one small crystal dish that Karl had given her that she cherished more than the others and never wanted to let go of because of the sweet memory that is attached to that piece of crystal. She feared she would have to exchange it if things got any worse.

The government allowed the towns' people to come in after the harvest was over to gather up any leftover food that was in the fields but much was bad or spoiled. Ralph and Alex went with their mother and opa to gather left over wheat in the field, most of it was on the ground. Alex learned to sift the dirt out with his hand as they gather as much of the grains as they could during their allotted time in the field. The wheat was used to make bread, soup, and cereal, even though it was sifted and picked through there would still be small bits of dirt and rocks that did not get removed, which made the food crunchy. Alex learned how to eat his food by taking a bite of food and without chewing washing it down with water to fill his stomach.

The winter was bitter cold with lots of wind and snow. It has been almost three years since there was any word from Karl. Josephine prayed for his safe return, but feared the worst since many people had died or just disappeared never to be found during or after the war. Liselotte talked to Michael and Krista about their father coming home one day to keep their hopes up until they knew for sure. Alex felt sad most days, he missed his papa and wanted him to come home, he wished that the American soldiers would bring him home and they would stay there so the Russian soldiers would leave.

The nights Alex heard his mother weeping in her bed, caused his heart to break. He would close his eyes tight so he would not cry also, but tears still spilled from his eyes as he laid there trying to fall back asleep. The next morning, he would find his mother and give her a hug and a kiss on the cheek. His mother's face always lit up with a smile when he kissed her and this helped him feel better.

All the children missed their fathers and there was nothing their mothers could do to take away the longing for their father. The only time that they felt better was when they were playing. Playing helped them to forget about the trouble all around them. Many nights Alex woke up with the same nightmares from the war and it caused him to scream out waking his brother and sister. Josephine always came into the bedroom and gather Alex into her arms and sat on the edge of the bed singing softly to her children until they all fell back to sleep.

The winter was over and the snow had finally melted, the air was warmed up and the spring flowers were just trying to push through the soil in the spring of 1946. Alex was playing a game in the living room with his brother and cousins. Ralph had made up a game using small pebbles he found in the backyard last fall. Liselotte and opa had gone to town to stand in the food line hoping to bring home some food. Oma went down to the farmer to see if she could exchange a rabbit for some eggs and potatoes. Josephine stood in the kitchen cleaning out one of the cupboards; she was home alone with the five children.

There was a loud knock on the front door. All the children froze from playing the game and looked at each other as fear pounded in their hearts. Josephine came quickly into the living room and put her finger on her lip motioning for the children to stay quiet. There was another knock on the door, this time louder and sounded more like pounding on the door. Two Russian soldiers stood outside the door. After the second knock one of the soldiers took his gun off his shoulder and pointed it at the door as he yelled, "Open the door or we will break it down."

Josephine hurried to the door as Ralph took Renate's hand and all the children lined up against the wall behind the door. Josephine slowly opened the front door; the soldier looked up and down at this small woman who stood less than five feet tall in stature and who stared up at them with determination in her eyes. Both soldiers put their guns back on their shoulder. The smaller soldier leaned in close to Josephine's face and said, "You're a petty one aren't you, is there any males living in this house with you." Josephine voice did not waiver as she told them an outright lie, "My husband is upstairs ill shall I go and get him for you?" The soldier stepped back away from Josephine and took his gun off his shoulder as he stared hard at her pointing the gun in her face. The larger soldier chuckled as if he was amused. Josephine did not take her eyes off the soldier as she prayed for help and protection for the children.

Alex moved away from the wall and moved in behind his mother and looked up at the soldier. One by one each of the children come from behind the door and stood around her legs. Renate went behind her mother and crawled out from under her long dress sticking her head out the front side of her dress looking up at soldier with her big blue eyes. The children clung to her as they hung onto her skirt in fear looking up at the two soldiers. Both soldiers took a step back from the door at the same time and looked at this small woman with all five small children around surrounding her. Suddenly they both began to laugh out loud. Josephine took a deep breath and Renate started to cry. The soldiers stopped laughing and pointed their gun back in Josephine's face. The shorter soldier fixed his eyes on Josephine and yelled out, "Is there any male living with you in this house?"

Fear gripped at Josephine's heart thinking she was caught in her lie, but she knew she could not let the fear show. She did not know what the soldiers might do to her and the children. There had been many stories in town where the Russian soldiers would tie up children and make them watch as soldiers would take turns raping their mother. The children pressed in closer to Josephine's legs, she took a deep breath and said as strongly as she could, "My father lives here, he has gone to town, but I expect him back any moment."

"Why has he gone to town?" the larger soldier demanded. Krista began to cry at the sound of his voice. Josephine had to raise her voice as she spoke clearly and loudly to be heard over the two crying girls, "With very little food to feed the children, my father went to town early this morning with my sister in-law to see if they would be able to get some food to fill the children's empty stomachs."

Not all Russian soldiers were the same, these two soldiers standing in front of Josephine loved children and would never rape women. Josephine kept her stare on the big soldier and counted her blessings when she saw the soldier's eyes filled with compassion when she mentioned the children, for he had a daughter the same age as Alex and always had a soft spot in his heart for children. With grace in his eyes the larger soldier looked down into the children's faces at their big eyes staring up at him. Then he grabbed the other soldier by the arm and pulled him aside and whispered something in their language into his ear. Then the big soldier stepped back up to the doorway and softly spoke to Josephine, "We will return another day when your father is at home, so we can speak with him directly." Letting out a sigh Josephine replied, "Thank you, kind sirs." Both soldiers turned and walked away.

Josephine knew in her heart that God had protected her and the children. As soon as the soldiers turned to walk away from the house, she pulled all the children inside the living room and quickly closed and locked the front door. She leaned her back up against the door and breathed as if someone had just knocked all the air out of her lungs. She kept repeating, "Thank you Lord!" over and over as she let herself slide down the door to the floor allowing tears to run down her face as the stress left her body. The children crowded up around Josephine and hugged her hoping to make her feel better as they too began to cry. Alex reached over touching a tear that ran down his mother's face and said, "Mommy it is okay, I will protect you from those bad men." She looked down at her young son and gave a slight smile to acknowledge his earnestness.

Josephine gently moved the children off her, kissing them on the check as she did. Then she stood up wiping away her own tears with the sleeve of her dress. She looked down at each of the children's tear stained faces, and realized they too had been weeping with her. She said to the children, "I need you to go upstairs and take a rest until opa comes home." The way Josephine looked at Alex he knew that his mother needed to have some time alone to sort through her thoughts. He led the way as each child followed without a word and marched up the stairs one by one to go rest in their rooms.

Alex stood in the bedroom doorway deep in thought as he was trying to figure what it was all about. He turned and walked back down the stairs, and went over to his mother wrapping his arms around her waist as he asked, "Will those soldiers come back and why do they want to see opa?" Josephine bent down and gathered Alex in her arms, knowing the fear deep in her children's hearts she gently answered, "Son, I don't know why they want to talk to your opa, but I do know that we are safe and you need to go upstairs and take a rest with your brother and sister." Alex kissed his mother on the cheek and then went obediently up the stairs and lay down with his brother and sister; they all quickly fell asleep.

Josephine sat on the sofa praying as her father and sister in-law came through the door. Liselotte shut the door as opa smiled and held up a bag full of food, and said, "Look we were able to get some food today and even some fruit." Opa sat the bags on the floor when he looked down at Josephine sitting on the sofa with tears running down her face. Concern took the smile away from him as he asked, "What happened, what is the matter?" Josephine looked up at her father and a new flood of tears filled her eyes as she told him what had happen while they were out.

Liselotte sat down next to Josephine on the sofa and put her arms around her shoulders. Both women looked up at opa. They could see anger in his eyes as he spoke out in a reassuring voice, "God's hand of protection is over this home and we will not fear, but put our trust in the Lord God Almighty." With those words a sense of peace came and the fear in Josephine's heart melted away; these words gave her the courage to go on another day and to keep looking after her children the best way she knew how.

Chapter 19 Home Invasion 1946

In the beginning when the Russian soldiers took possession of the East portion of Germany, it was common for the Russians to find a home where they wanted and take it over to set up a headquarters. If your house was chosen by the soldiers, they would come into the home and tell the people who lived there that they had only one room to live in and needed permission to come and go out of that room, making them prisoners in their own homes. If anyone in the home would try and defy the soldiers they were arrested and put in prison for their defiant act against the government; those who were arrested were tortured or killed.

The Russian soldiers who set up their headquarters in a home would also ransack the home looking for items of value or anything that would satisfy their needs. They had no thought or regards for the people who lived there. If a woman lived alone in a home with only children the kinder soldiers would lock the children in a closet while they had their way with their mother. These were horrible times for the people of East Germany.

Fear hung over the whole town of Suderode like a heavy dark cloak, the children did not understand what was going on, and the things they saw, no child should ever have to witness. The people who lived in East Germany knew they had to comply with every rule that was set before them by the new government or be punished if you did not obey. If the Russian soldiers heard anyone speaking anything against the government, the cruelty of the soldier's action or if they believed in God, that person, man, women or teenager was arrested on the spot and they were sent away. Alex was now six-years old and a deep-seated hate for the communist government filled in his heart, he did not understand everything but the hardness in his heart took away his tears.

The Russian government set up a reward program for anyone who would be willing to become a spy for them, telling on the people they knew. Since food, water and basic needs were of great shortage many people would align themselves with the government to get the food they needed for survival. The people did not know who to trust; even a family member could be a spy. Once someone was arrested the spy would get their reward of food. If they chose to be a point spy, they set these spies up in their own house and paid them money. Not only was there a great fear running deep, but now there was a lack of trust among the people to the point that even families were being divided. With the fear and division among the people, the communist government gained more power over the people.

Fall was in the air and the trees' leaves were already been dressed in their colors of orange and red. Opa sat on the sofa staring into space as his heart felt heavy. Josephine, Liselotte and oma were in the kitchen finishing up the dishes and talking about how they could make the little food they had left stretch until the next time the food lines were open. Opa felt worn out and prayed for wisdom to keep his family safe. Everything he had ever worked for was now taken away and his business was now in the control of the Russian soldiers. For the first time as he prayed a tear fell slowly ran down his face. He looked up and said, "God, where are you? We need your help!" Bowing his head again and closing his eyes a new peace filled his heart and he could restrain his fear for the sake of his family.

The day was warm and beautiful; opa had allowed the children to go out into the backyard to play for an hour. Alex was overjoyed as he and the children looked up at their opa and promised to stay within eye site of the kitchen window. Josephine stood by the kitchen window to make sure she could see all the children. She turned away from the window to help her mother put something away on the top shelf. When she turned back towards the window she did not see the children, she placed her hand on her heart and exclaimed, "I don't see the children." Liselotte rushed over to the window to look out. Fear struck both of their hearts like a knife as they hurried over to the kitchen door to go out into the backyard.

Since the back door could not be seen from the kitchen window they did not know the children were on the steps. Alex had found a treasure and after showing it to the other children they decided to take it into the house and show it to their mothers. Alex turned the door knob and pushed open the door just as his mother and aunt stood at the door. Josephine looked at Alex and all the other children in a line behind him on the steps ready to come into the kitchen and she let out a loud sigh of relief. She stepped aside and let the children come into the kitchen. Alex held up his cupped hands as he looked up at his mother to show her, with great excitement in his voice he exclaimed, "Mommy, mommy look what I found," He had found a little tree frog out by the big oak tree in the back yard. He slowly opened his hands so his mother could peek at the frog.

The moment Alex opened his hands the little frog jumped out hitting his mother on the nose as it sprung to the floor in its effort to get away. All the children began to giggle with delight and thought it was funny as they watched the little frog jump around the kitchen floor. Josephine did not think it was funny and jumped back while letting out a loud screech, "Alex, hurry pick up that frog and let it go outside, we don't need frogs in the house!"

This was the first time in a long time that joy filled all the children's hearts as they all ran around the kitchen trying to catch the little frog. Alex caught the frog just as it was about to take another leap and cupped it back in his hands. Josephine could not help but smile at the laughter of the children as she said, "Now, put that thing outside and all of you children go upstairs and wash your hands."

The kitchen door from the living room flew opened as opa walked in wanting to know what all the commotion was about. He looked at Josephine and then at the children and got a big grin spread across his face and winked at the children as they looked up at him. Alex was not happy that he could not keep the tree frog so he stuck out his lip in a pout as he pleaded, "Awe mommy, the frog is so little, why we can't keep him?" Josephine gave Alex one of her looks and he knew he better not ask twice as he headed for the back door.

Josephine looked around at each one of the children's faces that had now gone sad, she gave into them and said, "Go, play with the frog outside for a while, but you better not bring that frog back into the house!" All the children headed toward the back door. Their opa opened the door and lead the way outside as he and said, "Do you want me to build a house for your frog?" The children cheered in unison and jumping up and down saying, "Yes opa, yes!" They watched as he built the small house. Once the small house was built opa looked at his grandchildren's beaming faces. Alex put the little frog into the small wooden box covered with screen. Opa set the little house under the pouch steps and said, "Whenever you play with the frog you will need to wash your hands." The children followed their opa into the house to wash their hands.

Alex had just got into the bathroom to wash his hands when Krista ran over to the sink in front of him. Alex and the other children waited in line behind her to wash their hands. Krista washed her hands taking her time as she played with the lye soap and water. Alex was just about to tell Krista to hurry up when there was a loud knock on the front door and a couple of seconds later another knock which was even louder than the previous knock.

The knocking sounded just like when the soldiers had come to their house before the bombing. Alex knew this knock was the soldiers, so he whispered quietly in Krista ear, "Hurry up! The rest of us want to wash our hands so we can go down stairs and see who is at the door." Krista finished up quickly and whined, "I don't want to go down stairs, and I don't like the soldiers." Alex hurriedly washes his hands and he headed for the stairs wiping his wet hand on his pant as he went. He stood at the bottom of the stairs as he heard his opa open the door and said politely, "Can I help you?"

Alex froze in place there at the bottom of the stairs. Three soldiers pushed their way into the house almost knocking his opa off his feet. The soldiers looked around while one of the soldiers pointed his gun into opa's stomach and said him, "This house will be our new headquarters and it would be wise if you don't resist us, and don't give us any trouble then you and your family will not be harmed. Do you understand?" Opa stepped back shaking his head 'yes' as he said, "I understand." The soldier then put his gun back over his shoulder.

One by one each of the children stood behind Alex on the step and watched the scene unfold. Opa looked over and saw the children by the stairs and told them to sit on the sofa and not say a word. Alex led the way and the children sat in a row on the sofa with their hands folded on their laps. Josephine, Liselotte and oma were standing against the wall by the sofa as the soldiers moved through the house assessing it.

They watched as two of the soldiers pulled out large sacks and began to look through drawers and putting things in their sacks. Opa now stood on the wall next to oma and one soldier kept watch over the family with his gun pointed at opa. While the other soldiers continue to look around the room, one of the soldiers moved towards the kitchen and other went upstairs. There were loud crashing sounds in the kitchen and the upstairs floor clanged with things being dropped onto the floor. None of them dared move.

Soon the soldiers returned to the living room with their bags full. It was very hard for the family to just sit there and watch as the soldiers bagged anything they thought was valuable. Each soldier now had two sacks each of the family's stuff; they sat the sacks down on the floor with a loud bang. The soldier who was holding the gun spoke out in their language thinking that the family could not understand, but they could understand a few words that they had picked up since the soldiers had come to their town.

The soldier with the gun shouted out to opa, "Get your family and go into the kitchen this will be where you will live. Do you understand?" Opa shook his head 'yes' as he looked at his wife. Josephine and Liselotte moved to gather the children and they all move towards the kitchen. Opa turned to look back at the soldier with the gun and asked. "May we also use the backyard so the children will have a place to play?" The soldier was touched by the sad faces of the children and answered, "Yes, but we will be watching you from the windows and have guards posted at each side of the house, so do not try to leave." Opa said, "Thank you sir." Then he turned and followed his family into the kitchen quickly shut the kitchen door behind him.

They are now prisoners in their own home and great fear again fell upon everyone in the family from the youngest to the oldest. Josephine scanned the kitchen and what a sight it was to see. Broken dishes and other items lay all over the floor. Kitchen cabinet doors were left open and the cabinets were now empty. From what they saw the soldiers put anything they thought was of value and whatever small amount of food that was in the kitchen into their bags.

The soldiers had also unscrewed the light bulb and taken it. They removed the water faucet that was now missing from the kitchen sink and water was flowing into the sink. Fear gripped at opa's heart as he looked around the kitchen. Both Josephine and Liselotte looked around as tears ran down their faces. Krista and Renate began to cry and wrapped their arms around their mothers. Alex looked around the kitchen and then at his family's faces and became angry that those soldiers had made his family sad. He sat down on the floor next to the wall with his arms folded across his chest and his eye brows furrowed into a frown. He could still hear the soldiers in the next room milling around and talking in their own language.

The longer Alex sat there the madder he became at the soldiers for taking their food. He opened his mouth to protest and felt his opa's hand go lightly over his mouth and a finger went to his lips. Opa looked at Alex and his stern eyes, but Alex also saw fear in his opa's eyes. Opa whispered to Alex, "Do not say a word or the soldiers will come back into the kitchen." Alex looked up at his opa and shook his head 'yes' to acknowledge that he understood. His heart began to fill with fear as he sat there staring at his mother and sister. Opa slowly removed his hand from Alex's mouth. They all sat down on the floor, no one talked, but there was a slight whimpering from the girls as fear enveloped all of their hearts.

It was quiet in the kitchen except for a few left-over sniffles from the tears that had been shed. They could hear the soldiers talking in the other room. As Alex sat there he tried to figure out why the soldiers would take their food, lights, and water faucets, no matter how hard he thought about it he could not understand. The kitchen door suddenly swung open with a bang, Renate stared to cry again as one of the soldiers stepped into the room and looking straight into opa's face and he blurted out. "This is where you and your family will live until we leave. Now go upstairs and find some blankets for the children." Josephine and Liselotte got up and walked quickly passed the soldier who was still standing by the kitchen door. When they got upstairs they went from room to room quickly gathering the bedding along with some clothes that they rolled in the middle of the blankets so the soldiers would not notice.

As the two women moved from room to room they notice that each room had been rand sacked. In the last room Josephine suddenly stopped at the doorway and Liselotte bumped into her. There were two soldiers in the room pulling things out of the closet and dresser drawers. They both stopped what they were doing and looked at Josephine and Liselotte standing in the doorway. One of the soldiers stood up and rubbed his hand over his private area as he winked at them and said in German using a seductive voice, "Come on in ladies and we will show you some fun." Turning quickly, Josephine and Liselotte hurried down the stairs and rushed towards the kitchen. One of the soldiers whistled as he followed them down the stairs.

By the time the women reached the kitchen door, they were out of breath as they pushed open the door and rushed over to opa, with the soldier close behind them. Opa looked in his daughter and daughter in-law's eyes and saw the fear as the solder pushed his way into the kitchen and grabbed Josephine by the arm to take her back upstairs. The soldier who was standing guard in the kitchen must have been the commanding officer because he barked out a command in Russian and the soldier let go of his hold on her arm and left the kitchen. Josephine rubbed her arm to sooth the pain from the tight grip as she let out a sigh of relief.

Opa looked over at the officer and nodded his head in thanks. Josephine looked over at the officer with a crooked smile on her face and softly asked, "May we use the bathroom upstairs?" The soldier answered with a nod of his head and stated, "You must get my permission and I will be the escort for all of you when someone needs to use the bathroom, also you all must go to the bathroom at the same time." Then he left the kitchen making sure the door was shut.

There could be no modesty in the family since everyone had to use the toilet or bath with everyone in the bathroom. Out of respect for the women opa would always stand facing the door with his back to them. If they were not quick enough in using the bathroom the soldier who waited outside the door would pound on the door and say, "You have one minute to get done or I will break down the door.

Opa looked around the kitchen and in the cupboard for anything they had not taken, he found an old bucket under the kitchen sink that he set up for going to the toilet at night, so they wouldn't wake up the snoring soldier who guarded the kitchen door. Opa only wished he could go into every room of the house and see what else he could find to use for his family, but that was impossible.

Every room in the house was turned upside down from the soldiers pilfering and taking anything of value they could find. The officer set up his main command center in the living room, which was right off the kitchen. Most days and even into the late hours of the night the family could hear men's voices. It was hard to sleep and they were only allowed to go into the bathroom when no other soldiers were busy doing business with the officer. During the day when they needed to relieve themselves they would go outside behind the large oak tree in the backyard. The shovel from the shed leaned up against the tree that they used to throw dirt against the tree to cover up it up.

Their home had been under siege by the soldiers for over two weeks and the family had to survive by living in the kitchen and backyard. For some strange reason the soldiers never came into the backyard and did not see the rabbits and pigeons that were kept out in the shed. The food for the animals was getting low and they had to be feed grass and weeds.

The second day with no food oma went into the backyard and began picking dandelions' and nettles, she knew they were editable. With the dandelions and nettles she created soups, or salads with them. Opa found a big pot out in the shed for her and this is what she used to cook the soup. She hoped the soups she prepared would give strength to the children who were becoming weak and lethargic without food; Alex who was always was so full of energy didn't want to play; just sleep.

While they cleaned up the kitchen oma found some dishes that had not been broken. Once the soup was ready she took the bowls and filled them with the water soup. Everyone sat at the table. Sitting at the table the children looked down at the green soup with strings of nettles in it. Before they ate the dandelion salad and nettle soup, opa prayed over the food giving thanks to God for the provision. Alex looked down at the food that sat in front of him, his nose wrinkled up and then he leaned closer to smell the soup. Alex turned his nose up and crossed his arms and said, "Yuk!" Josephine looked over at Alex with compassion in her eyes and softly said, "I am sorry son, but this is all there is to eat." Alex sat there watching the others eat with his stomach growling.

The hunger pains in Alex's stomach made him reconsider; he moved his hands down and placed them on his growling stomach. He decided his tummy needed some food to make it quiet down and stop hurting. He was so hungry that even though the soup was bitter tasting and he would shake a little with each bitter bit he took, the soup filled his stomach and the hunger pain subsided. Alex had to learn to eat whatever was set in front of him even if it tasted bad so he could fill his empty tummy.

Early one morning Alex awoke to the sound of gun fire. Opa jumped up and looked around, he was not sure where the gun fire was coming from. Everyone was now awake looking around as a new fear filled their hearts. Then the gun fire stopped. There was a loud stomping noise as someone came down the stairs yelling curses in Russian. There was fear that rushed over the family as they huddled together and held their breath expecting the soldiers to bust into the kitchen at any moment and begin shooting. Renate began to cry.

Josephine held Renate tightly and rocking her and humming quietly in her ear. Opa stood up and walked over to the kitchen door, taking a deep breath he slowly opened it. Peering into the living room opa asked, "Is something wrong?" There were two soldiers sitting on the sofa and another one soldier stood in the center of the living room, he looked over at opa with a confused look on his face as he pointed up at the stairway and yelled in German with a heavy Russian accent, "It stole my cherries!" Opa was puzzled at what the soldier could be talking about and asked if he could go up and look at what it was that stole his cherries. The officer nodded and the soldier led the way up the stairs into the bathroom.

Opa was surprised at what he saw when he reached the bathroom. The toilet laid in pieces on the floor and water flooding out where the toilet had been. The soldier pointed at what was left of the toilet and stated, "I put my cherries in the water bowl to wash them, but when I pulled the handle up there to clean the cherries it stole my cherries." Opa was amazed that this soldier thought the toilet was the sink and quietly said, "I am sorry that happened, if you let me go out I will pick you some more cherries and show you where you can clean them as he pointed to the bathroom sink. But first please let me shut off the water and clean up this watery mess that is all over the floor."

The soldier stepped aside never taking his gun off opa as he watched opa turn off the water and begin to cleaned up the watery mess with a towel. A few minutes later the soldier turned and left going back down stairs. Opa felt a relief that the gun was not pointed at him but also a fear that he was unable to protect his family while he was in the bathroom cleaning up the mess. He listened and could hear the soldiers talking but was unable to understand what they were saying.

In the meantime, Oma had the kitchen door open just a slight crack to see what was happening in the living room. Alex crawled and sat on the floor next to oma's feet looking through the crack in the door with her. The soldier came down stairs and went over to the officer and quietly spoke into his ear. The officer rose to his feet and stated, "Gather up your stuff it is time to move on to another house, we are done here!" The soldiers began gathering up all their items along with the bags full of the things they had taken from the house. They did not say a word to opa or oma but just slug the bags over their shoulders and walked out of the house leaving the front door wide open as they left.

Oma waited a few minutes then slowly pushed open the kitchen door and walked over to the open front door with Alex following right behind her. Alex could see the soldiers go through the gate, which the soldiers also left open as they walk down the street. Oma let out a loud sigh. Alex looked up at her and asked, "Are the soldier's mad, will they come back?" Oma jumped and looked down at Alex in surprise; she had been concentrating on the soldiers and she did not even notice Alex was standing next to her. Leaving the door open she took Alex by the hand and led him over to the sofa and told him to sit there, she would be right back. Then she walked back and closed the front door, locking it before walking back to the kitchen.

When oma returned, she had Josephine, Liselotte and the children following her. Josephine turned to the children and told them to sit down on the sofa with Alex. They all obeyed. Five wide-eyed frightened children watched as Josephine followed their oma up the stairs. Oma did not know if her husband was alright and wanted to check and see if he was okay. Liselotte sat down on the chair across from the children and said, "Would you like me to tell you a story?" All the children changed their focus from the stairway to Liselotte as they all shook their head in agreement. She wanted to calm the children's fears by telling them the fairy tale story of Hansel and Gretel.

Oma peeked inside the bathroom door and saw opa on his hands and knees wiping up water from the floor. Opa then got up and kneeled over the bathtub to wring out a drenched towel. Liselotte had just begun her story when they heard oma let out a loud shriek and then she began to laugh. All the children looked up at her and Alex asked, "Is oma okay?" She answered, "I think so since she is laughing." Then she continued with her story.

At the sound of his wife's voice opa jumped up to his feet thinking something was wrong, he turned and saw his wife and daughter standing in the doorway. Tension left his face at the sight of them and he said, "Is everyone okay?" Oma chuckled and shook her head 'yes'. Josephine said as she looked at shattered pieces of toilet lying around the bathroom floor, "Oh no, now what are we going to do?" Josephine could not believe her eyes that someone would do such a thing as to shoot up a toilet bowl. Oma stopped laughing and walked over to opa giving him a hug and said, "The soldiers have left and not only have they ruined our toilet, they taken half of the house with them."

Opa let out a loud laugh in relief before telling oma and Josephine the story of what had happened to the toilet, "The soldier went next door and pick cherries from their cherry tree. Since the cherries were covered in dust from the dirt road the soldier wanted to wash the cherries before he ate them. Instead of putting the cherries in the sink, he put the cherries into the toilet bowl to wash them and I guess he did not know that if he pulled the chain on the wall that the toilet would flush the cherries down the toilet. The soldier became so angry at the toilet for taking his cherries that he took his gun and shot up the toilet"

Opa had a hard time keeping himself from laughing while he told the story about the cherries. Oma and Josephine also began to laugh, by the end of the story all of them were laughing and it felt as if the pressure from a pressure cooker has let out its steam as they continued to laugh. Josephine turned to go downstairs while oma took a towel to help opa clean up the water. Renate was asleep with her head lying on Ralph's lap when she walked into the living room. She looked at Liselotte with a smile on her face, and said, "You are not going to believe what happened, come up stairs and see what all the noise was about this morning." Renate woke up as soon as she heard her mother's voice. Josephine led the way up the stairs with every one following her to the bathroom.

On the way up the stairs Josephine stopped to relay the story of the cherries to Liselotte. Josephine allowed Liselotte to look in the bathroom first, her mouth dropped open with a gasp as she looked in amazement at the broken pieces of toilet laying everywhere. The children gathered around and looked inside the bathroom. Opa turned around when he heard Liselotte gasp and began to laugh out loud again, oma and Josephine also began to laugh. Alex looked at the toilet all broken into pieces and asked, "Why is this mess so funny opa, now we don't have a toilet?" Alex always wanted to fix something if it was broken; and in his mind, he could not see how to fix the toilet.

All the adults stopped laughing and looked at each other wondering how they could help this child who always wanted to make everything okay, not worry. Oma looked down at Alex with a smile on her face and was about to say something when opa interrupted her and said, "Sometimes life is hard and bad things happen, but when life is hard that is when we need to laugh out loud. When we laugh out loud it always helps us to feel better." Opa began to laugh again along with the other adults; one by one of the children begin to join in until everyone was laughing. Alex stopped laughing and held his stomach as he said, "Opa, you are right I do feel better now."

Josephine and Liselotte grabbed some more towels to help clean up the bathroom mess while the children sat outside the door chattering among themselves and watching the adults work. Once the bathroom was finished, Alex jumped up and asked, "Mommy, can we play outside for a while?" Josephine looked over at her father who shook his head 'yes.' Josephine replied to Alex, "Yes all of you may go out into the back yard, but remember to stay close to the window so I can see you. Alex headed for the stairs and the other children followed him towards the kitchen. Oma followed the children down the stairs and let out a sigh as she looked at her messy house.

Alex began to run as he got closer to the kitchen and just as he placed his hand on the kitchen door knob to open it oma snapped her fingers and said, "Alex slow down and do not run in the house." Alex listened and turned the door knob slowly as he opened it and all the children piled into the kitchen to go out the door.

Alex blinked his eyes as he looked up towards the kitchen window; the sun had just risen over the top of the mountain range and streamed brightly through the kitchen window. Oma took in a deep breath as a new-found peace came over her and she softly said, "This is going to be a beautiful day." Ralph opened the back door and hurried down the stairs as he shouted, "Not it!" and ran to hide. One by one the children followed out the door saying, "Not it" as they too sought for a place to hide. Alex stood by the door and turned towards his oma and asked, "Oma, will we have any food to eat this morning? I am hungry?" Oma eyes looked sad as she answered, "Alex, we will need to have nettle soup again today." Alex turned away without saying a word and went outside to look for Ralph and the others who went to hide for the game of hide-and-seek. Alex thought to himself, "Even though the soldiers were gone the food we have to eat is not real food."

Opa slowly walked down the stairs and surveyed his home, nothing was in its place and the home was in total disarray. The adults took turns watching the children as the others slowly began to clean up the mess. The first thing oma did was open all the windows to let in the fresh summer air. The cleanup began with the living room and then moved upstairs. It was Josephine's turn to watch the children; she walked over to the kitchen window to make sure they were all okay in the backyard. She smiled to herself as she watched the children playing tag. Watching the children play made her heart content with the thought that her children could play and forget for a while. Renate was tired and when Alex tagged her she fell to the ground and began to cry. Josephine went outside and gathered her into her arms to put her down for a nap.

The house cleaning would take days but most of the big messes were cleaned up. Opa and Liselotte went outside to find some nettles for making soup. They made a game of it and the children joined in. Oma and Josephine were in the kitchen organizing, oma had just filled the pot with water to heat up on the stove for the nettles when Renate screamed and began to cry. Josephine jumped, turned ran from the kitchen to find her daughter.

Renate had woken up and when she looked down the stairs and did not see anyone in the living room she thought that the soldiers had taken everyone away and she was all alone. Josephine hollered to Renate, "It is okay, I am coming." As soon as Renate heard her mother's voice she stopped crying and looked to see her mother coming up the stairs. She reached her arm out and Josephine gathered her daughter into her arms. She wrapped her arms tightly around her mother's neck as relief flooded her.

Even though Josephine's youngest child Renate was only four years old, she still knew the fear and the effects of war and what it was like living in a communist country. Fear is not a respecter of people; fear creeps into anyone's heart, young and old. It gave Josephine's heart the most pain when she would hear her children cry out in fear, yet all she could do to help ease the fear was to hold them and comfort them with her welcoming warm hugs, but she could not totally take away their fear.

Chapter 20 Stazi Police 1946

The new communist government had more laws than any other government. Everyone must obey the government laws and if they did not they were arrested. There was no freedom of speech and anyone who said anything against the government was arrested. The people kept to themselves and did not dare say a word against the new government even in private, because the government paid spies to turn people in for breaking even the smallest law. The school system began to teach the children the communist way of life and the Russian language. The government wanted to take the young minds and help them to understand why the communist ways are better.

The school leaders began to use the children as spies for them against their parents. The teachers would give a child a reward of food if during story time the child would tell if their parents were doing or saying something that was different than what they were taught at school. The children were innocent and they were hungry; they did not realize that what they shared to get food would have their parents arrested. If a child told the right story that child was rewarded with a large hot lunch and the other children were forced to sit and watch the child eat the food. If one of the other children asked for any food they would get punished.

Hunger was the number one problem for the children in East Germany, many of the children began to lie to get the free meal. They did not understand the outcome of what was about to happen to their family. The adults became angry with the government for using their own children against them, but fear kept them from speaking out against them. They could not take their children out of school because it was required by law that all children ages five-years old and older must attend school.

Alex who was just six years old got home from school and talked about what he had learned. Josephine just listened but did not say a word about it to Alex. The communist teaching was being ingrained into the children every day. It was not what she wanted her children to hear, but there was nothing she could do about it without being arrested. Alex shared that he needed her to join the government and registered as a communist as he was instructed by the teacher.

To become a communist a person you would have to believe that there is no god, and follow all the rules of the government, signing a document that would allow the government to own their children. They were promised that if they registered as a communist then their children would get a hot meal every day at school. The teachers were given a bonus for each parent that registered with the communist party. The children were instructed each day go home and tell their parents that if they would attend a class and sign a paper their parents would get work and have lots of money for food. Many of the parents listened to their children since they could not work unless they were a registered communist, they went to the class and signed the papers to feed their children.

The parents who did not attend the government class with their children were watched more closely by the Stazi police. Alex, Ralph, Michael and Krista did not say a word about their family to their teachers because they had seen what it was like to live with the Russian soldiers and they feared what they might do to them.

Alex out of the blue one night asked his mother as she tucked him into bed, "Mommy, when will the American soldiers come back?" He did not like the Russian soldiers because they were mean. She pulled the covers up under Alex chin and kissed him on the cheek before she answered, "Alex, I know this is hard for a young boy like you to understand but you must trust your opa and me that we will take care of you." Alex stared into his mother's eyes and did not answer. Josephine pushed his thick blond hair off his forehead, before she kissed him good night. Sadness filled Josephine's heart for her children as she left the bedroom.

The government took over churches and called them State Churches. The State Churches were run by pastors who had signed the agreement to serve the communist government and preach communist propaganda. If a pastor refused to cooperate with the Stazi police, they were arrested and that church was burned down. Pastors, who could not forsake their God and Christian beliefs, fled and went underground; they were sought out by the Stazi and if found were arrested. Not all people attended the State Churches for they would not give up their belief in God.

These people who believed in God tried to find out where the pastors were having their secret prayer meetings in what they call underground churches. The people had to be very secretive. The Stazi police put together a special force of undercover police to infiltrate the people who they knew had not signed the communist agreement and pledge their lives to the government. These undercover police would find out where some of the underground churches met and arrested the people. The people had to be very careful and became even more secretive; they moved their location for every meeting and created a secret knock and password to protect themselves.

Many people were arrested along with any leaders of any group who encouraged people to believe anything other than what the government approved of. When the teacher asked Alex's class if they heard anyone speaking against the government, Alex would pray in his head the "Our Father in Heaven" prayer. When he prayed, he felt stronger. With all he had seen and knew of this government, the fear was greater than the hunger in his stomach. When Alex attended school he always like sitting next to his friend Nicholas, but today Nicholas did not come to school.

Alex was sad all day and when he got home he cried to his mother and said, "Mommy Nicholas did not come to school, do you think he is gone like my friend Frank and papa?" Josephine heart ached as she pulled her son to herself to comfort him and she softly said, "Alex, I don't know where Nicholas is, but you need to be brave and keep quiet at school. Remember how I taught you to pray when you are afraid. For we always know God will take care of us."

Soon there was a great division of those who signed an agreement to pledge their allegiance to Communism government and those who did not. This caused a separation of those who had jobs and money and those who did not. Those who had jobs shunned and taunted those who were without. Those who did not sign the agreement were refused jobs if they did not present the papers given to them by the government.

People did not know who to trust. When they found someone they could trust, they would secretly trade things to help each other. It was hardest on the children who were teased and picked on by the other children. Alex had many scuffles with other boys who would pick on his little sister Renate just to make her cry and then they stood and laughed at her. This made Alex extremely angry and he would push the boys away from his sister and fight them off while a teacher watched until he thought Alex had enough.

Sometimes the older boys would bring a slice of bread to school and during recess they would throw it on the ground to see how many poor children ran to get it. Hunger ran rampant among those without money and a piece of bread was like gold to them. The older children would run and fight over the slice of bread until it was in small pieces and most of it was lost in crumbs on the ground. The boys who brought the slice of bread laughed with fun at the bloody noses. The teachers looked on and did nothing to stop it. Alex, Ralph and Michael would go home with their bumps and bruises from school and oma would take them aside and clean them up.

Time seem to drag by for Alex until he finally made new friends with two boys who also kept quiet in school but after school they would go into the woods just above the school and play games they made up. One day when they were playing hide-and-seek Alex found a cave; he slowly walked in and found a stockpile of leftover military stuff from the war. Alex ran out of the cave and called for his friends to come and see the treasure he had found. The three boys played soldiers with the guns and helmets they found in the cave. The boys decided to keep the cave a secret.

As Alex walked home from playing in the cave he began missing his papa. He longed to have his papa come back home. Alex's greatest fear that he held in his heart was that he would never see his papa again. Some of the other fathers who were missing were brought home dead. Alex was young but he knew his mother tried to be brave and strong when he asked her about his papa. Sometimes Alex would hear his mother crying herself to sleep and this made Alex cry too and he would look up at the ceiling and pray, "Please bring papa home soon."

Fall was filled with brilliant colors, the trees were dressed in bright red, orange and yellows leaves. The East Germany government began to train German men to operate the communist government laws and to make sure all the laws were followed. These German men became the German police that were named Stazies; each one of these men was rewarded with their own home and money. The Stazies began to bribe people with food and money if they spied on other people. These police arrested anyone without warning, people who did not follow the law in word and action or were turned in by others. Those arrested would be tortured to try and gather information about their friends and family. Once they were done the people were released back to their families. The arrest and torture became a great deterrent for the people to not speak their mind and a great fear of the government took a gripping hold on the people of East Germany.

Food and all goods were monitored and distributed by the Stazies, who increased prices. There were long lines for everything and there were no jobs for most of people to be able to earn money, this way the government could control the people. The communist government took over all business that had survived the war and slowly began to hire people to work for a very small wage per day; it did not matter if they worked eight hours or ten hours they were paid the same wage.

Unemployment was wide spread and many people wanted to work but found none. The government would announce a new job; people would stand in line for hours for the chance to get the job. If they were one of the lucky ones who were first in line they were given paperwork that they had to fill out and sign to be able to work. This paperwork would state that they would pledge their allegiance to the government, deny God and follow all the communist laws.

Since the people had no money and very little food, they felt they had no other choice but to agree and sign the papers. Many signed the papers just to work and provide for their families, but their hearts were not in it and they still held onto their beliefs quietly in their hearts.

When a job opening was announced, everyone that could work was in line to see if they could get one of the jobs at the government factories or stores to support their families. The lack of food and hunger will make people do things they would not do normally, even say they believe in something they do not believe just to feed their family. Opa became desperate and went to stand in line for a job, but when he reached the front of the line he was turned away and told he was too old to work. Josephine and Liselotte, along with other women whose husbands died or were lost in the war stood in the job lines. When Josephine reached the front of the line she was told, "Go home and take care of your children there is no place for women in the factory." Then the man stood up and yelled, "All women in this line need to go home, you will not find a job here!"

There was no money and no food; Alex and the other children were very hungry. Alex complained to his mother as he held his stomach, "Mommy my stomach hurts." Josephine pulled her son to herself and gave him a hug; her heart ached for her children. She prayed every day for the Lord to supply all their needs as He has said in the Bible. Many nights the children had to go to bed with empty stomachs. Josephine told them a story and would sing to them to help them fall asleep. After the children were asleep she would allow the tears to flow down her face as she walked to the bathroom to prepare for bed.

Many times, opa would go with Josephine or Liselotte out into the woods that were located about a mile from where they lived. They went deep into the woods to look for edible mushrooms, berries or plants to eat. Opa always prayed over the food on the table. There was only enough food to make one meal a day. All the children began to learn not to complain about being hungry and were thankful for the food that was prepared for and set before them each day. Alex did not know what he would eat or if there would be food tomorrow. As a child, he and the others learned how to live without enough food and they became accustomed to being hungry. Sometimes when he was hungry when he went to bed he would dream about the American Army Soldiers and eating a candy bar that they had given him.

In the summer when the berries were ready to be picked, opa took the children with him and Josephine to the woods. Each child had small buckets over their arms as they walked through the woods with opa and Josephine. There were many berries in the woods and Josephine explained which berries were good to eat and which ones would make them sick. She kept the children close to her as they picked berries; keeping a close eye on them making sure they did not choose and eat the wrong berries.

The first berries the children picked went straight into their mouths and not the buckets. Once Josephine thought the children had eaten enough berries she said, "Okay you have eaten enough, now fill up your buckets." Renate held up each berry and showed it to her mother shouting before putting it into her bucket, "Look mommy, I found another one." Josephine smiled at her daughter and said, "Great, now pick some more berries." Renate's bucket was always less than half full on their return home from the woods.

Monthly, the government would distribute a few coupons to families who did not work for the government. On each of the coupons was the name of the stores and the date and time the coupons could be used. Only once a month the people would be able to shop per their coupon date.

Josephine and her family's day per month was the tenth for food and the twentieth for clothes and shoes. Josephine stood in line with her father each month. If they got to the front of the line before the food ran out, they had to present their papers and coupon and once their name was crossed off the list they were given a few items of food. Often the food ran out and they had to wait a month before their next allotted time.

Josephine knew the baker's wife Ute from childhood, they went to school together. One day after the bakery closed Josephine knocked gently on the back door of the shop to talk with her friend. After the second knock on the door Ute slowly opened the door and saw Josephine standing there. Ute opened the door and invited Josephine to come in. Josephine entered and did not waste anytime stating her business as to why she was there. "Ute we have known each other for many years and I was wondering if I could come by in the evening to clean your kitchen floor, the only payment would be any flour or grain I find on the floor." Ute looked at her in surprise and then looked more carefully at Josephine's thin frame as she answered, "I think I can arrange that, but you must always come after closing." Josephine gave her friend a hug before departing and heading home.

Every evening Josephine would go and sweep the kitchen floor at the bakery shop, gathering up and placing the dirty into a scarf she had in her pocket and then stuffed the scarf back into her pocket to take home. Once she got the dirt home she shook out her scarf and sifted as much of the dirt as she could. At first there did not seem to be very much flour or grain, just dirt, but after a week or so more flour and grain appeared in the dirt. Josephine saved the left-over flour, grain and some small gravel that the flour clung to, so she could make bread. Alex ate his piece of bread and he would bite down on something hard, like dirt and tiny pieces of pebbles. However, the bread, more than anything filled his empty stomach and took away the huger pains.

The new government made a new law during harvest time; this law was to help those who did not get any food in the food lines for two months. They were given a voucher to take to the local farmers. The voucher allowed the families to go into the farmer's field and eat until you were full of whatever crops they grew in their fields at the time. No one was permitted to take any food with them when they left the fields. The famer searched the people even the children to see if they had any food stuffed in their clothing. If anyone was found with food they would be arrested and the children put in a government run home. Alex sat in the field with the other children eating a tomato in one hand and an onion in the other. Whenever they went into an orchard they could only eat the fruit that had fallen to the ground, good or bad, even with worms. Hunger will make a person eat anything just to fill their stomach.

This new government law also had a lottery at the end of each harvest. Those who were chosen in the lottery could go out into the fields once the reapers had finish in the fields. They could gather any remaining grain that may have been left over in the field and take it home. Josephine and her family's name had not yet been drawn in the lottery, but her neighbor Helga had. She had to sneak out after dark to give a loaf of bread to Josephine and her family. Josephine was overwhelmed with Helga's generosity and kindness.

While eating in the farmers' fields, the children were so hungry and many times they would eat too much. The children did not understand that eating so much when you were hungry would make their stomach hurt worst. On the way back home the children would throw up what they had eaten and were hungry all over again and there was no food. Alex could hear his mother pray as his opa carried the sickest child home, "Lord, please help the children to not over eat and throw up what they have eaten." Alex looked up at his mother and said, "Mommy doesn't God care that we are hungry. "Josephine patted Alex on the head but did not answer his question.

Two days had passed since they went into the farmer's field to eat and Alex woke up early just before dawn. He was so hungry his stomach hurt and he could not go back to sleep, so he got up and went to the kitchen to see if there was any food and he found none. He rubbed his hungry tummy as he remembered all the food he could eat was in the farmers' fields. A farmer lived near their house and He stood there in the kitchen and decided to go get some food from the farmer, since the farmer had more than enough food.

Alex slowly opened the kitchen door and walked barefoot around to the front yard and out the gate towards the farmers' field. His eyes lit up as he climbed up over the fence. Alex felt the soft wet dirt of the field squeeze in-between his toes as he walked into the field. He walked over where the tomato vines were and looked over all the tomatoes; he picked the biggest one he could find before sitting down to eat the tomato. He took a big bite and the juice of the tomato ran down his chin, it did not take him very long until he was looking for another tomato to eat.

Alex had just picked his third tomato to eat when a large hand went over his small hand and he heard a deep voice from behind him say, "I think that is enough. Where do you live?" Alex pointed towards his house; the famer picked him up and threw him over his shoulder to carry him home. The famer knocked loudly on the front door and Alex said, "Shh, everyone is still sleeping." The famer just looked at Alex with surprise. The front door opened and opa's mouth dropped open when he looked at the farmer and saw Alex hanging over his shoulder. The famer sounded irritated as he asked, "Does this child belong to you?" Opa stepped back to welcome the farmer in as he answered, "Yes, he does, where did you found him?" "He was sitting in my garden eating my tomatoes on a day that is not designated for sharing my crops." The farmer raised his voice as he talked and then followed with, "If the police were to catch him you know what would happen." Opa took Alex from the farmer as he kept apologizing and thanking the farmer for not turning them into the police. The farmer looked at opa with disgust and said, "Don't let it happen again," then he turned and left.

Opa stood Alex on the floor in front of him and bent down and in a very stern voice said, "Don't you ever go outside this house without asking me or your mother, do you understand me?" The tone in opa's voice made Alex eyes fill with tears, a tear single ran down his cheek as he shook his head yes. Opa gave him a smack on his rear-end and told him to go up to his room and not come down until his mother came to talk with him. Tears were running down Alex's face as he hurried up the stairs and jumped into bed; as soon as he laid his head down he began to cry loudly. Ralph woke up and wrapped his arm around his brother to comfort him as he asked, "What happened?" Alex told his brother the story as the crying subsided. Ralph said, "You know opa never gets mad you must be in big trouble." Alex just shook his head and closed his eyes to hopefully stop the tears that were beginning to fall all over again.

Chapter 21 Han's Return 1947

The winter was bitter cold with blowing snow and below zero temperatures. Josephine felt empty missing Karl as she climbed into bed. Her beautiful Germany lay in ruin from the war and had been torn in half. Now she and her children lived in a communist country, where food was scarce and everything was controlled by the government.

Winter had made it harder to find food and the children were getting too thin. Josephine did not choose this life but this is the life she had to live every single day. She wept into her pillow as she cried out to God, "Lord, I cannot do this any longer, it is too hard to be strong for the children and I need your help." A gentle peace enters Josephine's heart and she took a deep breath, it was this peace that caused her tears to stop and a new strength enter her as she fell asleep.

Some of the people who worked took advantage of those who did not have jobs by setting up a black market with prices three times as high as the store. The black market was underground and many people were so desperate in need they would decide to go to the black market to provide for their children and they would have to trade something of great value to get food. An increasing number of people became so desperate that they said they believed in the communist theory, denied God, and sign the pledge just to be able to provide food for their children.

All children in school from kindergarten to age 14 were forced to attend the state school and were forced to sign up to become "Young Pioneers" in the communist party. The government knew that they must reach the young and ingrain the communist message in their minds. Many of the children became brainwashed and when they were told they must spy on their parents to see if their parents obey the communist laws, they did.

Since the communists believe that there is no God, the government officials went from house to house collecting all Bibles and other books that did not agree with Communism, burning them in the street. The government also went door to door confiscating cameras and guns. If anyone resisted they were arrested and did not return to their households. Every time there was a knock on the door the people did not know what to expect.

The children were in school and all the chores were done. The family went to gather twigs and branches for the fireplace and Josephine was alone. Josephine sat on the sofa reading the Bible when she heard a knock on the door. Setting down her Bible she walked over to answer the door. She could tell by the heavy sound of the knocking that it was someone from the government. She slowly opened the door.

Two tall men dressed in dark suits looked down at her as said, "Do you own a Bible, camera or gun?" Josephine hands began to tremble since she did not know what they were going to do to her as she softly said, "Yes, I have a Bible, but no camera or gun." They pushed her aside and stepped into the house looking around. The blond-haired man said, "Get all the Bibles and bring them here." She turned to walk towards the sofa when the man with the mustache said, "You are not permitted to read the Bible!" Josephine handed them the Bible and they warned her that if they found out there were any other Bibles, cameras or guns in the house they all would be arrested. They turned and left heading for her neighbor's house. She quickly closed the door after they left and prayed for continued protection.

Alex's teacher stood in the front of the class room asking the children questions about their parents. Alex was staring down at his desk and did not look up to answer any of the questions. The next thing he heard was the teacher slapping a rod on his desk and yelling, "Alex do you understand that there is no God?" Alex looked up at the teacher as fear griped him and he shook his head 'yes' just as his opa had instructed him to do. The teacher turned and walked back up to the front of the class room. If a child reported to their teacher that their family attended another church than the State Church or if they read a Bible, that child would be rewarded. Henry who sat behind Alex stood to his feet and said, "My parents read their Bible every day." The teacher said, "Wonderful Henry you will get lunch and a toy today."

The teacher smiled at the class and said, "See children what will happen if you obey." Then the teacher said to Henry, "Go to the office and tell the principal about your parents and they will give you your reward." Henry got up and left the room to collect his reward, but he did not understand the outcome for his family. While Henry was enjoying his food, the Stazi police went to his home and arrested his family, they were put in jail for three days. The police tortured anyone if they did not tell them what they wanted to hear. That child was not allowed to go back to their family, but placed in a state run home for children.

The communist theory states there is no God and so all those who believed in God or spoke of God were breaking the law. All churches who confessed a faith in God were shut down and the pastor was arrested. The only way the church could survive was to go underground. Those who believed in God had to hide their Bibles under the floor boards or in the wall behind a picture. Alex's mother hid the other Bible under the mattress and then moved it behind a picture in the wall. She continued to read the Bible late in the night by candle light in the closet.

The underground church began to grow and had to be moved from house to house never in the same house twice to protect the people. Only two or three families could attend at a time and on different days so not to bring attention to the church. It was important to keep the underground church at night this way it was hoped the church meetings would not be detected by the police. The people knew it could be dangerous but chose to take the risk, even bringing their children out at night to attend a church meeting. Once a month Josephine gathered her children and after dark they would sneak out to go to a house to worship God.

Alex became bored and wanted to go out and play soccer like he used to, but his mother told him it was not safe. This answer did not satisfy him and he pressed, "When will it be safe to play outside again?" Josephine did not have an answer and said, "Alex you need to focus on your homework right now." He looked down at the floor and then slowly left the room to do his homework.

Josephine never imagined she would live in a country where there were so many rules. No one could speak out against the new government, all children five-years and older must attend school and become part of the red union, and no one was permitted to talk about God or attend church unless they attended the government State Church that proclaimed the propaganda of the government. Fear continued to oppress the people and no one could be trusted. This caused a deeper division among the people in this new world of Communism.

There was still no word from her husband Karl or her brother since the war had ended; she was giving up hope of ever see Karl again. There were so many who had gone missing. The children never stopped missing their fathers. Alex missed his daddy terribly and became angry and acted out. One night when Josephine tucked Alex into bed and began to say his prayers, Alex interrupted her, "Mommy is papa ever coming home?" Tears stung Josephine's eyes as she gently ran her hand through his thick blond hair as she answered, "Alex, I know your papa is thinking about you wherever he is. We need to keep praying for papa's safe return home." Josephine kissed Alex on the cheek and prayed.

There was a foreboding spirit that was all around those who did not agree to sign the communist contract. These people were taunted by those who had agreed to follow the communist government and they flaunted their money around them saying, "Look how stupid you are, just allow the government to take care of you." The children were hungry most of the time. At school the children had to listen to the teaching on the Communism and how much better their lives would be if they would tell their parents to come to the meetings.

Alex sat in class one day staring out the window day dreaming about playing soccer. The teacher walked over with his bamboo stick and rapped it across Alex's hands. He jumped and cried out. The teacher said, "Alex pay attention or you will get the strap." Alex sat up straight in his chair and folded his hand as he looked up at the teacher. The teacher walked back to the front of the class as Alex rubbed his hands. Often he would get confused about what the teacher taught him. At night, he asked his opa about what they taught him and why they did not go to the meetings and sign the communist papers. Opa tried to explain to a young boy all the dangers of the communist government.

The first of February came with a foot of new snow. Alex and his family began to adapt to their new lives. It was Saturday morning and there was no school for the children. Alex was hungry when he woke up and rubbed his stomach as he thought about the breakfast of homemade wheat cereal with dirt pieces in it, but he did not care he was just glad they had some food today. Alex washed up and went down for breakfast. Oma smiled at him as he walked into the kitchen and asked if he would go upstairs and get his brother for breakfast. He turned around and went back upstairs to find his brother in the bathroom washing up. Alex stood outside the bathroom door and said, "Ralph hurry up oma said breakfast is ready." Ralph wiped his hands and followed Alex down the stairs to the kitchen.

Alex always had a large glass of water to help wash down the grittiness of the cereal. Opa watched his five grandchildren eating their breakfast and asked, "How would you children like to go outside in the backyard and help me feed the rabbits and pigeons this morning? After we are done you can play in the snow for a little while?" Each child's face lit up with excitement, it had been such a long since they had been out in the back yard. The children chimed in unison, "Yes, opa, yes!" Oma excused herself and went to the neighbor's house to see if she could trade for food. Within five minutes after oma had left there was a loud knock on the front door. Opa looked up and his smile disappeared as he put his finger on his lip to let the children know they needed to be quiet.

Opa got up from his chair and left the kitchen, he walked slowly towards the front door not knowing what to expect. The children became somber and looked at their mothers with fear in their eyes; all the excitement of going outside to play had been forgotten. It had been a long time since they had heard someone pounding on the door. A flood of memories filled the children of the Russian soldiers and then the Stazi police who had come before and pounded on the front door. Renate began to cry and Josephine quickly took her upon her lap and rocked her as she whispered hushing sounds in her ear. Renate laid her head against her mother's breast and began sucking her thumb.

They overheard opa at the front door say, "Can I help you?" Two men stood at the door dressed in Russian soldier uniforms with guns slung over their shoulders. One of the soldiers asked, "Do you know a man named Hans?" As soon as Liselotte heard her husband's name she sprang to her feet hurried out of the kitchen toward the front door. Josephine put her finger up to her lips to signal to the children that they must still be quiet and not move. The children stared at the kitchen doorway to see what would happen next and then they heard opa say, "Yes, that is my son!"

The soldier held up a paper and pen in his right hand pushed it toward opa as he said, "Da, good, sign here!" Opa looked at the soldier first with a puzzled look and then he looked down at the paper for an explanation, but none was given. The soldier pointed to the paper and commanded, "You must sign paper." Liselotte stood behind opa peering over his shoulder watching as her father-in-law signed the paper. The soldier took the signed paper and put it back in the pouch that he had taken it from. The soldier then pointed towards a wagon that was parked in front of the house and said, "He is over there in the wagon." Not knowing if he was dead or alive, Liselotte pushed past the soldiers and ran out ahead of opa to see her husband.

The conditions for the German people were very bad after the Russians came in and set up a communist state. When the war was declared over, Hans journeyed towards home. On the way home, he decided to stop by his father's business and surprise his father. Hans was surprised when he walked into the door and found it full of Russian soldiers who were pilfering through everything. Hans could not believe his eyes as he yelled, "What are you doing here? Where is my father?"

Hans's voice startled the soldiers and they pulled out their guns and pointed them at him. Hans was arrested on the spot and they sent him to a prison camp over in Russia. During his stay in prison he was beaten so badly all his front teeth were missing. His feet were purple from being made to stand in cold water for hours. The Russians thought Hans was a spy and they were trying to draw information from him, information that he did not have. When the Russians were satisfied that he was not a spy, they decided to take him back to the city where they found him and see if they could find his family.

Hans was unconscious but alive, tears filled Liselotte eyes when she saw her husband lying there in the back of the wagon. She reached out and touched Han's leg and whispered his name as she fell on her knees next to the wagon. The soldier's voice interrupted Liselotte grieving thoughts as he blurted out, "Do you want us to take him in the house for you?" Opa turned from looking at his son and looked over at the soldier and said, "Yes please."

The soldiers pulled Hans out of the wagon and wrapped his arms around their necks as they dragged him to the house. Hans's feet made a pathway in the snow as they dragged on the ground. The soldiers dropped Hans onto the sofa and turned to leave. Liselotte said, "Thank you," as she moved Han's legs up onto the sofa. She went quickly upstairs to get a blanket. Opa followed the soldiers to the front door and shut the door behind them. Opa let out a long sigh as he looked down at his son; it grieved his heart at the sight his son just lying there unconscious.

Liselotte came down stairs with a blanket and tears were running down her face. They were tears of happiness that her husband was alive, but also tears of sadness at his condition. Josephine and the children patiently sat in the kitchen not knowing what was going on until opa came through the kitchen door and said to her, "Your brother is home but he is not in good shape." She held her hand over her mouth and the children did not understand what opa meant.

Michael sat up in his chair and asked, "Is my papa home?" Opa saw the excitement in Michael and Krista's eyes as he tried to explain to them that their papa was home but was very ill. Michael did not care as he asked, "Can Krista and I see him?" Opa answered, "I will let your mother decide when you can see your father." Just then Liselotte walked into the kitchen and said, "Come children and see your father, remember he is very ill and you will need to be quiet." Both children jumped out of their chairs and followed their mother into the living room. Everyone was glad that Hans was home. Sadness came over Alex, Ralph and Renate because their father was still missing.

Opa and Josephine were talking quietly in the kitchen to Alex, who had a lot of questions about why his papa did not come home. Oma was at the neighbors trading a small piece of jewelry for some potatoes; she was so excited that she could not only got potatoes but eggs also. Oma walked into the front door and saw her daughter in-law bent over someone on the sofa crying softly with her two grandchildren kneeling next to her.

Oma set down the bag of food and walked over to the sofa, she put her arm around her daughter in-law and looked down at who was lying on the sofa. Oma gasped and almost fainted as she cried out, "Oh my God!" Liselotte had to steady her so she would not fall backwards. Liselotte wrapped her arms around her mother in-laws neck and the both wept. Opa jumped to his feet and quickly walked into the living room as soon as he hears his wife cry out, he wrapped his arms around both his wife and daughter in-law holding them as his heart also was breaking.

Josephine carried Renate, as her sons slowly followed her out of the kitchen into the living room and stood at the edge of the sofa. She began to pray as they looked down at her brother. Michael and Krista began to cry out and weep with loud sobs, "Papa, Papa." Renate began to cry to join in with her cousins. Tears ran down all the women's faces at the sound of the children weeping. Tears stung opa's eyes as he looked down at his son. Ralph and Alex just stood there staring at their uncle

Hans was in shock. Suddenly they heard a moan come from Hans and he began blinking his eyes, everyone became still. Then Hans opened his eyes and saw his family, it was the most wonderful sight he had seen since the war began. It was his family that kept him going while he was in prison, love for his family caused him to try and live. Everyone stood froze as they stared down at Hans in amazement. Hans moaned as he reached up his arm to pull his wife to himself, he held her and she rested her head on his chest as tears began to flow again. Michael and Krista put their arms around their mother and a new-found sense joy flooded the room. Hans was home safe.

March came in with warm air and the winter snow begins to melt. The weather promised an early spring was on its way. Being home with his family was the best medicine for Hans. He grew stronger and stronger with each passing day until he was able to walk. Once Hans was strong enough, Josephine asked him if he had heard any word about Karl. He did not have an answer for his sister but promised he would do whatever he could to help find his brother-in-law Karl.

Alex was happy because the children had permission to play out in the backyard again. Having Hans home was wonderful for the whole family. They had to explain to Hans the entire rules they had to abide by under the communist government. There still was one thing that left a hole in their hearts, they did not know where Karl was or if he was even still alive. Josephine was strong during the day but at night her pillow was stained with tears as she longed for her family to be whole.

Hans waited until his parents were alone to talk to them about his plan. He cleared his throat before he spoke, "Mom and Dad can we go outside I need to talk to you? Both had a puzzled look on their face sensing something was not right with their son. Opa asked, "Okay let's get on our coats and go out in the backyard." Once outside they walked toward the oak tree. Hans began to tell them his plan on what he thought he should do to try and find Karl. As soon as Hans and his parents walked out the back door a hush came over the kitchen and the children climbed up onto the kitchen window seat to look out at them wondering what the big secret was. As Alex sat there looking at his grandparents and uncle standing under the oak tree talking, he began to wish again that the American soldiers would have never left and the men who took over their country would leave.

As soon as Hans and his parents walked back towards the house the children jumped down off the window seat and sat down at the kitchen table looking at the door. Josephine and Liselotte stood next to the table in anticipation as they waited for the door to open. The back door open and oma came in first; she looked as if she had been crying. Opa came in and Hans followed closing the door behind him. Hans stood by the door and looked at his wife and said, "I am going to see if I can find out what happened to Karl."

Michael and Krista began to cry and Liselotte ran over to her husband wrapping her arms around his neck as she cried, "No Hans, please do not go." He held his wife out with his arms and looked deeply into her eyes and firmly said, "I must go so that we can find out what has happened to Karl." Tears continued to run down her face as she nodded her head that she understood. Both children had their arms wrapped around their parents as they stood there together until all the tears were cried.

Chapter 22 Karl's Return 1947-1948

The day was bright and beautiful; the buds had just begun pushing out on the trees limbs and the spring flowers were blooming and sharing their colors with the world. The sun promised to be warm today and peace filled the room as Josephine sat at the kitchen window seat watching a bird hop around the yard hunting for worms in the grass. The children were in school and she was going to try and plant the onions the neighbor had given her a few weeks ago.

The bird had just found a worm and was tugging on it when there was a loud knock on the front door. Hans had left a few days earlier and she hoped it wasn't the Stazi police. Fear entered the house ever since the Stazi police continued to come into people's homes if they suspected anything was done against the government. The they would interrogate the people and if anyone complained they were arrested. Opa got up off the sofa and moved towards the door with his heart racing not knowing what to expect.

Anticipation filled the room as opa slowly opened the front door, he was surprised to see two man dressed in white standing at the door. One of the men said, "I have a man named Karl in the ambulance, he says he lives here, do you know him?" Josephine bolted towards the door shouting, "Yes, that is my husband." Moving past both the ambulance driver and her father, she ran out to the ambulance and tried to open the large back doors. Another man who was still sitting in the ambulance got out and helped her with the door.

Josephine gasped as she saw her husband's thin body; he laid there with his eyes closed. The man helped Josephine climb up into the ambulance; tears of joy began to running down her face when she saw that Karl was alive. His six-foot-four-inch frame was so thin that he could not walk on his own; his weight was only ninety-five pounds. Josephine knelt next to the gurney where Karl lay. She took his hand in hers and leaned over and kissed him on his dry chapped lips. Karl opened his eyes blinking them to get them to focus. Josephine stared into his eyes and spoke softly, "I missed you so very much." A smile spread across Karl face at the sight of his wife and he whispered, "I love you my sweet Josephine."

The other two men and opa arrived at the back of the ambulance, opa looked in the back of the ambulance and said, "Josephine come out of there and let the men bring him into the house." Opa helped Josephine out of the ambulance and stepped aside as the men pulled the gurney out of the back of the ambulance.

In the meantime, oma had made the living room sofa into a bed. Opa lead the way to the house with the men behind him, one man in the front of the gurney and the other man in the back. Josephine held Karl's hands as they moved towards the front door. When they reached the front door, the gurney would not fit through the front doorway. The men stepped back and sat the gurney on the ground trying to decide what to do next.

The men bent down and wrapped Karl's weak arms around their shoulders hoping Karl's legs would hold him up, but his legs were so skinny and weak that he could not stand. Even though he was over six-foot tall he looked so frail that it somehow made him look smaller. His feet hung loose as the men drug Karl towards the sofa. Oma took a deep breath of relief to see that her son in-law was alive and yelled out, "Thank God Karl is now safely home with us." Once the men laid Karl down on the sofa, oma tucked the blankets around him and gently kissed his cheek. Even though she did not like Karl at first she had grown to love Karl as if he were her own son. She whispered in his ear before moving away, "So glad you are home son." Karl smiled up at his mother in-law as she moved to allow Josephine to again kneel beside him. The room was quiet as they held hands and stared into each other's eyes for a long moment.

Josephine's heart was full of peace for the first time in many years. She looked over at the men who had brought her husband home and said, "Thank you for bringing him home." Opa walked the men to the door and closed it behind them. Josephine turns her attention back to her beloved husband; she began to stroke his hair back off his forehead her heart melting with love just knowing her beloved husband was alive.

Opa looked at oma and Liselotte and gave an order, "Come we need to give the children some privacy. Josephine and Karl were so engrossed looking at each other that they did not notice that everyone had left the room. Karl was exhausted from being moved and closed his eyes to sleep. Josephine bent over and gently kissed his lips, so thankful her husband had finally come home.

Ralph, Renate and Alex had no idea what they would find when they got home from school that day. Alex was day dreaming about playing in the woods when the school bell sounded letting the students know school was over for the day. He hurried from his seat to meet his sister in their usual place to walk home. He saw her standing there with their friends Wolfgang and Leona. As soon as Alex was close Wolfgang said, "Hurry up, the sooner we get home and do our homework and chores the sooner we can go out and play.

The children talked while they walked together towards their homes. Wolfgang gave Alex a slight punch in the arm and said, "Here is my street see you later." Wolfgang and Leona turned down the street and Alex and Renate continued to walk another block towards their house. It seemed to be a usual afternoon walk home from school. They played kick the rock back and forth as they walked.

Opa was standing on the front steps waiting for Alex and Renate to get home from school. They looked up at their opa's face as they turned into the path that led to the front of the house. Alex wondered why opa had a serious look on his face, since the only time he had that look was when he had something important to tell them. Alex and Renate walked up to the front steps and opa said, "Sit down on the step for a moment I need to talk to you before you go into the house." They looked at each other and then quickly sat down on the front step; they thought they were in trouble. Opa sat down between the two of them wrapping his arms around both of their shoulders.

Opa cleared his throat before saying, "Your father came home today." Renate screamed with excitement and both Alex and Renate tried to get up at the same time to run into the house, but opa held them down with his arms. He firmly said, "I need to talk to you before you see your father; he is very ill and needs lots of rest just like your uncle Hans did when he came home, do you remember? When you see him you need to be quiet and not bump him until he gets better, do you understand?" Alex and Renate could barely sit still as they agreed, "Yes, opa we understand, can we see papa now?" Opa lifted his arms from around Alex and Renate; their faces were beaming with a smile as they got up and hurried into the house.

Even after what opa had said on the front steps, Alex was still expecting his father to be sitting on the sofa waiting to embrace him, but what he saw was a very frail man covered in blankets. His smile went away at the sight of his father just lying there on the sofa. Karl's eyes were open watching for his children to come to him. Both Alex and Renate walked slowly over to greet their father.

A smile came to Karl at the sight of his two youngest children. He took his hand out of the blanket and reached for Renate's hand, but she quickly pulled her hand back and tears came to her eyes and threatened to fall as her lip quivered. Her only memory of her father was a picture that her mother had showed her.

Renate took a step back; papa did not look like his picture and she was afraid. Josephine saw the fear in her daughter's eyes and took Renate's hand and gently put it into her father's hand. Karl pulled his daughter into a hug and as she allowed the tears to fall and wet her father's shirt. Karl reached his free arm towards Alex, who stepped closer to his father taking him by the hand. Alex leaned in wrapping his arms around his father and said, "Papa, I am so glad you are home, I missed you so much."

Karl had always been a man of few words but he always told his children he loved them. Karl whispered into Alex's ear, "I love you son." A small tear escaped the corner of Alex's eye and ran down his nose as he leaned on his papa. Josephine interrupted the sweet moment and said, "Your father needs to rest now, you need to go and do your homework before your brother gets home to help you with the chores. After your chores, you can go out and play." Alex looked up at his mother and said, "I don't want to play, I want to stay with my papa." He thought that if he left his papa he might go away again.

The summer was warm and the children played outside whenever they could, but on many days Alex chose to spend his time sitting with his father and playing cards. It took weeks before Karl could even walk; he came back to his family only skin and bones. During Karl's recovery time, he did not talk about what happened to him and why he was unable to come home before now. Josephine worried about her beloved Karl and would give him his potion of food and half of her potion. Karl was not gaining any weight, but slowly with the extra food he began to gain some weight and his strength came back into his legs so that he could stand and soon began walking with a cane.

Hans had returned home two weeks after Karl came home and was relieved to find Karl alive. As Karl began to recover there was a new-found joy that filled everyone in the household now that they were all together again; especially Alex who loved spending time with his father.

One night after they had finished eating rabbit stew for dinner; Karl looked around the table at his family and said, "Please stay at the table I would like to share with you my journey in trying to come home." Everyone looked over at Karl; even five-year old Renate sat still as her father began to share his story.

Karl took a deep breath before he began, "I had just finished my routine inspection of a weapon factory and got into my truck to drive back to my base thinking about talking to my commander about going home. I drove along deep in thought until I came upon a road block in the road. I pulled my truck to a stop and looked at the two American soldiers standing at the front of the road block; they motioned for me to get out of the truck and had their guns pointed at me. I slowly exited the truck raising my hands so they would not shoot me. I was captured by the American Soldiers. After my arrest, another American soldier got out of a truck and pushed me into his truck. He started the truck and drove me to an American prison camp that was about an hour away."

Josephine gasped and put her hand over her heart. Alex's eyes grew big and he put his elbows on the table and cradled his head as he said, "Go on papa, what happened next?" Karl knew the children could not understand the meaning of what had happened as he continued, "The location of the prison camp was in the middle of an Army base that was set-up in Germany during World War II. The prison camp was a squared off area with a large fence that had a double roll of barrier wire across the top. Each prisoner as they entered the prison camp was given a blanket, along with a small metal cup and bowl. I took the items they offered me and a guard led me into a large dirt yard where other prisoners were already sitting on the ground. I noticed that the other prisoners were sitting in holes and wondered why. The guard pushed me forward and told me to find a place to sit. I learned from the other prisoners that I needed to dig a hole if I wanted to keep warm at night.

I was up most of the night digging a hole about six inches deep and seven-foot long. I finally lay down in the hole pulling the blanket over myself and fell asleep for a few hours. Early the next morning the commander of the prison came into the prison yard and all the prisoners were told to stand for inspection. After inspection, each prisoner was given one slice of bread and the guard filled our tin cups with water. After a few days of the same routine, I asked one of the prisoners if they ever gave them any more water or food. The prisoner just laughed at me and turned away. The nights were the hardest laying in our holes in the ground, trying to keep warm with the blanket that was given to us, hearing our stomach grumble with hunger. I thought of home and that helped me fall asleep."

Renate climbed down out of her chair and walked over to her father. Renate took her father's hand in hers as she said, "Papa I am glad you are home." Everyone smiled and Karl pulled her onto his lap as he continued telling his story. "One night in the middle of the night, one of the black American soldiers threw some food over the fence and quickly walked away. The first time this happened the first men who got to the food kept it for themselves.

The next morning, they were satisfied but after looking at the other prisoners they felt bad and told the others that they were sorry. After that, all the prisoners devised a plan to share any food that the nice soldiers threw over the fence. The food came about once a week and always by a black soldier. The black soldiers were the only soldiers that were kind to the prisoners and they only threw food over the fence at night when no one else was around. Most of the soldiers called us names."

Karl told his family that he was in the American prison camp for two years, during that time half of the prisoners had died of sickness. Karl had become so weak from lack of food that he could not get up out of the hole he dug in the dirt. The day came when the prison commanding officer came into the prison yard and said, "The war has been over and it is time for each of you to go home. We need to know where to take you." Everyone who survived was happy to go home. Karl thought about where he should go, the last letter he had received said that his wife and family had gone to her parents' house.

During his stay in prison Karl did not know that his country was divided nor did he know about the communist rule that his family was living under. The arrangements were made for each prisoner and they gave all the men a nice meal before loading them up in ambulances for their trip home. Father finished his story by saying, "I do not have any bad feelings towards the American soldiers or my time in the prison camp. War is war and men do things they would not normally do because of hate and prejudices." He looked around at his children and said, "Always remember not to hate anyone, because hate will change you."

It was a cool fall day even with the sun shining brightly in the sky. The wind tugged at the orange and red leaves on the trees and many of the leaves skated through the air before falling to the ground. A few months after Karl recovered the family moved a few blocks away from Josephine's parents into a house that they rented. Karl continue to gain health and began to look for work, but since he would not sign the form to pledge his allegiance to the communist government it took a long time to find a job; the job he finally found paid very little, but it was a job.

Hans also found a low paying job; with both men working there was some money for both households. But even with money the supply of food and other items in the store were mostly in short supply. The store shelves were often empty when Josephine would go the stores. Underground bartering became a way of life for those who did not agree to follow the communist belief. Many of the people who they called rebels were falsely accused of something and arrested. Shortage of food and the bad water made many people sick and the hospitals began to fill up with the ill people.

October was wet and rainy; it had been a long time since it rained this hard. Alex's seventh birthday was at the end of the week, the family was all together, but Alex did not feel right. After dinner, he asked to go to bed. Josephine thought that did not seem like her energetic son, so she went upstairs to check on Alex. The covers were up over Alex's head when Josephine walked into the bedroom. She pulled back the covers and Alex's face was flushed. Josephine laid her hand on Alex's forehead and he was burning up with fever. The next day Alex was too sick to get out of bed and the fever had not broken. Josephine thought if he rested he would get better; so she went to see if she could get some fresh eggs from the farmer down the street. She prayed as she walked down the street to the farmer's place, "Lord, please touch my son Alex and heal him of the fever, and please give me favor with the farmer to get some eggs." Josephine hurried home caring six large brown eggs in her basket she hoped that if she fed Alex some protein he would get better.

By the time Josephine had come home with the eggs and went upstairs to check on Alex, he was still burning up with fever and lay unconscious with labored breathing. Josephine panicked scooped Alex up in a blanket and carried his limp body down the stairs yelling, "I need to get Alex to the hospital." Oma and opa came running into the living room where Josephine began to cry as she looked down at her young son laying in her arms. Opa headed towards the door as he said, "I will see if the neighbor can take us to the hospital." Oma tried to keep Josephine calm as they waited for opa to return. When he returned, he said, "The neighbor is waiting in the car." Josephine and opa got into the neighbors' car and drove off to the hospital. Oma stayed home, so she would be there when the other children came home from school.

Josephine carried Alex into the hospital and she looked at the nurse at counter as she stated, "My son has a fever and is not responding." The nurse came from around the counter to check on Alex, after shaking Alex to see if he would wake up, the nurse hurried back behind the counter to push a button, soon two orderlies came and took Alex from Josephine's arms. Alex was admitted in the hospital and was diagnosed with typhoid fever. Alex lay in a comma for 6 months. Fear gripped Josephine and Karl's hearts as they were told only ten percent of the children as sick as Alex survived the fever. They visited the hospital as often as they were allowed by the staff.

Every night before going to sleep Josephine and Karl prayed for their son. Alex missed his first Christmas since his father came home. One morning Josephine turned to Karl and said her voice choking up with tears, "I cannot bear it if I lose my son." Karl pulled Josephine into his arms as she allowed the tears to flow. Karl understood for he too had thoughts of what it would be like to lose his son.

Renate heard her mother weeping and came into the kitchen, setting her school books on the table before asking, "Mommy when is Alex coming home?" Karl motion for Renate to come over to them and he pulled her into the embrace with her mother. Josephine looked down at her daughter and gained courage to go on. Karl released his wife and daughter and said to Renate, "You better go and find Ralph and get to school before you are late."

The spring of 1948, the trees were fully bloomed and the spring flowers filled the air with their fragrance. Alex slowly opened his eyes and blinked as he looked around, the sunlight flooded through the window into his hospital room. Alex's throat hurt and he had tubes in his arms and something was over his mouth. He did not know where he was and fear gripped his heart as he wondered where his parents were. Then he noticed a lady wearing all white with her mouth and nose covered with a white mask walking towards him. He was afraid and his throat hurt worse as he began to cry for his mother. More strangers came rushing into the room with white masks covering their mouth and nose also. The nurse began to take the tubes out of Alex's mouth and he gaged as she did. Everyone in the room looked happy and one of them said, "Wonderful he is awake."

The nurse took Alex's arm to check his pulse, he stared at her and looked at the others standing at the end of the bed staring at him. He thought that somehow the bad men had taken him away and he would never see his family again. The doctor came into the room to examine him, when the doctor touched Alex on the sides of the neck it hurt. Alex reached up his hands to pull the doctors hands off his neck, tears ran down his face as he tried to talk but his throat hurt badly and he could only make a squeaking noise. The doctor turned to the nurse and said, "This young lad has mumps, quarantine him and he shall not have any visitors until he is not contagious."

Alex put his hands around his neck and looked at the nurse with panic in his eyes. The nurse came over and explained that he was sick but would get better in a couple of weeks. Everyone left the room and Alex was alone and scared, he wanted to tell the nurse he wanted his mother, but couldn't because his voice would not come out. The nurse returned with a large bowl of ice cream. Alex had never eaten ice cream before. The ice cream tasted sweet and made his throat feel better. The nurse left the room again and Alex sat up in bed eating the ice cream, somehow the ice cream took away his fear. When the nurse returned, she took the empty bowl and told Alex to close his eyes and get some rest. Before the nurse left the room, Alex was asleep.

Alex woke to the nurse bringing him another bowl of ice cream; he sat up in bed and ate the ice cream. The nurse sat down in the chair next to his bed jotting notes as she watched him eat his ice cream. He looked at the nurse and said, "I want to go home to my mommy and papa." The nurse put down her notepad, rose from her chair and stood next to Alex. She looked intently into his eyes as she explained, "Alex until your neck gets better no one can come and see you and you cannot go home until you are all better. If your parents come you can look down at them through the window."

Alex's lip quivered and he began to feel sad as he thought about his mother; soon big tears ran down his face, he feared he would never see his family again. The nurse tried to comfort Alex, but was unsuccessful, so she took the bowl and left the room to return to her duties. Alex cried himself to sleep, he dreamed about being home and then about the war and then about papa coming home. The nurse was in the room when Alex woke up, he felt lost and alone. The nurse walked over and patted Alex's hand and said, "You will be going home before you know it." He was not comforted with her words and turned his head away from her. The nurse gave him a pencil and a pad to draw on before leaving the room. He looked down at the paper and pencil lying on his lap for a long moment. Then he took the pencil and began to draw his grandparents' house.

Alex had just finished his picture when the nurse came back into his hospital room and said, "Your parents are here, do you want to go over to the window and see them?" A smile spread across his face and his eyes lit up. The nurse helped him down from the bed and then took the chair to the window so he could stand on it to see out of the window. He climbed up on the chair and stood onto his tip toes so he could see down the three stories to the front of the hospital where his mother and father stood waving up at him. He did not think about his sore throat as he happily waved back to his parents. The ten minutes that his parents were there waving at Alex went by way too fast. His mother and father waved their final goodbye and began to walk away.

Alex's face went from a smile to a frown as he stood looking at the window hoping his parents would come back. He had tears in his eyes as he looked over at the nurse with a puzzled look on his face. The nurse walked over and lifted him off the chair and said, "You need to go back to bed and get some rest so you will get better. Your parents will be back tomorrow and you can see them again then." This did not make Alex feel any better, he was sad and wasn't sure he believed the nurse as he laid his head on his pillow, the nurse covered him up and left the room. He cried himself to sleep. That afternoon the nurse brought him a bowl of ice cream. He loved the ice cream and thought that was the best part of staying in the hospital.

The next morning at the same time the nurse came in and took Alex over to the window to wave at his parents who stood below waving up at him. He longed to leave the hospital and be with his family. Every time His parents waved their final good bye and walked away the nurse put him back into bed and was told to rest. Every day after he was put to bed he cried himself to sleep wanting to go home.

Alex continued to get stronger; he was given permission to get up and walk around his hospital room and he would push the chair up to the window so he could look out. He always hoped his parents would be standing there when he climbed up on the chair and looked out the window. If the nurse caught Alex up on the chair, he would get scolded and told he had to spend the rest of the day in bed. Ten days passed with the same routine every morning and afternoon until his fever and the mumps were completely healed.

Alex had just got back into bed after walking around his hospital room when the nurse came into the room and said, "I have a surprise for you!" He thought he might get an extra bowl of ice cream today; he sat up in bed as he eagerly waited for the nurse to come back with his ice cream. Instead of the nurse came back into the room and his father and mother followed her. Their faces shone with happiness as they looked at their son. He was so happy to see them he jumped down out of bed and ran over to them. Karl bent down and pulled him into a big hug and then scooped him up he sat him on the bed. Josephine walked over to the bed and kissed her son on the forehead before she opened a small bag she had brought with her. Josephine pull out some fresh clothes and said to Alex, "Let's get you out of those hospital pajamas and dressed you in the fresh clothes I bought with me."

Alex was so happy he undressed and dressed quickly. In the meantime, Karl was at the nurse's station signing the discharge paperwork, once he was done he returned to Alex's room and with a twinkle in his eyes said, "Son, let's go home!" Alex jumped down off the bed and took both his mother and father's hand and pulled them towards the door. He told the nurse thank you, as his mother had instructed him to do. Then he skipped happily down the hospital halls between his parents who held his hands tightly as they exited the hospital.

Alex was happy to be home with his family, food was still scarce and there was no ice cream, but none of that mattered to Alex, he just wanted to be home. By the time he came home from the hospital the school was on a two-week break. Ralph worked with Alex during the two weeks to help him with some school work to see if he could remember where he left off. It had been well over six months since he had attended school. Alex was unable to move up with his class and was held back to be able to catch up with what he had missed. Going back to school was good for Alex, except he did not like having to live with the secret that his family went to an underground church. Even at seven years old he knew he had to keep this secret to protect his family.

Chapter 23 The Accident 1948-1949

In the fall of 1948, the communist government controlled all business, schools and churches. The following laws were set in place and anyone who did not comply with these laws was considered a traitor and was arrested: First, every citizen who wanted to work had to sign an agreement to align with the communist government belief system. Second, all children must join the communist party and youth training program and attend school. And third, anyone was found who did not follow these rules they would be arrested and if they resisted arrest they could be shot. Many of the people who were arrested were sent to Russia to do hard labor in the Siberian prisons.

Alex was in the third grade when one of the Stazi police came into his class room and told the children that they were now all Young Pioneers and must learn everyday what it meant to be a good Pioneer. Alex along with the other third graders did not understand. Then the man handed out white shirts, blue shorts and a red square scarf to each child and said, "You must wear this white shirt, dark blue shorts and have the scarf tied around your neck to be able to come to school. If you do not have this uniform on when you come to school tomorrow the police will go to your home and speak to your parents." Alex looked at the uniform that sat on his desk; he picked up the red square scarf and thought how nice it was that the school gave them some new clothes. The school bell rang and class was dismissed.

Alex arrived home with his sister and they both had their new uniform in hand and walked into the kitchen to show their mother. Alex thought that the uniform was nice and he was happy to have them since the pants and shirt he now wore had been patched many times. Alex happily held up the uniform to show his mother, but when she saw the uniform she got a look of horror on her face. Alex drew his eyebrows together as a puzzled look came on his face; he thought for sure his mother would be happy. Ralph walked into the room with his uniform in his hand and said, "We were told by the Stazi police that we must wear these uniforms every day to school."

Karl walked into the room and Josephine looked up and said, "Ralph take your brother and sister upstairs I need to talk to your father." Alex looked back over his shoulder to watch his parents as he followed Ralph out of the kitchen. Karl was not happy about the uniforms and the children overheard their father say, "I don't like this either, but we need to follow the rules to keep the children safe." Alex stopped at the top of the stairs and pulled on Ralph's shirt sleeve as he asked, "Is someone going to hurt us?" Ralph looked down at his little brother and said, "Not if we wear our new uniforms to school and obey all the rules." The next morning the children all dressed in their uniforms and went off to school.

Josephine began to go to the State Church so that she would not bring attention to her and her family, but secretly at night she would attend an underground church meeting with other Christians. Josephine had a deep faith in God and decided since the children were getting indoctrinated with the communist propaganda at school every day she needed to take them to the underground church with her. One night after dinner Josephine sat her three children down to talk to them about the church. Ralph was twelve, Alex was eight and Renate was six years old.

The children sat in a row on the sofa looking up at their mother as she began to try to help them understand. "Children you know that we follow the rules of our government but in our hearts, we believe differently." The children shook their heads 'yes' before she continued. "I am going to take you with me to learn more about God, but you must never tell anyone that you are going to a special church." Renate asked, "Mommy will the police take us away if we do?" Josephine got choked up as she answered, "Yes dear they will." Alex stood up and said "I will never tell and I will never let anyone take Renate away." Josephine smiled down at her children and then knelt on both knees next to the sofa and pulled them into a hug. Even at eight-years old Alex knew he had to keep many secrets for fear of the Stazi police.

When the government set up a State Church, they also took a large portion of taxes out of workers' paychecks to support the State Church and the government. People were told that this is the church they must attend if they wanted to go to church. Even if you did not attend the State Church you still had to pay the taxes. The church only could teach what the government commanded them to teach.

Those who did not attend the State Church were being monitored more and followed at times. After a while the people began to accept the lifestyle of living in constant fear of the government. To the children life seemed normal, going to school and being careful what they said was just part of their lives.

Food became even scarcer for those who had not signed the communist agreement. With the lack of food and clean water more people were getting sick and dying of the fever. Karl and Hans had no choice but to sign the agreement so they could provide for their families. Karl did not like this new communist government and would never pledge his allegiance to it. To him, it was just a piece of paper.

Josephine and others would secretly barter for food and other household items, but anyone caught bartering was arrested; they had to be very careful. The food shortage lingered because of limited supplies that came into the towns and those who did not sign the agreement had to be last in line. Most of the food was being shipped in from Russia and there were weeks between shipments. The food lines were still long and once you got into the store the shelves were eighty percent empty. Opa planted a garden and still raised his rabbits and pigeons. He also traded some rabbits for a few chickens, which provided eggs and occasionally chicken for dinner.

In 1949, the communist government thought they had all the people under control and they began to lift the heavy hand of authority and allowed the people to move about more freely. People began to feel safe walking the streets without being harassed by the Stazi police. Children were permitted to play outside.

There were still empty shelves in the stores, but more food now since the war ended. The Russian government would not give money to help pay for improvements to any of the roads or buildings that were damaged from the war, so is all the people could do is clean up the rubble. All the roads had huge pot holes and most of the buildings which were still standing had windows broken out and bullet holes in them.

The communist government working with the Stazi police, devised a plan to help them gather information and keep things under control. If someone would spy on their neighbor or even family, they were rewarded with a brand new beautiful house built by the government. A greater division came among the people and fear hung in the air. People kept to themselves, they were polite, but they did not talk about anything except the weather or how their farm animals were doing.

In the fall of 1949, Hans figured out how to run his truck on wood fuel by reconfiguring the fuel tank. He used small wood kindling pieces that he would light. The heat fueled his truck with wood gases just the same as gasoline had done before. This was a wonderful since gasoline was controlled and rationed out by the government. Hans never took the truck to town and only use it in the early morning hours to try and keep it a secret. Karl built a wagon that attach to the back of the truck for hauling large pieces of wood down from the hills to be used for cooking and keeping the house warm in the winter months. Alex was always fascinated by how things worked. He stood back away from the truck when Hans was loading the truck with wood and lit it up. After a few minutes Hans started the truck and it hummed to life. Alex's eyes lit up with excitement every time the truck started.

Karl took his two sons Ralph and Alex with him when he went up into the woods to gather wood. Alex enjoyed going with his father; he always made it into some sort of adventure, like the twigs were snakes that he had to pick up without getting bit by them. Early every Saturday morning Karl woke the boys and they headed up the hill into the woods. Ralph and Alex had a wagon and Karl took the cart he had made. He led the way down the street and up the hill as the boys followed taking turns pulling each other in the wagon.

Once they got to the hill Ralph pulled and Alex pushed the wagon up the hill, they had to go almost to the top where most of the trees were located. Going home was the best part for the boys; they sat on top of the wood filled wagon. Ralph sat in the front and used his feet to steer the cart down the hill. To start the wagon motion Alex stood at the back of the cart and gave it a push before jumping on behind his brother. At the bottom of the hill both boys would laugh as they waited for their father to come the rest of the way down the hill.

This winter seemed to have a record snow fall. Karl rose early and looked out the bedroom window to see another foot of snow had fallen during the night. Karl dressed and went down stairs to check on the fire and add some more wood. He stirred the embers and threw in the last piece of wood before going outside to get more fire wood. Josephine came into the kitchen just as Karl had put on his coat; he smiled at her before going out the door. Karl slowly walked through the snow around to the side of the house where he stored their winter wood supply. He stopped in his tracks as he looked to where the wood was stored and not a single piece of wood was there.

Karl shook his head in disbelief as he tried to figure out what he was going to do. He walked up the back steps pounded the snow off his shoes before he opened the door and said to Josephine, "We have no wood someone has stolen it in the night. Get the boys up we will need to go up and get some wood." Josephine left the kitchen and went upstairs to wake the boys. Ralph did not want to get up and she had to shake him again as she said, "You need to get up now and help your father, someone has stolen the wood." Ralph's eyes popped open and he jumped out of bed.

Josephine bundled up the boys with as many clothes as she could and still allowed them to move. They did not have gloves so she put a couple of socks on their hands to protect their hands from the cold. Lastly she found two wool hats for the boys to wear. She knew the boys had to go and help Karl but wanted them to be warm in the snow. Alex was excited; he always loved playing in the snow. He walked into the kitchen first and said, "Papa after we get the wood can we play in the snow." He just smiled at his son as he put on his coat and hat.

Karl had rigged tin to make snow tires for the cart and wagon. The wind was blowing snow everywhere and the chill of the wind made the air temperature feel like it was below zero. He pulled the cart and struggled to get it up the hill. It was hard for the boys to push and pull the wagon up the hill in the snow too. Ralph looked up towards his father and said, "Papa I am cold." Karl stopped and turned around towards his sons and said, "Hurry as fast as you can to keep warm." By the time they arrived at the top of the hill with the cart and the wagon, Ralph was shaking with chills and his teeth were chattering. Karl told him, "Jump up and down while Alex and I gather up some twigs." Ralph began jumping up and down as Alex and Karl gathered twigs to make a fire.

Karl built a fire in the snow and told Ralph to stay by the fire while he and Alex took the cart up a little further and filled it with wood. It was difficult in the snow to find enough wood to fill the cart and Karl's hands were cold as he tried to hold the axe to cut the log pieces small enough to fit into the cart. When they returned to the fire Ralph had warmed up and said, "Can I help fill the wagon?" Karl said, "Let's just find some twigs for the wagon and then we will need to get back home.

While they were up in the woods, the temperature drop and the snow crunched under Ralph and Alex's feet as they found twigs to fill the wagon. In the meantime, Karl put out the fire; he wished he had not taken the boys out in this weather. The wagon was not very full but Karl said, "Boys that is enough we need to head home. Be careful going down the hill it is very slippery." Karl turned to make sure the fire was out.

By the time Karl had turned back around to pull his cart Ralph and Alex were on the wagon riding it down the hill like a sled. The boys had always ridden the wagon down the hill and did not understand that it was not safe this time. Karl yelled, "Ralph stops that wagon now!" The wind blew Karl's voice away from the boys and they could not hear him.

A moment later the wagon began to swivel, Ralph tried to steer and put his feet down to stop the wagon as Alex grabbed tighter around his stomach. Ralph tried with all his might to steer and stop the wagon with his feet; he could not, because the ground was too slippery. The wagon flipped into the air and threw both boys off it and they began to roll down the hill. The wagon landed upside down with twigs spread across the hillside. Karl dropped the handle of his cart and ran as fast as he could to his sons. Alex landed face down just to the left of a big tree and Ralph landed face up under the tree.

Neither Ralph nor Alex moved they just laid there in the cold snow. Karl's heart was pounding loudly in his chest as he saw his sons lying still. He was just about to where Alex laid when he sat up in the snow; blood was running from his nose. Alex looked over at his brother who was not moving. Karl went past Alex and over to Ralph, he touched his cheek. Ralph opened his eyes and looked up at his father. Ralph raised his hands to his head and cried out, "Papa my head hurts." There was a cut on the side of Ralph's head that was pulsing out blood at the pace of his heart beat. Karl quickly took off his coat and ripped his shirt off popping all the buttons. Taking the shirt, he wrapped it as tight as he could around Ralph's head. Alex sat there in shock and fear watching not knowing what to do next. Karl pulled his handkerchief out of his pocket and wiped Alex's bloody nose and said, "Hold this on your nose. Stay here and do not move." Ralph closed his eyes and Alex sat there watching his father put on his coat and then he walked back up the hill.

Karl hurried up the hill to where the wagon had been tipped over. He picked up the wagon and carried it down to where Ralph and Alex were waiting. He had to leave his cart full of wood at the top of the hill; he hoped it would still be there when he returned, but doubted it would be. None of that mattered right now; the only thing that mattered was getting his boys home. By the time Karl got back down to the boys the shirt wrapped around Ralph's head was red with blood and Ralph was passed out. Karl sat Alex in the wagon with his legs hanging over the edge so that he could lay Ralph head on Alex's lap as he laid him into the wagon. Karl hurried home through the snow that had begun to fall again. The only thing that mattered was the safety of his children. Alex looked down at his brother's bandaged head and asked, "Papa Ralph's head is all red is he going to be okay?" Karl did not answer he just kept moving toward the house.

The house was in sight, Karl pulled the wagon into the front of the house and said to Alex, "You wait here and I will come back for you." Alex shook his head 'yes' as his eyes followed his father's movement. Karl gathered Ralph into his arms and carried him into the house. Josephine had been watching for them from the window and opened the door and pointed to the sofa so that Karl could lay Ralph down. Then he went back outside and picked up Alex and carried him up the slippery steps.

Alex looked intently at his father as they entered the house and he saw his brother lying still on the sofa. He asked, "Is Ralph going to be alright?" Karl pulled Alex into a hug and said, "Yes, son." Josephine had gotten some towels and water. She was kneeling over Ralph examining his wound; she looked up at Karl and said, "He is going to need stitches." They could not drive to the next town to the hospital for the snow was too deep and besides there was no wood to fuel the truck.

Alex sat on a chair in the living room watching his parents. Karl said, "I know Hans was a medic in the Army, I will walk over and get him." Josephine just shook her head as she took a fresh towel and began to firmly wrap it around Ralph's head; he suddenly woke up and let out a loud cry. Josephine went to get two blankets, one she wrapped around him to help him warm up.

Josephine finally turned her attention to Alex whose eyes were filled with tears even though he did not cry out loud. She took the other blanket and wrapped it around his shoulders. She saw the dry blood in his nostrils and a big scrap on his forehead. Alex sat brave in the chair as his mother took a clean rag and wiped his nose and mouth. Then she cleaned up the wound on his forehead and covered it with a piece of gauze. At the sound of Ralph's crying out Renate hurried into the living room and sat down next to Alex who wrapped his arm around his little sister.

Karl and Hans came into the house and Hans walked straight over to Ralph, after examining Ralph's head he opened his medical kit. He gave Ralph a leather band and told him to bite on it. Ralph bit firmly on the leather band and cried as his head was stitched up. Alex pulled Renate closer as she cried in sympathy for Ralph. Karl knew everything was under control and he needed to walk back up the hill to see if he would be able to find the cart full of wood. He decided to take the wagon and find some wood to bring back in case he could not find the cart. He walked past the tree where the blood of his children stained the snow; a chill ran up his spine at the sight.

Once Karl got to where the wagon had scattered the twigs he left the wagon there and continued to walk up the hill towards the cart of wood he left, as he had suspected the cart that was full of wood was missing. He walked back down the hill a little dishearten not only did they take the wood but now his axe and cart for hauling wood was gone too. He began to pick up the twigs and looked for other wood to fill the wagon. He was thankful for the small amount of wood that would help keep his family warm until he could go and get some more. He was also thankful that his sons were both home and safe. He whistled a hymn as he pulled the wagon toward home.

Josephine had been waiting for Karl to come back home with the wood. The house had cooled off since the log that Karl had placed on the fire that morning was burnt out. The fire was out and there was no more wood to keep the house warm. Josephine gathered extra blankets to bundle up the children. Ralph was asleep on the sofa while Alex and Renate snuggled together to keep warm. She kept looking out the window for Karl.

Karl stomped his boots to get the excess snow off his boots before going into the house. Josephine stopped what she was doing and went to open the door; He stood there with a bundle of wood in his arms. Josephine moved out of the way and Karl came in and started a fire in the fire place and another one in the kitchen stove. Josephine put a kettle of water on the stove to heat it up so she could bath Ralph to help warm him up. Karl took Josephine into his arms, after kissing her he asked, "How is Ralph doing?" She sighed as she answered, "He is resting now, but I am keeping a close watch on him."

The water was hot and Josephine went upstairs to draw a bath while Karl carried Ralph upstairs; he was still groggy from his head injury. As soon as the bath was done Josephine put him into bed and he fell right to sleep. She whispered to Karl, "If Ralph keeps sleeping like this we will need to find a way to get him to the doctor tomorrow. Karl looked at her and said, "I will need to make another trip up into the woods and get some more wood so we can start up the truck tomorrow. Josephine had a worried look on her face as she said, "Please be careful."

Karl went downstairs and put on his boots and coat. Alex got up and went over to his father and asked, "Papa where are you going?" Karl looked down and studied the gauze on his son's forehead and said, "I need to get some more wood." Alex went to get his coat as he said, "Papa I'll go with you." Karl knelt next to Alex and said, "Not this time, I need you to stay home and help your mother in case she needs anything." Alex was disappointed as he shook his head in agreement. Karl walked out the door just as Josephine came down the stairs.

Alex ran over to his mother and said, "Papa is going to get some wood and told me to take care of you." Josephine smiled and rubbed the top of his thick blond hair. He went to play with his sister. A couple of hours later Karl came home with another wagon full of wood. It had just gotten dark outside and Josephine was so relieved to see Him walk through the door. He took off his coat and said, "I think we have enough wood for two days; I will need to figure out a way to build another cart for hauling wood." Alex walked over to his father and pulled on his shirt and asked, "Papa can I help you build it?" Both Karl and Josephine chuckled as Karl answered, "Of course you can."

The next morning the sun was out and it had stopped snowing. The ground always looked bright as the sun reflected off the snow. Josephine went to check on Ralph, when she came into the bedroom he was sitting up in bed talking to Alex. Great relief flooded her at the sight of her son sitting up. Alex looked up at his mother and said, "Look mommy Ralph is all better." She walked over to the bed and felt Ralph's forehead before saying, "That is good but he will still need to rest today."

The economy was not doing well and many people were being laid off. Karl got laid off, but he did find a part time security guard job, working a couple of days a week. Most days there was only enough food for one meal a day. Josephine decided that lunch would be the meal they would always eat. On the days Karl worked Josephine packed him a lunch to take with him. Since Alex had typhoid fever he would get sick easily, but even when he was sick Alex never lost his appetite and was hungry all the time. Karl always saved a small piece of his lunch to give to Alex when he got home from work in hopes to help him become stronger and hopefully stay healthy.

Josephine continued to trade any items she could spare for food or trade sewing for food. One day the neighbor lady needed a dress altered and asked Josephine if she would sew it for a dozen eggs. Josephine gladly completed the alterations on the dress and took it over to the neighbor's house. The neighbor was so pleased with the work Josephine had done that she gave her two dozen eggs in exchange. Josephine was so excited that she wanted to surprise her family by cooking eggs for dinner that night. It had been sometime since they had two meals in one day. She looked at the clock it was almost time for Karl to come home from work. She took out a frying pan to heat it up as she scrambled the eggs in a bowl. Pouring the eggs into the frying pan and mixing them, the eggs were almost done when she decided to go outside and get some chives.

Alex and Renate were upstairs doing their homework. Alex lifted his head and took in a deep breath and licked his lips as the most wonderful smell filled the room. Renate rubbed her stomach and said, "I am hungry." Alex said, "Me too." They both slowly got up and crept down the stairs following the smell. Alex gently pushed open the kitchen door and a notice that the back door was open but his mother was not in the kitchen. They went over to the stove and looked at the eggs that were simmering in a frying pan. Alex reached up and pulled a piece of egg out with his finger and popped it into his mouth and Renate did the same. Even though it was burning their mouths it did not matter because they were too hungry to care as they continued to eat the eggs right out of the hot pan.

Neither of them heard their mother coming in the back door with a handful of chives from the garden. Josephine could not believe her eyes as she saw her two young children eating the eggs right out of the frying pan, she raised her voice and hollered, "Alex and Renate!" Both jumped around to look at their mother and then they put their hands over their mouth to hide the food in their mouths.

Josephine walked over to her two children and said as she stirred the eggs, "What do you think the two of you are doing? There are more than the two of you who need to eat." Josephine put the chives down and gave Alex and Renate a swat on the bottom and said, "Now go to your room, you had your dinner!" Renate began to cry as they went upstairs to their room. Alex walked over to the bed and sat down with his arms crossed, he was mad that he would not get any more eggs. As children, they did not understand what they had done wrong, all they knew was they were hungry for food most of the time.

Even with the little money that Karl earned there was not enough money for food and bills. Every time they had enough money to go to the store to purchase food most of the store shelves were empty. When you have money and you still cannot get the food you need, the money did not mean anything. Karl went out late at night to the back of restaurants and go into the garbage cans in hopes of finding some food scraps. As Karl did this he thought back to before the war and never imaged that he would ever dig through garbage cans for food.

Since the children were little Josephine took them into the woods and educated the children of what berries and mushrooms were good and which ones were poisonous. Mushrooms have lots of edible varieties. If they found a rare truffle mushroom they could sell them and earn money. The truffles grew underground under some trees in the woods. They never know which tree though. Alex began to learn that finding these truffle mushrooms meant he would be able to earn money when they sold them to the restaurants in town.

Some of the children of spies who had plenty of food and money would take a slice of bread to a group of children who did not have enough food or as they called them, second class citizens. Usually the oldest child in the group held the bread up in the air and shouted, "Who's hungry?" Then they thought it was great fun as they encouraged the hungry children to fight over the bread while they watched and shouted, "I got a penny for anyone who gets the biggest piece of bread." Of course, the oldest hungry child would be able to fight off the younger ones and get the bread.

One hot summer afternoon Alex was with a group of boys playing soccer when they saw the rich kids walking towards them. They stopped playing soccer and all just stood there watching the boys approach them. One of the boys held up a piece of bread and threw the bread in the air, as he shouted, "Who ever get the largest piece of bread will also get a penny."

Alex was fast, so he was the first one to the bread. He grabbed the bread up from the ground just as two of the older boys in the group grabbed him and the larger boy punched Alex in the mouth, while the other one grabbed the bread out of Alex hand. The rich boys cheered and laughed as they walked away without paying the penny to the winner. Alex took the handkerchief out of his pocket and wiped the blood from his mouth as he slowly walked home.

Alex promised himself that he would learn to fight so that he would be able to win a fight and not be beaten up. At the end of summer flyers were posted everywhere advertising boxing lessons for five bank notes a week. Alex had no money but knew he needed to learn how to fight. He pulled one of the flyers off the wall and crumpled it into his pocket. He said to himself as he walked home, "I have to make some money so that I can pay for those boxing lessons."

He went straight to his room when he got home and pulled the small old wooden box from under the bed. This box held what he called his treasures, odd color rocks and a small rusty pocket knife he found in one of the caves up in the hills. Alex reached into his pocket and pulled out the crumpled flyer and put it into his box before sliding it back under the bed.

Alex sat on the floor next to the bed pondering how to earn money to take the boxing lessons when he remembered the truffle mushrooms. He went into the kitchen and lifted the window seat and pulled out a small bag. He put the bag into his pocket and walked out into the woods and began digging under trees to find truffle mushrooms. After digging for an hour, he found two small truffle mushrooms. He put the truffles into his bag and walked into town and went to the first restaurant he came to. Alex knocked on the back door of the restaurant until the cook came to the door.

Alex opened his bag and pulled out the larger of the two truffles and held it up to the cook as he asked, "How much will you give me for this truffle mushroom?" The cook bent over and carefully looked at the truffle before he answered Alex, "Five bank notes." Alex beamed and said, "Okay." The cook went back into the restaurant and returned with the money. The cook said to as he gave Alex the five bank notes, "Anytime you find truffle mushrooms you come here and I will buy them from you."

Alex was pleased with himself as he walked home; he was excited to give his mother the other truffle. Alex opened the door and looked for his mother who was upstairs cleaning the bathroom. Alex entered the bathroom and held up the bag and said, "Mommy, look what I found?" Josephine walked over and gazed into the bag and smiled as she said, "Alex, what a wonderful surprise." She took the bag and gave Alex a hug. He walked over to the bathroom sink to wash his dirty hands that he got from digging in the woods. Alex had enough money to take his first boxing lessons but he did not tell his mother, he kept it a secret. He decided that finding these truffle mushrooms would not only help him but would also help his family, so he went out as often as he could to look for more truffle mushrooms.

The next few years went by without any problems for Alex. He went to school, picked berries and mushrooms, dug for truffle mushrooms in the woods, took boxing lessons and played with his friends. The woods were the children's playground. They would climb trees and play hide-and-seek and investigate caves that they came upon to see if they could find any lost treasures from the war. Alex always got excited when they found a cave where they could play the treasure hunt game; finding a treasure was what Alex liked the most. The best treasures that Alex found so far was a pocket knife and small star that came from a soldier's uniform.

One sunny afternoon Alex and Renate were out in the woods looking for berries to pick and take home. They just finished filling the bottom of their buckets and were in search for more berry bushes when Alex looked up and saw some string hanging down from a large tree. Alex put down his bucket and climbed up the tree. Renate stood at the bottom of the tree watching him move up past the first layer of branches. He held the string in his hand as he moved slowly up the tree, just past the fourth row of branches he saw a large white cloth strung across the branches. Alex moved around the tree pulling the cloth into a ball so he could take it with him down the tree. The cloth fabric was very soft and as he pulled it to gather it up some of the branches tore small holes here and there in the cloth.

Alex tucked most of the fabric under his arm and slowly climbed down the tree to where Renate was waiting. As soon as he touched the ground she asked as she touched the fabric, "What is this?" Alex said, "I am not sure but we need to go home and show mother." Forgetting about picking any more berries she picked up the two buckets and followed Alex out of the woods toward home. Once they got home she stopped abruptly as she remembered they did not have very many berries in their buckets and thought their mother would be angry with them.

Josephine heard them walk up the porch steps and opened the door. She looked at Alex holding the white cloth and Renate had a guilty look on her face. He held up the cloth and said, "Mommy, look what we found in the woods. Josephine took the cloth and smiled at Alex and Renate and said, "Alex this is wonderful." Renate spoke up and with a quiver in her voice, "Mommy, we did not get very many berries. Josephine patted her on the head and said, "That's okay, you did the right thing to bring this right home, someone could have tried to take it from you, this cloth is made of silk." Alex asked, "What is it?" Josephine answered, "It is a parachute left over from the war."

Over the next few weeks Josephine took the white silk, cut it into pieces and stained the pieces with berries, walnuts and grass. Josephine and her mother pulled strings of threads out of each fabric to use as she sewed the fabric together. Josephine made Ralph and Alex two shirts and Renate a dress. Out of the leftover fabric she made a quilt. This was the first new clothe they had since the war. Alex was excited to get his blue and green shirts. Renate wanted to wear her new dress every day. Seeing her children enjoy their new clothes made Josephine happy and thankful for her ability to sew.

It was a hot summer day and Alex had finished all his chores. His two best friends, Peter and Wolfgang along with two other boys went up into the woods to play the treasure hunt game. Up the hill in the woods a slight breeze blew through the trees, which made the air feel cooler. Alex led the way as they walked up higher and deeper into the woods; they had never gone this far up before. Peter pointed and yelled, "Cave up there on the left!" All the boys followed Peter's pointing finger. Excitement filled them when they found this new cave to search for treasures. Since Peter found the cave he was the one to lead the way into the cave. Wolfgang had a candle and matches in the bag he brought with him; he gave the candle to Peter and lit it so the cave would not be pitch dark as they searched for treasures.

The candle made a dim light in the dark cave. Just after they entered the cave it broke into two paths. Peter stopped and turned towards the others and asked, "Which way should we go." Wolfgang said, "Since the cave was on the left, let's go left." That made sense to the others and they followed Peter into the left path of the cave. The path opened into another large opening in the cave. The boy's eyes opened wide as they saw weapons left over from the war lying along the side of the cave wall. There were guns, ammunition, knives, helmets and hand grenade. The boys had never seen a hand grenade and did not know the danger. The boys were filled with delight as they looked at their new-found treasure.

The older boy said, "Come on let's take some of the treasures home. They put ammunition and knives into their bags. They each put on a helmet and slung a gun over their shoulder. Alex had a foreboding about the hand grenades and did not take one, but the others put at least one in their bag. They walked down the hill and marched into town like conquering soldiers. The oldest boy who was eleven stopped and took the hand grenade out of his bag. He began throwing it up in the air and catching it like a ball.

The boys parted ways to go home each to their own houses. A couple of minutes later there was a loud boom and then the boy with the hand grenade was screaming. Alex turned around and noticed that the boy had blown off his left hand and arm, blood was spirting everywhere. Alex screamed at the sight and neighbors came out to see what was going on. Tears were streaming down Alex's face as he ran home as quickly as he could, losing the helmet off his head as he ran. The neighbors gave aid to the hurt boy.

Alex ran up the steps to the front door, he opened it up and closed it hard behind him; he did not know what to do. He just stood there with his back against the door breathing hard. Josephine was in the kitchen and jumped at the loud noise. She came running into the living room wiping her hands on a towel. Josephine saw the terror on Alex's face; his face was as white as a sheet and she said, "What is the matter? Are you feeling okay?"

Alex did not say a word; he stared at his mother and held up the gun and bag up to her. Josephine could not believe her eyes as she looked at the gun, then she lost her composure as she yelled at Alex, "Where did you get that gun?" She took a deep breath to regain her compose as fear gripped at her. She walked over and took the gun and the bag from Alex and sat it on a nearby table. Then she took him by the hand and led him to the sofa. Alex's nine-year old shoulders shook as he put his face in his hands and cried. Josephine wrapped her arms around him softly said, "Alex tell me what happened."

Alex tried to stop crying as he told his mother through his shaky voice what had happened. When he came to the part about the ball blowing his friends arm off he began to cry harder. Josephine thought he might throw up. She pulled him even closer as she hummed to comfort him. Once he calmed down she took him upstairs to rest on his bed until his father got home. Alex cried himself to sleep. As she left the room she could not believe the trauma her son had gone through today and she knew this might trigger the nightmares again, the ones he had during the war.

Josephine heard the front door open and close, and then she heard Ralph and Renate talking down stairs. She looked at her watch before going down stairs to tell the children your brother is not feeling well. Ralph said, "I was looking for Alex everywhere, a kid from school got hurt really bad." Josephine saw the concern in Ralph and Renate's eyes and said, "Alex is safe, we will talk about this when your father comes home."

Karl came home about an hour later and Josephine met him at the door. He looked at her exhausted face and sad eyes with concern and said, "What's wrong?" Josephine took Karl by the hand and shut the door. She told him what had happened to Alex that day. Karl hugged Josephine and said, "I will go and talk to him and hopefully he will understand why war weapons are not toys." She stepped back from Karl and shook her head as she wiped a single tear that ran down her cheek away. He leaned down and kissed her before heading up the stairs.

Alex was awake and staring at the ceiling when Karl walked into the bedroom. He looked down at his son who was visibly shaken. His thick blond hair was matted to the side of his head wet from his tears. Karl sat on the side of the bed and cleared his throat before he spoke sternly but quietly, "Son, I am sorry for what happen to your friend, but I need to tell you that the round ball is called a hand grenade and that they are a weapon just like a bomb. The knife and gun are also weapons that can hurt people and they are not toys. Do you understand?"

Alex looked in his father's face and saw a fear in his father's eyes he had never seen before. His lower lip trembled as he shook his head that he understood. Then Karl stressed in a very loud tone of voice, "You may never go into that cave again!" Alex reached up and put his arms around his father's neck to give him a hug and said into his ear, "I'm sorry papa, I won't go there again." Karl wrapped his arms around his young son and wished he could erase from Alex's mind all the things he has seen since the war.

After a few days Alex was almost back to normal. He decided not to go back up in the woods for a while to play, but to only look for mushrooms that he could sell. He always had to be busy doing something and wanted to find more ways to make money. Alex became quite good at taking things and fixing them for his mother or to sell for money. One day Alex was sitting on his bed doing his school home work when he heard his mother scream. Alex ran to the bathroom and saw water shooting out of the bathroom sink faucet. Josephine stood with her clothes wet as she held the faucet to try and stop the water. Alex pulled a hand towel from the rack and put it over the leak, while Josephine went under the sink and turned off the water.

Once the water had stopped Alex turned the faucet handle and it fell off into his hand. Alex stared at the handle for a few minutes while Josephine changed her clothes. An idea popped into his mind to wrap the small piece of wire that he had found around the faucet and then try to put the handle back on. He pulled the wire from his pants pocket and after he wrapped it around the inside of the faucet he put it on and slowly turned the handle until it was tight before he hollered, "Mommy come and see if you turn on the water if it will leak." She slowly turned on the water and only a small dripple came out of the faucet. She reached up and turned the handle a little tighter and the drip stopped. She patted Alex on the head as she praised her son, "Good job Alex."

Every Saturday Alex and Ralph would walk down to the dump and look for broken items that Alex could use to make something that his family could use or that he could sell. Alex found old broke bicycles and parts lying around the dump. The boys gathered up the old bike and parts to take home. Once they got the old broken bikes and parts home Alex took apart the old bikes and then he laid out all the parts. After a while he could build a new bicycle that worked out of all the many parts. Alex saved the other parts of the bicycle until he had enough for another working bicycle. The first bike he gave to his brother and then he made one for his sister. Once he had all the parts for another bicycle he built it for himself. As he built his new bike he got very excited since this was the first time he had his own bicycle.

Alex also collected old tires and old leather belts from the dump. He took the tires and cut the tire into four pieces and then decided to cut the old leather belts into pieces. Alex stood and looked at all the pieces that lay out on the lawn. He cut a piece of tire the size of his foot and then went to find the jar of old screws he found. Alex reached in and pulled out four small screws. He assembled the pieces by putting enough of the leather belt across the top of the tire piece and he used the screw to secure the belt to the tire. He slipped his foot into the tire and a smile came to his face. He walked around the yard as excitement filled him.

He went into the house to find his mother. She was sitting on the sofa mending a pair of socks. He stood in front of her and said, "Look mommy I made a pair of shoes." Josephine looked up and Alex began to walk around the living room. Josephine stood up and asked, "Can you make more of these." He said, "Yes." Alex was so creative and could fix anything that Josephine began to call Alex her little fix-it man. They sold these tire shoes to make money for their needs.

Chapter 24 The Escape 1950-1953

In the early 1950's, an uprising began to try and overthrow the communist government. Karl and many others became angry with the government and they began to band together in secrete underground meetings to plan a revolution against the government. He kept his involvement in the meetings a secret from his family for he knew if he told even Josephine his family might not be safe. It was dangerous for him, but he felt that it was important to not give into this harsh new government and their treatment of the people. Karl hated the communist way of life and how his family could not be free to worship God or even get a good paying job without favors to the government officials.

The Stazi police began to suspect something was not right and they began to keep an eye on men whom they called radicals. The fall of 1953, began warmer than normal; even the breeze was warm as it blew leaves down from the trees. The Stazi police suspected a handful of men whom they began to monitor very closely. Karl was one of the men on their list.

Early October was when Karl noticed he and his families were being watched. He hurried up the street to work and noticed that a man in a black suit was following him. This worried him. That day Josephine noticed that the police were standing outside their house watching. When she went out to go to the neighbor's house one of the policeman stood in front of her path and asked, "Do you know where your husband is?" Josephine looked intently into the policeman's eyes as she answered, "Yes, he is at work!" The policeman stepped aside and let her pass.

Karl came home from work and noticed the same man in black following him home. He walked up the steps and opened the door closing it quickly behind him. Then he peeked out the window curtains to see if he was still there. He was. Josephine walked into the living room and he quickly pushed the curtains back in place and then turned and walks over to her. As they embraced Josephine whispered in his ear, "Karl what is going on the police were here asking questions today?"

Karl's heart skipped a beat as fear for his family stabbed at his heart. He took Josephine's by the hand and led her upstairs to the bathroom shutting and locking the door. She noticed the fear on her husband's face and how his jar twitched as he looked at her. Tears began to sting her eyes, she had to blink to keep the tears from falling.

Karl placed his hands on her shoulders and looked deeply into her eyes as he whispered, "Josephine, I need to go away so you and the children will be safe. I need you to keep acting normal then in a couple of months if you can, try to escape to the other side." She could no longer hold back the tears and they began to run down her face as she realized what her husband was saying. She did not say a word as Karl pulled her to himself and just held her until he could feel the tension leave her body.

The next morning Alex sat at the kitchen table with his sister and brother making plans for what he would do tomorrow for his birthday. Karl walked into the kitchen and was not his chipper self. Alex looked up at his father as he walked over to the table and gave each child a hug and a kiss. Then he walked over to Josephine and embraced her before giving her an extra-long kiss. He picked up his lunch pail off the counter and headed out the door for work just like he did every day. Alex watched his father leave the kitchen and thought something doesn't seem right with his father today. Alex was staring at the door when he heard his mother say, "It's time to go to school." Alex turned toward his mother and asked, "Will papa be back for my birthday tomorrow?"

It surprised Josephine that he could sense something was different. She did not answer right away instead she picked up the children's lunch pails and handed a lunch pail to each of her children. As Josephine kissed Alex goodbye and sent him out the door for school she said with her voice filled with emotion, "I hope your father will be here for your birthday, now you better hurry so you won't be late for school." Josephine could not tell no one about Karl, not even her parents who could tell something was different about their daughter and Karl was not home.

Alex ran to catch up with his brother and sister. Karl did not come home that night and when Alex got up the next morning his father was not there. His heart dropped and his countenance became sad as he knew he would have another birthday without his father being home. Josephine noticed the sadness on his face and tried to cheer him up. She gave him a cheerful peck on the forehead and said, "Happy Birthday Alex!" Alex heart was sad and he walked slower than normal to school, Renate kept saying, "Hurry up or we will be late."

Day after day the Stazi police followed Josephine and watched all her movements. She told the children that they could no longer go into the woods to play and instructed them they must come straight home from school. She feared the police would take one of her children away from her. She never mentioned a word about why their father left or why the police were watching them. The children were old enough to know something was not right; Ralph was seventeen, Alex thirteen and Renate eleven years old. They saw the fear in their mother's eyes, but they did not question her, they just obeyed.

A few weeks after Karl had left the children were getting ready for bed when there was a loud knock on the front door. The children came into the living room as Josephine slowly opened the door and asked, "Can I help you?" Two Stazi policemen stood at the door and darted their eyes around the room. One of the policeman asked, "Where is your husband, he has not been at work the past few weeks and we need to know his whereabouts." Josephine spoke quickly, "I do not know where Karl is, he left for work and never returned home." The short stocky policeman looked in her eyes as if to see if she was telling the truth, then he shouted in her face, "I don't believe you?" Fear griped Josephine heart as she just keeps staring into his eyes.

Alex's eyes grew big as the policemen pushed their way into their home and searched for his father. Josephine waited by the door for them to return to the living room. She said once they returned, "Please leave us I need to get my children to bed." The taller policeman pushed his hat back on his head and looked over at the children standing in the corner in their pajamas. That seemed to satisfy the policemen and they bid Josephine goodnight. She was thankful as she watched them get into their car. She turned and let out a sigh of relief as she closed the door. She looked over at her frighten children and said, "It is time for bed." Alex asked his mother as she tucked him into bed, "Is papa ever coming home again?" Josephine pushed Alex's hair off his forehead and kissed him goodnight, then she said, "All we can do is hope and pray." He felt sad as he closed his eyes to sleep, but sleep did not come right away, he thought about the war when his papa was gone.

Police watched their house daily, but for some reason they did not come knocking on the door again nor did they want to come into the house to search for Karl. Josephine was relieved, but feared they would find out she lied to them. She began a ritual of taking the children for a walk every evening. She was trying to figure out a way to leave without the police stopping her.

She had to devise a plan to escape. She decided it would be best to leave on one of their nightly walks. The children had no idea what Josephine was planning; this was the only way she could leave without putting her children at risk. The colder the weather got she noticed that the police did not stand outside her house at night, but made rounds every now and then. She decided that in December she would leave late in the night and head for the border with the children.

Late one night in early December 1953, it was cold and windy but the first snow had not fallen yet. Josephine did not say a word as she handed Renate and Alex their coats. Alex and Renate put on their coats and Josephine said, "You will need to bundle up tonight to keep warm as we walk." Taking Ralph's coat over to him as he sat on the sofa reading a book, he did not get up to get his coat. He just sat there and looked up at her and said, "Mother, I am not going for a walk on a cold winter night they say there is a risk of snow." Josephine pressed for Ralph to go with them on their family walk. She raised her voice as she said, "We all need to go together tonight." Ralph still refused to go and said, "I am old enough to make my own decisions and I am not going!" Josephine could not understand why he was being so disrespectful; she thought it must be his friend at work named Otto; ever since he has been seeing him Ralph was changing. Josephine's heart sunk for she knew she had to go tonight or not at all. She would have to leave her eldest son behind trusting that opa and oma would take care of him.

Grief filled Josephine's heart as she walked over and looked out the window making sure it was clear of policeman. It took weeks for Josephine to get up the nerve to leave and now with Ralph refusing to go it made it even harder to leave. She walked over to the sofa and bent down to give Ralph a hug before leaving. She did not dare let Ralph know or take anything with them; just the clothes on their backs in case they got stopped by the police. One more look out the window and the three of them stepped out of the house shut the door behind them and walked down the street. The streets seemed very quiet tonight except for the wind howling through the trees. Alex had his hands stuffed deep in his pockets to keep them warm. Renate walked close to Josephine and had one hand stuffed into her mother's coat pocket and the other in her own.

They walked for a long time in silence she kept looking around and changing directions in hopes that no one would be following them. Alex thought they were walking in large circles around the town. Josephine looked around before stopping under a large oak tree; she looked down at Alex and Renate faces and saw that their cheeks were red from the cold. She put a hand on each of her children's shoulders but did not look at them she kept darting her eyes around to make sure no one was watching them. Her voice was tight as she whispered, "We are going to try and find your father tonight." Alex looked at his mother with a puzzled look as she pointed and explained, "We are going to cross that field and there will be a watch tower with lights that move from side to side. Then we will come to some barbed wire with tin cans hanging from it. We must crawl under the wire on our stomachs until we get to the other side. Do not touch the wire or the cans or you will get hurt. Do you understand?"

Alex and Renate had fear in their eyes as they looked at their mother and shook their heads that they had understood, even though they truly did not. They began to walk through the field. The flood light was on the other side as they walked quickly through the field and came to the barb wire. Josephine instructed the children to lie down on their stomachs as she looked towards the tower and the lights were still on the other side. Renate was scared while she instructed them through her stained voice, "Go and do not stop crawling no matter what, just keep going until you get to the other side of the barb wire." Then get up and run as fast as you can to the nearest tree and I will meet you there." Renate looked like she was going to cry when Alex reached over and took her hand and pulled her closer to the barb wire, letting go of her hand he laid on his stomach and began to move under the barb wire. Renate lay on her stomach and began to crawl following close behind Alex. Josephine stood for a moment and watched her children move under the barb wire. Josephine looked up and saw the lights of the watch tower moving towards them. She went down on her stomach and began to crawl under the barb wire behind her children.

When Alex and Renate got out from under the wire and they stood, Alex took Renate by the hand and they began running towards a grove of fir trees. Josephine was close behind her children and ready to get out from under the barb wire when her leg hit the tin cans and they made a loud clanging noise. Alex heard the noise of the clanging tin cans but did not look back he continue to run towards the trees with his sister. The sirens went off and the spot light began to move towards Josephine as she jumped to her feet and began to run towards her children. The spot light was on Josephine and the sound of gun fire came towards her. Josephine moved quickly to the right as she yelled to her children, "Keep running and don't stop!"

The gun fire scared both Alex and Renate as they came to a very large fir tree; its branches touched the ground. They crawled under the fir tree branches and turned to look out from under the branches towards their mother. They could see their mother running back and forth towards them as she tried to avoid the spot light. The gun fire was making flashes of light in the dark. Fear got the best of Alex and Renate as they saw the light move on their mother and then she darted away again. Both Alex and Renate began to cry and their eyes became blurry hindering their view, Alex pulled his sister closer, they did not know what would happen to their mother. Suddenly they felt an arm wrap around them as Josephine pulled them closer towards the tree trunk.

The communist watch guards could not cross over from the East to the West side of Germany; it was their job to try to kill any person who tried to escape but not chase them. The spot light stopped on the fir tree and lit it up. Josephine wrapped her arms tighter around each child and whispered, "Lay flat on your stomachs, keep your heads down and do not move!" She was thankful that the branches of the fir tree touched the ground. Gun fire began to spray into the tree. Renate began crying loudly into the dirt that lay against her face. They were all shaking with fear as a shot hit the tree trunk just above their heads. A few more shots and then the only sound was the siren blaring into the night. The light disappeared from the fir tree. Josephine and the children did not move; they lay in the same position for what seemed to be forever to Alex.

The siren finally stopped and it became quiet. The spot light went back to its original movement of slowly going from side to side. The three of them laid there listening for some time before Alex whispered, "Mommy my nose itches from the dirt may I scratch it?" Josephine moved her arm so that Alex arm was released to scratch his nose. Josephine whispered, "Okay you can sit up against the tree trunk." After the spotlight left the tree it was dark, they had to adjust their eyes to the darkness. A light snow began to fall and the moon light lit it up as it hit the ground. Renate's face was covered in muddy dirt spots from her tears. Josephine pulled a handkerchief out of her pocket and wipes her face. Josephine prayed out loud, "Thank you God, for your protection and for the full moon's light on the snow." Her prayer brought a sense of peace to the three of them.

They sat there quietly in the dark watching the ground fill with snow. Renate began to shake with cold and moved closer to her mother to get warm. Josephine decided to move over and look out from under the tree branches to see if the snow had stopped. There was about three inches of fresh snow on the ground, but the snow had stopped. She looked up at the full bright moon. There was a slight breeze that made the air crisp and cold. Josephine knew that to keep warm they needed to keep moving.

She pulled her head back under the fir tree branches and said, "We need to walk again." Renate asked, "Mommy, are we going home to get some clothes and my ragdoll that papa gave me?" Josephine sighed as she explained, "Renate we can never go back home or the police will take us away." Renate began to cry again, "I am cold and tired, I want to go home, and I want my ragdoll." She wrapped her arms around her daughter trying to comfort her as she said, "I know and I wished we could go home too, but we cannot, you must trust me."

Alex moved toward the fir tree branches and stuck his head out to see what was out there, pulling his head back under the tree he said, "We are in the forest, if we cannot go home, will we get lost in the forest?" Josephine looked out from under the tree branches to make sure the spot light was on the other side before leading the way out from under the fir tree. They stood up and the wind caused a chilled to run through their bodies. Josephine took Alex and Renate by the hand before answering Alex's question, "Alex, we must trust God and let the stars guide us and lead the way out of the forest." She looked down at Alex and his blond hair and face was full of dirt from lying under the tree. They walked hand in hand deeper into the woods as Josephine prayed in her heart for direction.

Josephine felt the money in her pocket that Karl had given her before he left. The thoughts of Karl made the chilly air feel a bit warmer. She led the children through the snow-covered ground moving as quickly as the children could go, she knew they needed to keep moving and prayed that they would not get frostbite on their cold feet. Alex's thirteen-year old boy voice cracked as he said, "Mommy my feet are freezing and tired, I need to rest." Josephine debated what to do. Up ahead she saw a very large fir tree with lots of branches hanging low to the ground, she looked at Alex and said, "Okay we can take a break and try to warm up. See that big fir tree over there; we can rest under it for a while."

Alex began running to get under the tree. Josephine and Renate slid in under the tree branches after Alex. She motioned for them to go close to the tree trunk. They huddled together to keep warm, they had their backs up against the tree truck and their feet pulled in to put their coats over their legs. Renate laid her head on her mother's shoulder and fell asleep. Alex leaned his head back on the tree truck and soon he also was asleep. Josephine looked down at her watch, it was almost 3 am. She too was tired, but chose to stay alert to keep watch over her sleeping children. It had begun to lightly snow again. Josephine sat watching the snow falling gently to the ground and listened to the sound of an owl in the top of the tree. The falling snow lulled Josephine to sleep.

Josephine awoke with a start and saw that the night sky was lit by the early dawn. She looked at her watch, it was almost 6 am. It looked like another three inches of snow had fallen to the ground. Josephine shook Alex and Renate to wake them. Alex rubbed his empty stomach before he crawled out from under the tree branches. He stood next to the fir tree stomping his feet in the snow. Josephine and Renate came out from under the tree, Josephine looked around and noticed that to the left the trees began to thin which meant that the forest was coming to an end. She said, "This way, I think we will find a town." The sky was clear and the sun was just under the top of the mountain. It lit up the sky so the mountain took on a glow of orange.

At first Alex ran ahead picking up snow and forms it into snowballs then throwing them at trees as Josephine and Renate followed behind. He stopped and stood waiting for Josephine to catch up before he said, "I am hungry do you think we can get some food when we get to the town?" Josephine knew her children were hungry since it had been almost twenty-four hours since the last time they had eaten. Her heart prayed as she answered Alex, "I hope so." Renate pointed ahead and said, "Look there is a dirty path in the snow over there and I see some lights way over there." Josephine looked towards where Renate's finger was pointing and said, "Wonderful." Alex ran ahead and led the way down the path just as the sun began to rise over the mountain and fill the sky with red and pink colors, it looked so peaceful.

The path turned into a dirt road that was wet from the snow. The dirt road widened and turned into a cobblestone road with a few houses not far down the road. Josephine looked at the sign posted near the road that read, "Welcome to the City of Duisburg." The smell of fresh baked bread filled the air as they came close to a bakery. Alex's stomach growled and his mouth began to water. She stopped in front of the baker and said, "Wait here I am going to see if I can buy us some rolls" The children waited outside in anticipation of eating a fresh made roll. Josephine came out of the bakery shop and had no rolls.

Alex had a puzzled look on his face as he looked at his mother's empty hands and asked, "Where are the rolls? Renate whined, "I'm hungry." Josephine heart sunk as she answered the pleading faces of her children, "I am sorry, but the money we have is for East Germany and it does not work in West Germany, so we cannot buy any rolls. The baker told me to go to the City Hall that is a few blocks away from here and they would show us where we can get food and a place to stay." This news gave Alex and Renate hope as they followed their mother through the streets of Duisburg towards City Hall.

Alex looked up and down the street and did not see any police with guns. He stopped and looked in the different shop windows as he trailed behind his mother and sister as they walked ahead towards City Hall; the shops were full of merchandise unlike the shops where he grew up. Alex thought to himself, "This new place is going to be a wonderful adventure I think I will like being here in West Germany." A sense of peace filled him and the thought of finding his father entered his mind. Josephine stopped walking in front of a large white building with lots of steps leading up to the door. She looked at Alex and Renate and said, "Wait here at the bottom of the steps while I go inside and talk to the people and see if we can get some food." She began climbing up the snow-covered steps towards the door, with each step she had to rest a moment; she was exhausted from escaping the East side of Germany and then their long walk to town. Alex and Renate began bouncing up and down to keep warm as they watched their mother disappear behind the big door.

Josephine took a long time in the building and Alex wanted to sit down as they waited. He took his foot and ran it across the bottom step to remove the snow so the two of them could sit down while they waited. People began to fill the streets on their way to work. They watched the people rush by them but none of them even looking their way. Alex reached over and wrapped his arm around Renate's shivering body. They were cold, tired and hungry as they waited on the bottom of the steps for their mother's return.

For the first time since they left they had time to think of their brother Ralph who they left behind. After he graduated from school at age 15, he got a job. They didn't see him as often but now they were greatly missing him. Their mother told them that opa and oma would look after him. She promised that they would all be together again someday but first they had to find their father.

Renate looked over at Alex and said through her chattering teeth, "Alex, I am scared, what if mommy never comes back." Alex being thirteen tried to be brave for his little sister, even though he too was afraid: he pulled her closer and whispered, "It's going to be okay, mother will come back." Just as Alex finished those words Josephine came walking down the steps towards them. She looked more tired and there was sadness in her eyes as she spoke, "Children, a car is going to come and take us to a place where people like us who have escaped from the East side can live. They call us refugees. The lady said this place is where we can find help until I can find a job; I just pray your father will be able to find us there."

A big black car pulled up to the curb. Josephine said, "Come children this is our ride." She sat up front with the driver and Alex and Renate climbed into the back seat. The car was warm and it felt good as the car drove to the other side of town. Alex looked out the window and watched as they passed shops opening and people moving along the sidewalks. They drove out of town to a large fenced off area with lots of buildings made from old stones. The six-foot fence had barbed wire strung across the top of it. There was a large gate that was pulled shut across the entrance. On the gate was a large sign with the word spray painted in red across the words underneath, "CLOSED." The car stopped at the gate and the driver got out and pushed open the gate. Then he drove through the gate before getting out of the car and closing the gate behind them. Even though the car was warm, a chill hit Josephine as the driver slid back into the car.

Alex looked at the barbed wire on the top of the fence and an eerie feeling ran up his spine, he shuttered at the memory from yesterday of having to crawl under the barbed wire and then the gun fire shooting through the air as he watched his mother running towards the fir tree where they were hiding. Escaping from East Germany was something Alex would never forget.

Alex looked around as the car drove towards the buildings and he asked the driver, "What is this place?" The driver answered in a robot tone of voice, "At the beginning of World War II, this place was called a concentration camp where the Jews were gathered up by Hitler's men and put in prison, but now it is a refugee camp." Silence fell in the car as Alex thought about what was said. Alex figured that this must have been the place where they took his childhood friend Frank and family when they took them away. Deep sadness filled his heart as they drove closer to the buildings.

The car slowed and pulled up a dirt street where there was a row of buildings. The car stopped in front of the largest building on that street, it had a sign posted on the large double doors that said, "OFFICE." Alex stepped out of the car onto the dirt road which was now muddy from the wet snow. Josephine thanked the driver for the ride as she got out of the car. The car drove off as soon as the car door shut. She looked up at the building just as it began to snow lightly. She turned towards Alex and Renate and said, "Stay close and follow me inside, we can see if they can help us."

Josephine led the way up the four steps, she stopped and took a deep breath before opened the large double doors. Once inside the doors there was a long hallway with another set of double doors at the end of the hall. Their shoes squeaked on the freshly scrubs floor as they walked down the hall. A wooden bench sat on the side of the wall next to the second set of double doors. Josephine pointed to the bench and said, "Sit down on the bench and wait for me to return."

Alex looked around as he walked over to the bench to sit down, the floor shined from being polished and his voice echoed when he said, "Okay mother." Josephine made sure the children were sitting on the bench before putting her fingers to her lips to tell them that they needed to be quiet while they waited. Alex watched his mother disappeared behind the set of double doors. She was gone for a long time and he got tired of sitting on the bench so he got up and stood next to the bench. As soon as he heard footsteps coming towards the door he quickly moved back to sitting on the bench.

Josephine followed a lady out of the double doors; she was well dressed in very nice clothes. The lady walked towards Alex and Renate, with a note pad and pen in her hand. She stood in front of the bench and looked down at Alex and Renate making notes on her note pad, while Josephine stood behind her watching and waiting. She turned abruptly and almost ran into Josephine as she headed back towards the double doors. Josephine gave Alex and Renate what they called "the look" before following the lady through the double doors.

Josephine did not come back for what seemed to Alex like forever. Renate laid her head on the arm of the bench and fell asleep. Alex sat, bouncing his foot on the floor and the whole bench began to shake. He stopped as soon as he saw his mother coming through the double doors; she walked over and shook Renate to wake her up and said, "Come we must go to another building in the back. They both immediately were on their feet and followed their mother back down the hall and out the double door where they first entered the building. The morning air was crisp and the sun was trying to peek out from behind a layer of heavy clouds. Walking around behind the building they saw another building which also had double doors on it. They stood at the door for a moment before Josephine knocked on the door.

There was the sound of clicking of heels as someone approached the door. A very stern looking lady wearing large rimmed round glasses opened the door. She looked down at Josephine standing there with her two dirty children. Without saying a word, the lady extended her arm pointing through the open door signaling for them to follow her. She turned and Josephine followed her into the building. Alex and Renate lined up behind their mother to follow her in a line just like ducklings would follow the mother duck.

The room they entered was very large room and dark, Alex blinked to adjust his eyes to the darkness. There was a blanket hanging from the ceiling and there were rows in between the blankets. Alex wondered what the large room was used for before it became a refugee city. Alex learned that the people that West Germany people called the refugees were "people from the other side."

As they wandered around the aisles of blankets Alex noticed names pinned to the outside of the blankets, he could hear people quietly talking behind each one. The lady abruptly stopped causing Alex to bump into his sister, which made Renate turn and push Alex back. They had stopped in front of one of the blankets. The lady pulled back the blanket and pointed for us to enter. Josephine entered the room whose walls were made of blankets the children nervously followed their mother into the room.

The lady stood and watched as the three of them looked around the room. The blanket room was dark with a soft glow of light that came from the ceiling high above the blankets. With the glow of the light Alex observed that the room had three cots and a small table with a flashlight sitting in the middle of it. The blankets were the walls that separated families' living spaces. There was one living space per family; the size of their new home was an eight-by-eight square foot space. This building of blankets was the refugee camp for those who had escaped from East Germany. Renate held her nose and complained loudly, "This place is dark, small and it smells." Josephine looked at Renate with "the look." Renate walked over and sat down on one of the cots crossed her arms over her chest; she did not dare say another word.

The lady closed the blanket and pinned a sign on the outside of the blanket with their last name on it. Pushing back the curtain again the lady pointed to show Josephine the sign with her last name and said in a soft voice, "Welcome to your new home, we serve one meal a day at 6:00 p.m. The meal is served in white building next door. If you are not there by 6:15 p.m. the door will be closed and locked and there will be no more food until the next day at 6 p.m. There is an outhouse for your use around the back of the building. Josephine shook her head that she understood and then smiled at the lady and said, "Thank you for your kindness." Then the lady turned to leave and closed the blanket door behind her. They could hear the clicking of the lady's steps as she walked away. A baby was crying from one of the other blanket rooms.

It was now noon and they had not eaten since the day before, they were all hungry, but more tired than hungry. Josephine looked at her two tired children covered in dirt from lying under the tree the night before, she explained what they needed to do, "We are going to take a rest now, close your eyes and think about papa and how we will someday find him and be able to be together again, and then we will go to dinner." Renate was the first one to unroll the blanket that was on the bottom of the cot she sat on. Both Alex and Renate were asleep in a matter of minutes. Josephine lay on her cot and closed her eyes, images of what had happen during the last twenty-four hours filled her mind. She prayed silently, a prayer of thanksgiving for the safe arrival to this place of refuge, she prayed for Ralph to be safe. She prayed for wisdom and protection as she too drifted off to sleep.

Alex woke up and sat up on his cot, he heard people talking as they walked down the aisle between the blankets past their room. Josephine woke up and looked at her watch. She jumped out of bed and woke Renate by shaking her on the shoulder. Renate stretched and looked up at her mother with a look that said, "Where am I?"

Josephine looked down at her and expressed in an urgent whisper, "It is time for dinner we need to go now." Alex and Renate stood in the middle of the room with their stomach rumbling with hunger. Josephine pulled the blanket to see a line of people. A woman with a small child stepped back to allow Josephine and her children to step in front of her, they followed the line of people to the exit. By the time they got outside there was a long line waiting to enter the white building to eat.

The same lady who showed them to their room stood in front of the door of the white building. She looked at her watch and right at 6:00 p.m. she rang a bell and opened the large double door to allow the people to file into the huge dining room filled with tables. The smell of food made Renate and Alex hungry stomach growl. They followed the line to where the food was served.

Once they sat down at a table Alex tasted his food and ate it way too fast; he thought that this was the best food he had ever eaten. After he was done eating and waiting for his sister and mother to finish he looked around the room full of people. Every table was full; there were mostly women and lots of children. Alex wondered how each family got to the refugee housing. Josephine finished eating and got up and went to get a wet cloth from the kitchen crew to wash her children's face and hands.

After the meal, they walked back to their room made of blankets. Alex stared at their last name pinned to the blanket outside of their room and thought about his father. He wondered if his father might be there somewhere in another room. Karl had left two months before his family escaped from East Germany to the West side to search for him and their freedom. Alex pushed back the blanket and entered the small blanket room; he walked over and sat down on his cot. He sat there in deep thought for a long time before he turned towards mother and asked, "Mother, do you know when we will find papa? Do you think he is in one of these blanket rooms?"

Josephine just sat there quiet for a moment and then Alex could hear his mother's voice as she tried to keep her tears from falling in front of her children. Then she cleared her throat and spoke softly, "I do not know when we will find your father, but I do know we will!" The confidence in his mother's voice calmed both Alex and Renate. Josephine wanted her children to rest, but Alex wanted to investigate to see if his father was in the refugee camp somewhere.

Josephine saw the adventure in his eyes and sternly said, "Alex lay down on your cot and I will tell you a story. Alex and Renate both climbed under the blankets on their cots. Josephine lay down on her cot and began to tell her children a story that began with, "Once upon a time in a faraway country lived a very special family……. Both Alex and Renate had drifted off to sleep before hearing the end of the story. This was their first day of freedom, but not the end of their struggles.

Chapter 25 Refugees 1953-1954

Alex awoke early the next morning full of fear and with sweat on his brow, he had dreamed of the escape. Josephine woke as she heard him cry out in his sleep. The room was still dim as he opened his eyes and felt his mother's hand push his hair back off his forehead; this small gesture told Alex that he was safe. Then she walked over to wake Renate from her sound sleep. She rubbed her eyes and looks confused. Josephine quietly said, "We need to get up so we can be in line early. The lady told me last night that we could get a shower and fresh clothes this morning."

Both the children got up off their cots and folded the blanket down to the bottom of the cot as Josephine waited by the door made of blanket. She led the way around the maze of blankets to the exit. The sun was already up and bright to their eyes; the snow sparkled in the sunlight. The sky was blue with no clouds. Josephine pointed to another building across from theirs and then led the way; there was a line of five families waiting to enter the building and shower.

The door opened and an older lady with a clipboard took the name of the next person in line and they entered the building with her. Josephine, Alex and Renate now stood at the front of the line and it would be there turn to enter the building. The large door swung open and the older lady said, "Names and ages!" Josephine answered, "Josephine age forty-three, Alex age thirteen and Renate age eleven." After writing the information on her clipboard she turned and they quickly followed her into the building.

The inside of the building smelled musty and had many doors off the main entrance. The lady opened a door that was filled with clothes, a heavy set older man sat at a table looking through the papers that were set in front of him. The lady handed the man the paper off her clipboard. The room was filled with stacks of clothing lying in different piles on the floor, there was a sign posted on the wall of the type and size of the clothing above each pile.

Josephine walked around the room and found the piles of clothes set out for each sex and age group. She said to Alex and Renate, "Pick out a change of clothes and meet me in the center of the room. The man looked up over his glasses that set on the end of his nose watched them as them moved around the room. Renate was the last one to find the clothes that she wanted to wear; she turned to meet Alex and her mother in the center of the room. Josephine led the way over to the table and laid the clothing in piles in front of the man. They waited as the man took each piece of clothing and wrote in on the paper, once he was done, he pushed a button under the table that let out a loud buzz noise. He looked up over his glasses and said, "Wait here, Frau Laume she will take you to the showers."

The door opened and Frau Laume entered and with a command said, "Follow me!" Josephine and the children followed her out of the room and a couple of doors down she opened another door. The room was steamy and a young woman with a pleasant smile sat at a table folding towels, boxes sat behind her filled with packages of toothpaste, toothbrush, mouth wash and a comb. Frau Laume handed her the same paper that had Josephine's information and left the room.

The young woman smiled as she looked up at Josephine and handed each of them a towel and one of the packets from the boxes behind her. Josephine was thankful for the pleasantness of the young women and softly said, "Thank you for your kindness." The young woman looked down and marked the paper before she said, "There are six showers through that door over there. Please take your showers and place your old clothes and towels in the bins labeled as such. Then return to me so I can check you out." Renate and Alex followed Josephine through the door.

Alex stepped into the shower and notice that there was no bar soap, instead a large tub with a pump held the soap. He took his shower, got dressed and combed his hair. He walked over and put his towels and clothes in the correct bin and then he stood waiting for his mother and sister to come out. They came out and put their towel and clothes in the bins. Josephine led the way back to where the young woman was sitting. The young women looked up and said, "You will be allowed to shower and get new clothes every two days." Josephine nodded her head and said, "Thank you."

Just then Frau Laume entered the room and directed them to where the exit was. Once outside Josephine shielded her eyes from the sun as she said, "Alex and Renate, I am going to take you to your new school. While you are in school I am going to look for work, we can only stay here for a short while." Alex looked down at his clothes and said, "We don't have on the uniforms for school." Josephine looked up and down at Alex new clothes and then she smiled and said, "They do not wear uniforms at this school and I think you look fine in your new clothes."

Alex was hungry as they walked to school. The school was a large brick building with lots of windows, the grounds of the school were well kept. A few children were standing on the steps that led up to the school main entrance door. A tall skinny boy looked Alex up and down as Alex approached him. As he passed by the boy jeered, "Refugees!" Alex tried to ignore the skinny boy as he walked up to the door. Once inside the school building they walked down a hall to the office, Alex could hear the children in the halls whispering as they walked by them.

Josephine opened the office door and a lady dressed in a plain blue dress with her hair pulled up in a bun on the top of her head and a pencil stuck through her bun stood behind a counter. She smiled at Josephine as they approached the counter. Josephine pulled out the children's birth certificates (she had sewn into the lining of her coat before escaping) and the letter she got from the lady at the refugee camp. The lady in the blue dress gave Josephine a welcoming smile as she took the papers. After filling out more paperwork for Alex and Renate to begin school, the lady handed her back the papers she had brought and said, "Welcome, we have a meal program for all refugee children and they will be fed breakfast and lunch." Both Alex and Renate smiled when they heard this news.

Josephine left to look for work and felt that her children would be safe and fed while she was away. She pulled the paper out of her pocket that was given her with the directions and a recommendation to the clothing factory to hire her. She walked briskly the two miles to the clothing factory. She stopped and looked again at the directions and then turned right at the next corner; there it was a very large brick building. She pushed open the door of the clothing factory and walked into a large reception area.

The woman at the desk asked, "Can I help you?" Josephine answered as she showed the recommendation paper to the women, "I was told I could find work here." The women pointed and said, "Have a seat over there and I will call the manager." Before Josephine could sit down a tall older man walked into the room and asked, "Do you have any paperwork for me?" She handed him the recommendation letter and waited for him. The man looked at the letter and then looked at Josephine's small size before reaching out to shake her hand. He smiled and said, "Welcome, I will take you to the sewing room."

The new life for Josephine, Alex and Renate had begun in this new place; they had food and a small blanket room to live in. Life was very hard for the three of them, but not as hard as where they had left. They were refugees and strangers in their own country. Josephine worried about Ralph, who she had to leave behind and wondered if Karl had even made it when he escaped. School for Alex and Renate was a place to study and the teachers were nice compared to the old school where the teachers would have a child hold out their hands and hit them with a ruler if they thought the child was not following the rules.

Alex being thirteen and the new kid in school found it difficult to fit in. The other children made fun of and teased all the refugee children. He did not like it when a couple of the boys pushed Renate and called her names. Alex began to fight with these boys, he wanted to protect her. Both Alex and Renate felt like outcasts and did not know why the others did not like them and were so mean to them. Alex became angry and fought a lot as he tried to prove himself and protect Renate. Josephine cleaned up Alex's wounds from his fighting scrapes and tried to help him understand that he needed to try and find another way to express himself.

A few months passed and Josephine was able save some money. She knew she had a limited time to stay at the refugee camp; they could only be there four months. She did not like that Alex was angry all the time. She hoped that once she had enough money to move to their own apartment that things would get better for her children. She did not know how to get in touch with Karl and prayed every night he was somehow safe and would find them. Alex missed his big brother Ralph and wished he was there to talk to.

When Alex saw his mother's worried and tired face it made him angrier that they had to leave Ralph behind and that they did not know where his father was. Every night before going to sleep Josephine prayed for the safety and protection of Ralph and Karl. After the prayer Alex always ask, "Will father come for us soon?" Josephine replied with the same words every night, "God will keep both your father and Ralph safe." Somehow these words brought Alex peace and he could fall asleep dreaming about his brother and that his father had found them.

It had been a long day; Josephine could not concentrate at work. Her thoughts of still not having enough money to rent an apartment and she had to leave the refugee camp in three-weeks. Worry filled her while these thoughts bombarded her mind. She pricked her finger several times while sewing that day. Josephine was tired when she got off work; she hurried towards the refugee camp. She was so focused on the money dilemma as she walked; she thought she heard Karl's voice. She stopped walking and listened, she heard his familiar voice again, "Josephine is that you?" It sounded like it was coming from across the street. She turned her head to look across the street and there she saw Karl. She had to blink her eyes to make sure what she saw was real.

The moment she looked over at Karl he began to run across the street and took her into his strong arms, picking her up off her feet and swinging her around while he whispered in in her ear, "Josephine, my Josephine, I am so glad I found you." Karl sat Josephine back down on her feet and they stood in the middle of the sidewalk holding each other not wanting to let go. People walked around them and stared as they passed.

Holding hands Karl leads Josephine to a park bench where they could talk. They sat on the bench holding hands for a long moment before Josephine reached up and ran her finger along his jaw line, "Karl, I was so concerned for you, I did not know if you made it across." Her voice trailed off as she looked down. Karl lifted up her chin and looked deep in her beautiful green eyes as he said, "I have looked for you every day since I have arrived here 6 months ago. I prayed every day that you and the children would be able to safely come to me. Are the children okay?" Josephine answered with a tone of sadness in her voice, "Yes, all but our eldest son, he refused to come, he was working for the Russians who took over my father's business." Karl replied, "What! He is only 17 years old!"

Tears filled Josephine's eyes as she took Karl's hands in hers and said, "I did not know what else to do except leave him and take the rest of us for what Ralph thought was just a night walk, I did not want him to know we were leaving in case the police questioned him." Karl stiffens, but shook his head that he understood even though he did not like that his family was still apart. Josephine stood up and said, "Alex asks about you every night and Renate longs for her papa. Come and I will take you to them." Karl stood up from the bench and they walked hand in hand towards the refugee camp.

Alex and Renate got home from school into their blanket room to wait for their mother to get off work and began doing their homework as they did every school day. They took turns holding the flashlight on the school work. They were busy doing their homework with their backs towards the blanket door. Alex was helping Renate with a math problem and they did not hear as Josephine and Karl entered the room.

Karl cleared his throat to get the children's attention and as he did Alex dropped the flashlight on the table and both children turned around. Alex and Renate were on their feet and ran to their father wrapping their arms around him. Renate began to cry, "Papa, papa you found us." Karl bent down and wrapped his arms around both Alex and Renate; he looked Alex in the face and said, "Son, I am so proud of you and how brave you are." Then he whispered in Renate ear, "I love you baby girl."

Josephine stood there with tears streaming down her face as she watched her children and her husband's reunion. Karl was glad to see his children again, but was concern for his eldest son who was left behind. It saddened Karl's heart to think he may never see Ralph again. Josephine pulled her handkerchief out of her sleeve and wiped the tears from her face. Karl stood up and looked around the small blanket room and then said with a twinkle in his eye, "This room is nice, but I have an apartment that I want to take you to today. Gather up your things so we can go and see it." Both Alex and Renate jumped up and down before going over and packing up their homework. Josephine gathered the few things she had and said, "We will need to check out at the office before we leave."

Josephine stood at the doorway to their blanket room holding back the blanket door as she scanned the room to make sure they had everything. Renate put her book bag over her shoulder as she grabbed both her parent's hands. Josephine felt like a weight had been taken off her as they walked towards the office building. Karl opened one of the large double doors and they walked down the hallway towards the main office.

Alex and Renate sat on the bench outside the office door as they waited for the return of their parents. A new sense of peace filled Alex's heart and somehow he knew everything was going okay, his father was home. Many times, during Alex's short life his father has come and then left for a long time before returning, it seemed different this time. Karl and Josephine stepped out of the office and Karl had a bag filled with stuff. Alex asked, "What is in the bag." Karl smiled as he answered, "A going away gift from the woman in the office."

The sunshine seemed extra bright as they walked toward their new home. The walk was quite long since Karl lived on the other side of town. Renate complained that her feet hurt and she needed a rest. Karl stopped and looked down on his eleven-year old daughter with compassion. He decided since it was only a few more blocks to the apartment he would carry her. He handed the gift bag to Josephine. Alex looked at his sister and said, "You are such a big baby." Karl hushed him and said, "Here take Renate's book bag." Karl carried her piggy back as they walked the rest of the way to the apartment.

Karl stopped outside of a large apartment building; Josephine looked up at it and said, "This is very nice." Karl looked up and said, "We are on the second floor." Alex stood and looked up at the building with a smile on his face. Karl set Renate on her feet and said, "Okay, follow me." He took a key out of his pocket before taking the gift bag from Josephine and then opened the door, there was a spiral stair case leading up to the second floor. He led the way up the stairs and opened the door to their apartment. Renate ran in through the open door and twirled around singing, "This is our new home!"

The apartment was sparsely furnished with a sofa and a table with four chairs. It felt warm and inviting; Alex walked around taking in just how big the apartment was compared to the refugee camp. He turned toward a hall where he saw three doors and then he walked down the hall to investigate the doors. One door led to a bathroom and the other two doors were bedrooms. The first bedroom was large with a window seat and a large bed in the center of the room, a small table stood on the right side of the bed with a small lamp in the center. The other bedroom was somewhat smaller with a single bed; it also had a small table with a lamp in the center.

Alex thought to himself as he walked into the smaller room, "This room is perfect for me." Karl knew his son's thought process and walked over and placed his hand on his shoulder as he said, "Son, your sister will be sleeping in here and you will be sleeping on the sofa in the living room." Alex was disappointed as he turned to look at his father. But just having his father home would be worth sleeping on the sofa. Alex said to his father as he walked out of the bedroom, "Okay, I will sleep on the sofa." Alex walked back into the living room and looked at the sofa, and then he saw another door that led off the living room. Alex walked over and opened the door to a large kitchen with a window that looked out onto another set of apartments that stood only a few feet away.

Karl walked into the kitchen and sat the gift bag on the counter, Josephine followed him into the kitchen and said, "Karl this will do fine." Alex had so many questions about why his father left them. Karl knew he needed to share with his family why he had to leave so quickly and hear their story of how they escaped from the East. He said, "Let's go and sit in the living room and talk for a while. Karl sat on the sofa between Alex and Renate. Josephine pulled up a chair and sat across from them. Alex asked, "Father, why did you have to leave? Will you leave again?"

Karl could sense the fear in his son, so he wrapped his arm around him as he began to explain, "Son I had to leave, but I promise I will not be leaving again." Karl could feel Alex's shoulders relax as he went on to tell them how the pastor of the underground church helped him escape and that he was able to get a new papers and find work as a security guard. He had looked for them every day and found the apartment a few weeks ago.

When Karl finished, he asked no one in particular if they would like to share their journey out of the east side. It was silent for a moment before Alex said, "Mother took us on our nightly walk and it was very cold. Ralph did not want to go out into the cold. For a while a man followed us and then he was gone. Mother led us up to a place with a high tower with lights and a barbed wire fence. I was scared as Renate and I crawl under the barbed wire and ran to hide under a big tree. Then we heard gun fire and saw their flashes of lights in the darkness as we waited for mother to find us under the tree." Renate began to weep at the memory and tears filled Josephine's eyes.

Karl wrapped his arms around both of his children and bowed his head to pray. He thanked God for their safety and for bringing them back together again, then he prayed for protection of Ralph and that God would bring him to them.

Karl then rose from the sofa and walking over to Josephine and gave her a hug before saying, "I will make us a warm meal of potato soup and bread; you must be hunger." They all followed him to the kitchen. He would not allow Josephine to help prepare the food. She turned towards the children and said, "Alex and Renate, you can finish their homework while we wait." Karl was happy to have his family in their new home and he whistled while he prepared their meal. The children listened to their mother and fathers discuss their hopes and dreams for their future together as they ate their meal. For the first time in Alex's life he felt his stomach was full and he felt safe in their new home with the warmth of his loving family surrounding him.

Alex woke up early the next morning, he sat up on the sofa and his feet touched the cold floor. He rubbed his eyes and looked around the room, a smile spread across his face as he realized that he had not just dreamt that his father had come and brought them to their new home, it was real. He could hear talking in the kitchen; it was his mother and father talking quietly about Ralph and what they should do. Karl raised his voice slightly as he said, "Since we all live here now and Ralph is not yet twenty-one, we will send a letter to your parents asking them to arrange the papers for him to come and visit his ill mother in West German." Josephine said, "That is a wonderful idea, I will prepare the letter today."

Alex got up and walked towards the kitchen. Both parents looked at their son as he entered the kitchen. Karl was ready for work and grabbed his lunch before kissing Josephine and ruffled Alex's hair as he headed out the door to work. There was a content look on Josephine's face as she turned to Alex and said, "Go and wake your sister, we will need to get ready to take you to your new school today before I go to work."

Alex's heart dropped at the mention of another new school. He slumped his shoulders as he walked out of the kitchen door towards his sister's room. The covers were up over Renate's head when Alex shook her to wake her up. She stretched her arms over her head and said, "I love my new bed, I slept so well." Alex pretended not to hear her as he walked towards the door and said, "You better get up and get ready we are going to a new school today." Then he walked out of the room and closed the door behind him.

After breakfast Josephine looked at her watch, it was getting late, she handed Alex and Renate each a packed lunch and said, "It is time to go." The new school was only a few blocks away from the apartment. As they walked toward the school Renate said to Alex, "Maybe the children in this school will be nicer than the ones at the other." Alex wanted to believe that would be the case, but he doubted it. They stopped in front of the new school; it was a three-story brick building with a flight of stairs that lead up to the entrance door. Josephine looked at Alex and Renate and followed their eyes to see what they were looking at. A couple of big boys were glaring at them. She turned back to Alex and Renate and said, "Come we need to get you checked in so I can get to work."

Renate followed Josephine up the steps and Alex trailed behind glaring at the boys as he passed by them. Josephine opened the entrance door and led the way down the hall to the main office. The hall was filled with children going to their classes. The lady at the desk wore thick glasses and had red orange hair pulled back in a bun, she looked up and said, "Can I help you?" Josephine replied, "Yes, we just moved her and I need to register my children for school."

Once the paperwork was completed the lady said, "I will take care of the children and show them to their rooms." Josephine turned towards Alex and took his hand in hers, she pressed a house key into the palm of his hand as she said, "Walk straight home after school and do your homework, your father and I will be home right after work." Josephine waved goodbye as she left for work. The lady returned to her desk to get something while Alex and Renate stood in the office waiting. The school bell rang, the lady walked towards them, she had a bright smile on her face as she said, "Okay children, it is time to go and meet your new teachers and friends."

They followed the lady out the office into the hallway. This time the hallway was quiet since classes had just begun. The first door they came to was Renate's classroom. Alex waited outside while the lady took Renate inside and introduce her to the teacher. The lady quickly returned and smiled at Alex and she said, "Now it is your turn." They walked up a flight of stairs and turned to the right, the lady stopped in front of the first door. He followed the lady into his new classroom.

The whole class became silent as all eyes were on Alex. The teacher was a tall skinny man who stood as the lady approached his desk. She said to the teacher, "This is your new student Alex." Then she left the room as the teacher said, "Class this is Alex, please help him to feel welcome." All the students said in unison, "Welcome Alex." The teacher pointed to a chair in the front row next to a pretty girl with long blonde hair. The teacher gave Alex a math book and continued with his lesson. Alex thought to himself, "Wow, everyone seems nicer at this school.'

The bell rang for break and all the children rushed out of the room except the girl sitting next to Alex, she turned and asked, "Would like me to be show around the school during the break." He couldn't believe it, someone was being nice to him and it was a girl with beautiful eyes and a great smile. Alex stood up and almost knocking over his desk, then he stuttered out an answer to the girl, "Y-Yes, thank you, w-what is your name?"

She blushed and looked away as she said, "Erika." Alex's heart melted at the sound of her voice. Alex and Erika walked through the halls and she pointed out the restrooms and cafeteria. A group of boys walked over to them and said to Erika without looking at Alex, "What are you doing with one of those kids from over there?" Erika pointed her finger at the boy who was talking and said, "That is none of your business." He scowled at Alex as he said, "We will see you after school." The boy turned and walked away with the other boys giving Alex an up and down look before they followed the boy.

Alex knew what the boy meant; when they said, they would see him after school. They wanted to fight, that saddened Alex's heart, and he did not want to keep fighting. He missed his friends from his old school back in East Germany. Sometimes he just wanted to go back there where he could go to school and have friends again. The bell rang for class to begin; Erika led Alex back toward the class. The group of boys passed him in the hallway and the biggest boy pushed Alex as he passed by. He was getting angry and could not concentrate on his school work the rest of the day.

The final school bell rang and it was time to go home. Erika and Alex walked to the front of the school steps without saying a word to each other. Alex turned to Erika and said, "My sister is waiting down at the bottom of the steps for me." Erika looked down at Renate and then said as she walked down the steps, "I will see you tomorrow." Alex answered, "Sure, see you tomorrow." Renate looked at Alex with a puzzled look as he slowly walked down the steps. He looked across from the steps and saw the boys waiting for him under a tree that stood in front of the school. Once Alex reached his sister he told her to wait on the bottom of the steps, as he nodded his head toward the group of boys under the tree. She nodded back as she watched Alex head towards the boys, she understood, since Alex had been in many fights before.

Alex walked over towards the boys with his head held high. The biggest boy stood about a foot taller than Alex and he looked him up and down as he approached the tree. The big boy walked over and pushed Alex to the ground and said, "Go back where you came from and stay away from Erika!" The other boys laughed at Alex and before he could get to his feet they held Alex down on the ground as the big boy hit him in the face and stomach several times.

They let Alex go and walked away laughing. Alex laid there hurting with his nose bleeding. Renate ran over to him and knelt next to her brother as she said, "Are you okay?" She pulled a handkerchief out of her pocket and wiped at the blood that was flowing out of his nose and down his cheek. Alex slowly sat up with a grunt as he held his stomach; he grabbed the handkerchief from her and said, "What do you think?"

Alex hated that he had to fight all the time, but this time it was not a fair fight, since the boys held him down so that he could not fight back. That made him even madder and he began to think about the boxing class' poster that he saw in a window of one of the buildings he walked past on the way to school. He had taken a few lessons in East Germany, but thought he needed more. He sat there on the ground holding the handkerchief up to his nose and thought about how he was going to get the money to take the boxing lessons when Renate interrupted him by saying, "We need to be home doing our homework before mother gets home from work."

Renate gave Alex her hand and helped him to his feet. It was painful for Alex to walk so they slowly walked towards home. He stopped in front of the window where the boxing poster was taped; he stood staring at the poster. Renate kept walking for about a half of block before turning around and seeing Alex standing, looking in the store window. Renate put her free hand on her hip and said, "Alex what are you doing?" He turned and looked at his sister and then slowing began to walk towards her. Once he was caught up to her Alex said, "I need to learn how to box better."

Alex held his stomach as he slowly climbs the steps up to the apartment; he pulled the key out of his pocket and opened the door. They were surprised to see their father standing in the middle of the living room waiting for them. Karl took one look at his son and his swollen face to know something was wrong. He walked over and helped his son to the sofa. Alex sat down and Karl bent down to examine Alex's face. He stood up and said, "We need to clean you up before your mother gets home." As he took care of Alex's face Renate told him how the big boy pushed Alex down, then the other boys held him down so the big boy could beat him up. Father looked sternly at Alex and said, "The big boy is the bully and leader of that group of boys, unless you can beat him in a fight you will be fighting the rest of your time at school."

Alex looked up at his father and said, "Papa he is as tall as you. Can I take boxing lessons?" Karl looked down at Alex serious face and said, "Yes, you will need to do whatever it takes to win the fight against that boy if you don't want to keep getting beat up, but remember boxing is for defending yourself only."

Karl heard the key in the door and he walked over to meet Josephine at the door. Alex sat on the sofa doing his homework and tried not to look up at his mother, but he could hear his parents whispering. Josephine walked over to the sofa and sat down next to Alex, he turned to look at his mother. Josephine lifted his chin to examine at his face. A sad look filled her eyes as she got up without saying a word and went into the kitchen.

Karl followed her into the kitchen leaving Alex alone with his thoughts. He stood up and put his homework into his book bag a little harder than necessary, he wished he did not have to fight, that way he would not disappoint his mother. Alex said to himself, "I wish Ralph was here he would know what to do." The thought of his big brother brought sadness to his heart and tears stung his eyes at the thought that he might not ever see his brother again.

A week later Alex's face was healed up from the fight, but he did not sleep well at night since his bruised ribs were still sore. Karl had signed him up for boxing lessons. He was up early; he was excited since after school today he would take his first boxing lesson. He swore to himself that he would not pick a fight, but if someone started a fight he would finish it. Alex got up from the sofa; he folded his bedding and put it away before heading to the bathroom. The smell of food filled Alex's nostrils as he came out of the bathroom. Alex entered the kitchen surprised to see everyone had already begun eating. He sat down and enjoyed eating his breakfast of eggs, toast and peppermint tea. He thought about the time when he did not have enough food but now his stomach was full. He was thankful that now they had three meals a day.

Karl left for work and Alex went to get his book bag for school. Josephine looked at her watch and said, "It is time to go Alex, do you have your key to get in after school?" He felt his pocket and said, "Yes." Josephine continued, "After you walk Renate home you can go and take your boxing lesson, then come straight home." She handed Alex and Renate their lunches before they all were out the door.

On the way to school Renate told Alex about her new friend Else and how she wished he could find a friend also. While she talked about her new friend, Alex thought about Erika. She was so pretty, and then his thoughts went to the group of boys and the words of the big boy who told him to stay away from her. The school bell rang just as Alex and Renate entered the building. They departed ways and each one went to their class.

Alex walked into the classroom and sat in his chair next to Erika without looking at her. His teacher was turned away from the class writing on the chalkboard, Erika whisper, "Good Morning Alex." He looked over at her and smiled as the teacher turned and called the class to order. Then Alex turned around and looked over his shoulder at the big boy in the back of the room who was frowning at him. Alex quickly turned back around and looked at the teacher. During each class break time he rushed out the classroom and did not look or talk to Erika.

When the last school bell rang at the end of the day, Erika reached across and grabbed Alex arm before he got up out of his chair. She looked at Alex and she said, "Did I do something wrong?" The class room cleared out except for the teacher who sat at his desk grading papers. Alex's heart melted as he laid his hand on Erika hand and said, "No, I just don't want to fight."

Erika smiled and pulled her hand away as she said, "Oh, Manfred isn't so bad when he isn't around his group; he has to be tough, because when he first came to school here everyone picked on him because he is so tall. Manfred had to beat everyone up who picked on him and now everyone respects him and will help him fight." Alex looked Erika in the eyes and nodded his head to let her know that he understood. He got up from his chair and said, "I've got to go, my sister is waiting for me out front." Erika smiled and got up and walked with him out of the classroom.

Alex froze as he saw the group of boys waiting under the tree for him to come out. Alex said to Erika, "I will see you tomorrow," he hurried down the stairs to his sister. The group of boys began yelling names at Alex and Renate as they turned to walk home. He told himself unless someone started a fight with him he would not fight. But if they start a fight he would take Manfred out before the others could grab him.

Alex and Renate walked in silence all the way home, each of them deep in their own thoughts. They walked up the steps of their apartment, Renate stopped and said, "Alex, will they every stop calling us names?" Her words made him even madder at Manfred and his group. He opened the door and let Renate into the apartment and said, "I hope they will stop. I need to go to my boxing lesson now, remember to do your homework right away." He shut the door and hurried down the steps to go take his first boxing lesson.

The next morning as Renate and Alex walked to school Alex told himself that if Manfred started a fight he was going to make sure he won and Manfred would be the one lying on the ground next time. The school day went by as usual but after school every day Manfred and his group stood under the tree and taunted Alex and Renate by calling them names. Alex ignored the group of boys as he walked home with Renate. Other than the teasing, school was good. Alex liked his teacher and after class Erika always waited for him to walk her out of the school building.

Alex had a big crush on Erika. One day as they walked down the hall at the end of the school day Erika stopped and said, "Do you want to be my boyfriend?" He looked at her in surprise, he couldn't believe his ears. He smiled and said, "Yes, that would be great." He reached over and took Erika's hand as they walked out of the building. Renate looked up at them walking down the step hand in hand.

Someone else noticed Alex and Erika holding hands. Manfred and his group of boys walked over towards Alex and yelled at him, "Get your hands off my girlfriend!" Erika yelled back, "I am not your girl!" Alex let go of Erika's hand as the group moved closer. He told Erika and Renate to go back up the steps that he would deal with Manfred; both girls walked back up the steps. He stood with his head held high as Manfred approached. Manfred pushed Alex in the chest and said, "Didn't you hear what I said, Erika is my girlfriend." Manfred raised his arm and swung the first punch; Alex ducked down and from that position he sprang up and jumped as high as he could, landing a punch directly on Manfred's nose.

The other boys stepped back and stared in amazement because nobody had ever hit Manfred in the face. Manfred held his hand to his face and when he saw the blood on his hand he ran away with the other boys close behind. Alex's hand hurt but he did not care he gave Manfred what he deserved. Erika walked down the steps and took Alex's swollen hand in hers and said, "Thank you." Alex looked deeply in her eyes not sure what Erika meant.

Erika release his hand as he said, "Renate and I need to get home, but I will see you tomorrow." Erika leaned over and kissed Alex on the cheek before turning to go. He felt no more pain in his hand just butterflies in his stomach. Renate said as they headed home, "Wow, she must really like you." They walked home and Alex felt better than he had felt for as he could remember.

Not only did Manfred get what he deserved but Alex got a kiss from the most beautiful girl he had ever seen. Karl was just getting home from work when Alex and Renate came up the street; they saw their father standing on the steps and waited for them. Renate ran up to him and said, "Papa, Alex is a hero, he punched the biggest bully in the nose and he has a girlfriend." Karl raised his eyebrows and he looked over at Alex, then Karl looked down at his swollen hand and said, "We better get in and take care of that hand of yours."

After Alex punched Manfred in the nose, Manfred and his group never said another word to Alex or Renate again. As a matter of fact, whenever Manfred saw Alex he would turn around and walk the other direction. They finally had peace and made new friends at their school. Alex and Erika became boyfriend and girlfriend; they walked hand in hand out on the school grounds and Alex walked Erika home after school. Renate found a new best friend named Brigitte and they would do everything together at school and on days off from school. After doing their chores Renate would go and visit Brigitte and Alex would go see Erika. Life finally seemed right to Alex, except for his brother Ralph not able to be with them.

Right before Alex's birthday a new boy started school and was in his class. Jonny's father had found a new job in their town. Jonny was very short for his age and some of the other children began calling him names. Alex was moved with compassion for Jonny and became his friend. He enjoyed hanging out with Jonny and did not spend as much time with Erika. She did not like that because she wanted Alex to spend all his time just with her.

One day after class Erika pulled Alex aside and said, "I don't want to be your girlfriend any longer, Fredrick is now my new boyfriend." Alex was stunned and his heart broke at this news. He turned and walked away, taking a big breath in order not to cry. He walked over to where Jonny was waiting for him. As Alex walked he looked back at Erika who walked over to Fredrick and kissed him. Jonny asked Alex, "What was that all about?" Alex tried to smile as he said, "Erika has a new boyfriend." Jonny looked at Alex with a puzzled look on his face and then he slapped Alex on the back and said, "Let's go see if you can come over to my house for supper."

Alex was doing well in school. His father had found a good job and they had enough food and could purchase some brand-new clothes. Jonny was an only child of an elderly couple who adopted him and after the war they ended up on the west side of Germany. Jonny's parents worked hard to build a new life for their son Jonny. His parents had enough money to live in their very own house. Jonny's parents were very kind to Alex and always fed him every time he came to visit.

One day Alex and Jonny were sitting at Jonny's kitchen table when Jonny's father came into the kitchen and said, "When you boys are done come out back, I want to show you something." Alex could hardly concentrate on his school work to finish it. He closed his school book and looked over at Jonny. Then he got up off his chair and walked towards the kitchen window as he said, "Let's go and see what your father is talking about."

Jonny's father looked up as he saw the two boys coming out of the house and said, "Wait there by that tree." Jonny's father walked over to the shed and pulled out a brand-new bicycle and said, "Son, I want you to have this bike for doing so well in school." Jonny looked at his father and said, "Thank you Papa!" as he took the bike from him and sat on the seat. Both boys were admiring Jonny's new bike and did not notice his father leave. Alex turned his head as he heard Jonny's father call his name, "Alex, this bike is for you." Alex couldn't believe his eyes as he looked over at Jonny's old bike with a ribbon tired to the handle bars. Alex did not know what to do; he looked at Jonny before walking over to Jonny's father. He said, "Thank you!" Alex was so excited all he wanted to do was leave and show his new bike to his family.

As Alex rode his new bike home he looked up and the sun was just setting behind the western hills and as he looked in the sky he thought the red and orange colors that streaked across the sky seem to have more depth of color tonight. When he got home he jumped off his bike and leaned it up against the side of the apartment building. He took two steps at a time up the stairs that led to his apartment. He pushed opened the door and burst into the living room and with excitement if his voice he said, "Come, look what Jonny's father gave me." Karl looked up from reading the daily newspaper and said, "Calm down son."

Josephine and Renate came into the living room from the kitchen to see what all the commotion was about. Renate wondered why her brother was slightly out of breath and his face was beaming. Karl stood up and said, "Okay son lead the way." Alex went down the stairs as quickly as he could, once outside he climbed on his new bike and stood there with his legs bracing himself on each side while he waited for his family. Renate was the first one out the door. With wide eyes, she said, "Wow, can I ride it?" He looked at her and with a big grin on his face he said teasingly, "Maybe later I will let you to ride my new bike." Karl and Josephine just smiled as they stood on the front steps watching the happy faces of their children.

Jonny and Alex began to ride their bikes every day; they loved to ride for miles. Early on Saturday mornings' Jonny rode his bike over to Alex's house to pick him up for their bike riding adventures. Jonny knocked on the door in the boy's secret code, three raps pause and then two raps. Alex jumped up from the sofa and went to the door to let him in. Jonny always greeted Alex's family with a handshake before the left.

Both of Jonny's parents smoked and on one of their long bike trips they stopped along a country road and parked their bikes. Jonny reached in his pocket and pulled out a pack of cigarettes. He told Alex that his parents did not care if he smoked. Then he pulled a cigarette out of the package and offered Alex his first cigarette. He coughed as he began smoking with Jonny. After that the boys always did their homework over at Jonny's house so they could smoke. Alex liked smoking with Jonny who always had a supply of cigarettes for them both.

Summer was here, Jonny and Alex were off on one of their Saturday bike riding adventures. The sun was warm on Alex's face as they rode their bikes down the street. He heard the birds chirping in the tree tops and there was a slight breeze blowing through the trees. Jonny turned to Alex and said, "Today, I think we will go over to Holland and look at the boats."

Alex thought that was a wonderful adventure and he shook his head to agree and a big smile spread across his face. Then Alex said, "On your mark get set go!" The boys raced their bike to the corner. Both boys laughed as the first one got to the corner and slowed down to wait for the other one. Alex was usually the first rider to the corner. It seemed like forever since Alex had escaped from the east side of Germany. He was happy living in West Germany and he love spending time with his friend Jonny.

It was about a four-hour bike ride to Finlo Holland and being boys they did not think to take a lunch with them. By the time they pulled up to the waterfront both boys were famished, Alex said, "I am hungry, how about you." Jonny rubbed his stomach and said, "Yes, me too." They looked up and down the street; on one side of the street was a rail with benches in front of them that over looked the river.

There were boats docked on the edge of the water and others boats were sailing around the lake. On the other side of the street were rows of shops, it was the bakery shop that drew Alex's attention. The aroma of fresh bread filled the air; Alex pointed and said, "Let's go get some fresh bread." They pulled their bikes up in front of the bakery and walked inside the bakery where Jonny had purchased a couple of rolls. The store next door to the bakery was a delicatessen where Jonny bought them each some slices of cheese. They walked their bikes back across the street and sat on a bench to watch the boats as they ate their lunch.

Before heading back towards home, Jonny bought a couple of packs of cigarettes that they hid under their bike seats so they could cross the border back into Germany. Once they got to the German border the border patrol officer asked, "Do you have anything to declare?" They both shook their heads no, but they must have looked guilty because he searched both them and their bikes finding the cigarettes. He told them they were too young to smoke and they would have to pay a fine next time as he confiscated their cigarettes.

Chapter 26 America 1955-1961

The East Germany's revolution against the communist government failed and all those involved who were not able to escape were captured and executed as a traitor, except those who committed suicide before they were arrested. Mail between East and West Germany was very slow since the East German officials still read every letter before sending it on. They also opened every package taking out what they wanted themselves before giving it to the people.

The letter Josephine sent to her parents requesting that they ask the government official to allow her son Ralph to have a five-day pass to the West side so he could visit his very ill mother took weeks to get there. Josephine was not truthfully ill, but she thought that would be the only way they would let Ralph out of East Germany.

A month has passed since she sent the letter. She feared her letter would not reach her parents. Josephine knew her parents would worry about her, but she could not give them a clue, except for the same code she used on all her letters during the war. The code was a letter 'K' at the bottom of each of her letters, this code would let her parents know that she and the children were okay. Josephine prayed her mother would remember the code and not worry.

Josephine's parents had just finished breakfast when there was a loud knock on the door. Oma wondered who would be at their door this early in the morning; opa went to answer the door. An officer of the government stood at the door. Opa and oma looked at him as he pulled a letter and a bunch of papers out of his bag. Then the man said, "Please sign here and follow all the instructions on the forms." He signed the paper before taking the letter and papers from the man. He thanked him for delivering the letter. The man looked at him before turning to leave. Opa noticed that the letter was from Josephine and it had already been opened. He handed the letter to oma and shut the door.

They looked at each other before walking over and sitting on the sofa. Oma pulled the letter out of the envelope and began to read it out loud to opa, "To my dearest parents, I am very ill and would ask you to see if the government would allow my son Ralph to come and visit me before I die." Oma placed her hand over her heart and let out a gasp before she noticed the signature and the secret code they had established during the war. The letter was signed, "Forever and always your daughter, Josephine K." Both oma and opa let out a sigh of relief when they saw the code letting them know that their daughter was well.

Opa looked at the papers he had in his hand, they were papers giving permission for Ralph to go to West Germany for a five-day visit and he needed to be at the border this Saturday by ten in the morning. The rest of the papers were forms to have Ralph fill out and take with him when he went to the border to cross. Opa was thankful that the government had read the letter and had already brought the papers approving Ralph's visit. He looked at oma and said, "Thank God for His favor, I am not sure how we got this letter and the favor but thankful we did." Oma shook her head in agreement and gave him a hug.

They could hardly wait to tell Ralph when he got home from work. Oma knew she had to write a very careful letter back to her daughter for Ralph to take with him when he left. She wanted to make sure that when Ralph went through security to cross the border and they searched from head to toe there would be nothing that questioned he might be a security risk and arrest him. Ralph's grandparents both knew they could not tell him the truth, but only that his mother was very ill and that he was given permission to go and visit her.

Ralph came home from work tired but happy his work day was almost over. Ralph went into the kitchen and put his lunch bucket on the table. His grandparents were sitting at the table and looking at him as he walked into the kitchen. Ralph stared at his opa with a puzzled look on his face and said, "What?" Oma spoke up first and said, "A man came to the door today and brought us this letter from your mother saying she is very ill. Because your mother is so ill the government is allowing you to go and visit your mother." Ralph's heart felt heavy and sadness filled him as he thought about the war and all they had been through as a family and now his mother might die before he could see her again.

Oma looked at Ralph and saw the sadness engulf him; she got up and wrapped her arms around him. Opa spoke up, "You need to leave Saturday morning." Ralph felt like crying and being happy all at the same time. He did not want his grandparents to see him cry, so he was brave and held his tears. He was wise for being only nineteen-years old, he had to swallow hard before he could say to his grandparents, "Thank you both for all you have done for me since my mother left." Then he turned and walked out of the kitchen to prepare for his trip. One single tear ran down his cheek as he closed his small bag.

Ralph had one more day at work before leaving. At work that day he went to the office to request the time off to visit his mother. He liked his job and the people he worked with he was confused about the communist teaching and about not believing in God or even if there was a God. But he remembered his mother's prayers and what she had taught him about God. He had seen the hand of God's protection during the war, but he just did not know what to think about God now. That night as Ralph laid in bed trying to go to sleep he thought about his mother and tears slipped down the sides of his face and fell unto his pillow. For the first time since Ralph's mother had left he prayed, "God if you are out there please let my mother be okay so that I can see her again." A peace entered his heart and he fell asleep.

The morning air was already warming up as Alex and his family stood waiting for the arrival of Ralph's train. Alex did not think he would be this excited to see his brother again as he looked down the tracks to see a train coming towards the station. At 1:00 p.m. sharp the train horn sounded as it pulled into the station. Josephine and Karl watched the train doors as anticipation filled them to be able to hug their son again. Karl pointed towards the back of the train and said, "There he is." Alex looked and saw his brother step down off the train with a very small bag in his hand; Josephine was already running towards her son with open arms.

Ralph bent down to hug his mother at the same time he looked up at the rest of his family waiting to greet him. He saw his father standing there and relief came to him at the sight of his father. Then Ralph realized something and with a puzzled look on his face he said to his mother, "You don't look very ill to me." Josephine smiled as she explained, "I missed you so much and needed to see you, your father will explain everything to you later. On the way home Ralph told them about his grandparents, his job and how everything was the same in East Germany as before.

Karl listened to Ralph talk but his mind was on going to the authorities that very afternoon to make arrangement for Ralph to stay in West Germany. Ralph was under twenty-one and Karl would not allow him to return to the East side. He chose not to say anything about his plan to any of his family, just in case his request was denied and they would all be disappointed. Josephine had already prepared a pot of soup before they left to for the train station.

Ralph finished his bowl of soup and was surprise when his mother asked him if he wanted seconds. He could never get his stomach full in East Germany because of the food shortage. After the meal Karl cleared his throat to get his family's attention before saying, "I need to go into town this afternoon and would like you children to show your brother around town today." Ralph turned towards his father and said, "I would like that." Alex chimed in, "You have got to meet my friend Jonny."

That evening they sat around the dinner table eating open faced sandwiches and talking about their day. Ralph and Alex talked about his friend Jonny and riding bikes with him tomorrow. Karl cleared his throat and said, "Ralph you are not going back to the East side, I got the papers signed today to keep you here with your family." Ralph stood up and protested, "But what about my job and my friends?" Josephine reached over and took Ralph's hand and said, "You will find a new job and new friends, and the most important thing is that we are all together, I thank God for bringing back to us." Ralph pulled his hand away and crossed his arm and said, "You lied to me to get me here, I don't want to stay here and I don't believe in your God!" Karl interrupted, "Son, you do not talk to your mother like that, you are under twenty-one and are under my authority and until then and you will not return to the East side." Ralph plopped himself back down in his chair and stared at his plate. The room filled with silence as they finished their meal.

Ralph had found a job and a girlfriend and even though he was going to be twenty-one in a few months he did not plan on going back to the East side. Alex only had a little more time left at school before he graduated and then he would go to a trade school. The time went by fast and Alex enrolled at KRUPP Trade School to become a master auto mechanic. School had classes in the morning and hands-on training in the afternoon. He was excited to take the training and spend eight-hour days at school, six days a week, with at least two hours of homework every night. School was a lot of work and he would be glad when the four years was over.

His father thought he should go for one more year beyond the four and become an engineer and he encouraged Alex to continue his education. Alex thought about his father's words, but he thought he had enough school and just wanted to be done with his four years and begin a full-time job. Alex's dreamed of owning an auto repair business someday.

Christmas of 1958, Ralph announced his engagement to his girlfriend Brigitte. Ralph and Brigitte planned to marry in early spring. Josephine was so excited for her son and his fiancé; her thoughts wandered back to her own wedding with Karl, as the rest of the family listened to Brigitte explain some of the couples' wedding plans. Josephine and Karl's wedding seemed a life time ago to her, their marriage had been filled with many trials and sorrows. A smile spread across Josephine's face as she thought, "After twenty-five years together life finally seemed normal again for the first time since their first Christmas together." Josephine's thoughts came back to the present as Ralph stood and said, "Brigitte and I need to get going." Karl stood and said, "I am so happy for the both of you."

Renate left right after Christmas to go to school down by Frankfurt; she was excited to become a lab assistant. Alex completed his training and started working and earning his own money. He hoped to move out on his own by the spring of 1959, but wanted to purchase a new car before that. Alex worked very hard and within a couple of months of getting his new job he purchased his first car, a used Mercedes sedan. It was a beautiful car and he was proud of it. After driving the car for a couple of months he decided to use his car to earn extra money by driving tourists sightseeing around the city and nearby country side. He liked being a tour guide.

The end of April, Alex decided he had saved enough money to move out on his own. He found a fully furnished studio apartment a few blocks from his parents' home. He loved the freedom of living on his own, but still spent every Sunday going to his parents for family dinners. He would never take his family for granted for they had been through so much together. Every Sunday he looked forward to spending time with his family. Alex's wages increase every six months and he began to have his clothes tailor made. For the first time in Alex's life he had more than enough and enjoyed buying things for his parents' home. He thought to himself, "Life is great."

One Sunday just as they finished eating Karl stood up from the table with excitement in his eyes as he spoke, "I have some very good news." He paused and looked at each one sitting around the table before he went on to explain, "I got a job promotion and they are transferring me to Paderborn. It is a large city to the north and I will be getting a large pay increase." Josephine already knew as she said, "Karl, I think this is a great opportunity for us." Renate who had just finished school and was looking for work said, "Perhaps I can get a job up there also." Ralph had his job with the Bayer Company and had moved into a nice apartment with his beautiful wife.

Alex knew he could not move with his job. Karl sat down and said, "All your mother and I ask is that at least once a month all of you come up for Sunday lunch. The all agreed and Alex said, "Father this is wonderful news and a great opportunity for you." Ralph took his wife's hand, stood up and said, "I also have an announcement to make." Ralph looked down at Brigitte before he said, "We are going to have a baby." Josephine clapped her hands with excitement and everyone in the house was filled with joy and celebration at the good news.

Alex had a license to drive large trucks, so he agreed to drive a moving truck for his parents. While he drove his car to pick up the moving truck, the others waited and finished some last-minute packing. Josephine would hardly allow Brigitte to do anything knowing she was pregnant. She said to Brigitte, "You need to be careful of lifting while you are pregnant."

Alex pulled the truck up in front of the apartment building. He opened the back of the truck for loading and looked up at the clear sky and was grateful that the rain they forecasted had not shown up. He walked up the steps and opened the door to find boxes everywhere around the door ready to be moved. Ralph and Karl began picking up boxes and heading toward the truck, Alex bent down and picked up a box following them out the door. The women were busy cleaning the apartment.

Karl had secured a two-bedroom apartment in a small town just outside of Paderborn. It was about a two hour drive up to the little town of Schlangen. Karl and Josephine led the way driving his car. Renate rode in the truck with Alex, and Ralph and Brigitte followed behind the truck as they caravanned to Schlangen. The hours passed quickly as Renate talked nonstop about her school and what it was like living with their spinster aunt while she was away at school. Alex told Renate about his job and how much he loved driving tourists around and learning about the countries his passengers lived in. He slowed the truck down to turn off the freeway and head the few miles more to his parents' apartment. Renate looked over at Alex and studied him for a moment before saying, "Someday I want to go and visit all those countries." Alex smiled and said, "Someday I want to live in America."

Alex enjoyed his work as an auto mechanic, but enjoyed even more his job as tour guide. Every Saturday morning, he had arranged to drive German speaking tourists around the city and country side. He chose to drive only tourists who spoke German because he did not speak any other language except for the Russian he was forced to learn while living in East Germany. He refused to speak Russian in West Germany because he did not want people to know he escaped from the East side.

There were many German speaking tourists from around the world. Alex love listening to the tourists' stories about where they were from, but the tourists that were most interesting to him were those from America. He still had fond memories of the American soldiers who were kind to him. Ever since he was a little boy and the American soldiers left and the Russians came into what now is call East Germany he said to himself, "One day I want to go to America and explore that great country."

The summer of 1960, was hot but always seemed to have just enough of a breeze to keep things tolerable. Alex booked a wonderful older couple for a weekend tour to the Black Forest down in the southern area. The couple not only paid for Alex's time but also paid for his overnight stay while they were in the Black Forest. The elderly couple shared much and Alex was very interested in it. Otto and his wife moved from Germany to America right before the war began. They had lived in America for over twelve years and owned a German sausage store in Portland, Oregon. They made their own sausage and imported specialty items in from German to sell in their store. Otto and his wife took a liking to Alex as they got to know him.

During the hours Alex spent with Otto and his wife he learned a lot about them and their family, they had three children who were young and did not come on this trip with them. Alex began to ask questions about what it was like to live in America. Otto placed his hand on Alex shoulder and said, "Son, if you every want to come and visit America you can come to stay with us." Alex smiled as he looked at Otto in surprise and said, "What if I want to live there?" Otto smiled back and said, "Well, in that case my wife and I will sponsor you to live in America."

Alex could not believe his ears as he stared at Otto with a look of amazement on his face, he could not speak for the longest time. Otto said, "Alex, are you alright?" Alex reached his hand out and took Otto's hand in his and shook it as he said, "Yes, thank you, I am more than alright." Otto reached into his pocket and pulled out one of his business cards and gave it to him and said, "Here is my contact information if you decide you want to come to live in America."

Over the next few months Alex could not stop thinking about Otto and his wife from America. He would hold the business card in his hand and say to himself; "Someday I am going to America." One night while He sat staring at the business card, he picked up the phone and dialed the number on the business card. He got nervous as the phone rang and was just about to hang up when he heard Otto's voice on the other end of the phone, "Hello, Hello." Alex cleared His throat and answered, "Hello, this is Alex from Germany." Otto answered, "Oh, yes, I remember, the young man that drove my wife and I around the country." Alex answered, "Yes, that is me; I have a question to ask you. When you were here in Germany and gave me your business card and said, if I ever wanted to come to America just let you know. Well, I want to come and live in America, does your offer still stand, will you will help me come to America?"

The phone went silent for a few moments and Alex thought Otto had hung up. Then he heard Otto say, "Alex, I would love to sponsor you to come to America, I will need to do some paperwork on my end and you will need to fill out paperwork over there. When are you considering coming?" He answered with excitement in his voice, "Next year!" "Well good then, keep in touch and I will begin my paperwork over here. Talk to you soon, goodbye." Alex was beaming as he said, "Thank you Otto and goodbye." He held the phone in his hand staring at it amazed by the conversation. He finally hung up the phone and jumped up off the sofa with excitement, he walked over to look out the window into the dark street below. His thoughts went to his parents; he had just turned twenty a couple of months ago and knew he needed to be twenty-one to legally leave the country. He thought to himself, "I need a plan of how to tell my parents my plan to go to America."

Alex decided that when he went to his parents' house for Christmas he would tell his family about Otto and his family. Once he finished he would talk about Otto's offer to sponsor him to come to America. Alex knew he had to convince his father, since before his twenty-first birthday he would be unable to leave Germany without his father's consent. Alex felt good about his plan as he finished his work week.

With the money from Karl's new job Josephine could celebrate Christmas the way she used to before the war. Josephine spent the week of Christmas preparing cookies and she always made her very special cake that she only made once a year. The cake consisted of seven layers, first layer was a thin layer of a cookie mixture and then alternated with a chocolate layer, with the last layer being cookie mixture, and then the cake would be coated in chocolate. Karl loved this cake and always looked forward to having some.

The weather was cold and crisp as Alex loaded his overnight bag and Christmas gifts into the trunk of his car. The air smelled as if it may snow, He loved having snow for Christmas. He hopped into his car and drove to the first gas station to fill up before heading north to his parents' house. The sun played peekaboo with the clouds as Alex drove the two hours. His thoughts wandered in and out of how he would begin to tell his parents about America, he said out loud, "Father and Mother I have some wonderful news, no, that won't work. I would like to tell you about a new friend name Otto." Alex stopped himself and focused on the road as he came to the exit off the freeway that leads to his parents' house. The closer Alex got to his parents' house he decided to not bring up his news until after they finished their main meal.

Alex pulled into the parking area across the street from his parents' apartment. He looked around and said to himself, "It looks like everyone is here," since he saw his brother and sister's cars in the parking area. Alex got out of the car and walked around to the trunk, he bent over to gather the Christmas gifts. He heard Renate holler down from the balcony, "Hey, do you need some help?" He bumped his head on the truck lid as he moved out of the trunk with the gifts. He looked up at his sister and yelled back, "No, I got it, but would you get the door for me?"

Alex walked with his overnight bag slung over his shoulder and his arms loaded with the gifts. He walked carefully so as not to drop any of the packages. Renate was waiting with the door open; she gave Alex a hug before taking a couple of packages out of his hands. She led the way up the spiral staircase up to the apartment. Ralph was waiting at the top of the stairs with the door open. The smell of all the holiday baked goods and cooking filled Alex's senses, his mother's cooking was one of the reasons he tried to come home whenever he could.

Josephine came out of the kitchen wiping her hands on her apron, she looked at Alex and pointed towards the spare bedroom and said, "Put the gifts in there, also I booked a room for you at the bed and breakfast across the street." He said, "Thank you mother," as he walked towards the spare room to put the gifts there. Then he walked into the living room and looked around, he saw the undecorated Christmas tree in the corner and the table filled with empty Christmas plates waiting to be filled.

Alex always loved the family traditions his mother began again since they started their new life with his father here in the West. Ralph walked up to Alex and said, "Don't you love Christmas time when we can celebrate with the whole family?" He shook his head in agreement. Then Ralph asked, "How is work going?" Alex turned to look at his brother before he answered, "Fine and how is married life going?" Ralph just smiled and walked over and sat on the sofa; Alex followed him and they talked for a while about many things in general. Karl came into the room and said, "Boys I need your help to bring up the Christmas decorations from the basement and put them in the spare bedroom." Both sons looked up at the same time and said in unison, "Sure." They both were instantly on their feet and followed their father out the door and down the steps toward the basement.

Going down to the basement, Alex's thoughts returned to how he was going to express to his parents his desire to let him go to America before he was twenty-one. Heading back up the stairs with their arms filled with boxes of Christmas decorations, Karl said, "Alex you seem to have a lot on your mind today is everything okay?" He answered, "I am just thinking about how much I love being here with my family on Christmas." Ralph added, "With the baby coming next month there is just so much to be thankful for." Alex felt bad for lying to his father and still planned to talk to his parents after the main meal. He did not want to begin the conversation in the middle of the stairwell. Once they put the decorations into the spare room Josephine said, "It's time for your walk before church. The men bundled up in their coats and went on their Christmas Eve annual walk leaving the women behind.

The tradition Josephine had was that everyone would meet for Christmas Eve service at the church for the six o'clock service. The men would walk and later meet the women at the church when the service began. The women would stay behind and decorate the tree, put out the gifts and fill the Christmas plates with cookies fruit and nuts before heading to the church. After church, everyone would walk home together and find that the Christ Child had decorated the tree, filled the Christmas plates with goodies and left gifts under the tree while they were at church.

After church, they walked home singing Christmas Carols. The streets were decorated for Christmas and in the dark the Christmas lights set off a beautiful glow around the small town. Even though they did not have any young children with them this Christmas, Alex was going to enjoy every moment of the joy of spending time with his family. When he goes to America he was not sure if he could come back the following Christmas. Once they reached the apartment Karl unlocked the door and Josephine led the way up the stairs.

After taking off and hanging their coats Josephine said, "Renate and Brigitte help me bring the food into the living room." The men went into the living room where they had put up a table and set it for dinner. The tree was decorated with gifts lined up around the bottom of the tree. The Christmas plates were brimming with candy, fruit and nuts. Alex stood at the entrance of the living room taking in the sight. Karl walked over and lit the candles on the tree and then went to see if Josephine needed any more help.

They all sat down at the table to have a wonderful light dinner. After dinner Karl stood up and turned off the lights and then said, "Come gather around the tree." The room was filled with a soft glow of the candles that flickered on the Christmas tree. Karl began and they all joined in and sang Silent Night, the room felt so peaceful. As they sang, their thoughts and prayers went to oma and opa and their other loved ones in East Germany. Once the song was over Josephine walked over and turned on the light.

They exchanged gifts and ate from their Christmas plates enjoying great conversation. Sadness began to fill Alex as he walked over to the Christmas tree and stared at the candles that were more than half burnt down. His thoughts reflected how much he would miss his family when he moved to America. But the adventurer in Alex told him that he must go and explore this new land. He turned to go over to the bed and breakfast, giving each family member an extra-long hug before going out the door.

On Christmas morning Alex woke early to find a layer of fresh snow covered the ground and his car. He said to himself, "Wonderful a white Christmas, now everything is perfect." He decided to take a walk before going over to his parents' house for breakfast. The snow crunched beneath Alex's feet as he took a walk towards the church. His thoughts were planning his talk with his family about moving to America.

When Alex returned, his mother had breakfast ready and everyone was waiting for Alex to arrive before they began eating. The conversation at the breakfast table was about the soon arrival of Ralph and Brigitte's baby. Josephine is very excited about the birth of her first grandchild and she asked, "What names are you thinking of for the baby?" Brigitte answered, "We like Wolfgang for a boy and Sabine for a girl." Josephine smiled and said, "Wonderful names."

Talking about the baby seemed to make everyone happy, so Alex decided while everyone was in such a good mood he would tell his family about his plans to move to America now instead of at lunch. He cleared his throat to get his families attention. Then he began to tell them about Otto and his wife from America, everyone was interested until He ended with "I want to go and live in America." Josephine's eyes got big as she placed her hand on her heart. Karl looked Alex straight in the eyes and stared for a long moment before saying, "Son you are not going anywhere until you are twenty-one years old!"

The mood around the table changed and silence fell over the room as everyone stared at Alex in disbelief. He stood up and looked around the table and then finally looking directly into his father's eyes said, "If I can't go this spring then I will go in October. Either way I am going to America." He excused himself from the table and went outside for another walk. Sadness filled Alex's heart that he had upset everyone at the table and ruined Christmas for his parents. He was set in his mind that he was going since Otto said he had finished his paperwork and could sponsor him to come to America. He said out loud, "I was going to America no matter what; this was my dream since I first talked with the American soldiers during the war."

After Alex walked out the door and Karl wrapped his arms around Josephine who was now weeping softly, Ralph and Brigitte just sat there in silence. Josephine looked up at Karl with tears running down her cheeks and said, "Oh Karl, I just now got all of our family back together and with the new baby coming, everything seemed so perfect for the first time in many years."

He looked down at his beautiful wife and said, "I know my sweet Josephine, but our son is a very strong willed young man and he will go either way." Josephine shook her head in agreement and softly said, "I know and that's what makes me so sad." He looked at his son Ralph and his wife and then back at Josephine and said, "When Alex gets back I will tell him we will allow him go in the spring if he has his heart set on America."

Josephine took a deep breath and wiped her tear stained face before she took her glass and raised it for a toast, "To our son Alex and his adventure to America, with hopes he will return home soon, and to our new grandchild's birth." Everyone toasted and the mood lightened, the conversation moved back to the new baby's arrival in January.

As Alex walked around town he prayed for a way to convince his parents to let him go sooner than later. What if they did not allow him to go in the spring? How would he tell Otto who had already said the paperwork in America was ready to sponsor him for coming in the spring? Alex walked past the pond and stood watching two swans swimming around. He shivered in the cold fresh air and his feet were icy cold; he looked down at his watch and decided he needed to get back since he had been walking around for several hours. When Alex arrived back at his parents' apartment, he hesitated at the door before going up the stairs.

Alex was surprised when he opened the apartment door to hear laughter; he wondered what had happened to change the mood. He walked into the living room and everyone in the room went silent. They all fixed their eyes on him as he walked into the room. Karl walked over and put his arm around Alex shoulder and said, "It is time to celebrate." Alex had a puzzled look on his face as his father opened a bottle of champagne and poured it into the glasses that were arranged on the table.

Karl handed Alex a glass and then lifted his glass in a toast and said, "To Alex who is going to America." Everyone lifted their glasses in a toast. Alex could not believe his ears and it took him a few minutes to realize what was happening before he lifted his glass. He did not understand the change in his parents' attitude towards him going to America and dared not ask. He was happy that everyone had accepted his plan.

In January of 1961, Alex needed to fill out the paperwork for America. He and his father had to travel to Hamburg to apply for the visa because that is where Alex was born. It was snowing heavily as he drove with his father to Hamburg; the snow plow had been out earlier and plowed the roads making the road safer to drive as they made the four-hour trip. They arrived in Hamburg just after noon and decided to get some lunch before heading over to City Hall. They found a nice little restaurant a few blocks away. During lunch Karl got a serious look on his face and asked, "Son are you sure this is what you want to do, America is a long way?"

Alex looked up at his father and swallowed the bit of food that he was chewing before he answered, "Father, I understand your concern, but this is something I need to do." Karl looked deeply into his son's eyes and a smile spread across his face as he recalled how strong willed his son was. Karl spoke softly, "I know son I just needed to make sure."

Karl followed Alex up the stairs that lead to the City Hall; they entered a large atrium that had a statute of Michael Angelo in a fountain that stood in the middle of a polished marble floor. Around the atrium were office doors; they walked around looking at the name plates on each door until they found the one labeled "German Counsel." Karl opened the door for Alex and followed him over to a desk. The desk clerk was an older woman; she was looking down reading something when they walked up to the window. The woman looked up over her glasses and asked, "May I help you?" Alex answered, "Yes, I would like to apply for a visa to go to America." She looked from Alex to Karl who was standing behind Alex and then quickly said, "Let me get you the paperwork."

When the woman returned to the desk she had a large stack of papers for them to fill out. Alex looked at the stack of papers and said, "That's a lot of paperwork." The woman pointed over to the corner of the room where there was a small table with three chairs around it and said, "You can fill out the paperwork over there and then return it to me once you are done."

Karl took the paperwork from the woman and thanked her, and they walked over to the small table. It took over two hours to complete everything. Karl waited at the table while Alex took the pile of paperwork back to the woman. She looked up over her glasses as he approached the counter. He handed the woman the paperwork and said, "I think you will find everything in order." The woman flipped quickly through the paperwork before saying, "We will get back to you in about three weeks." Alex was disappointed he wanted an answer today, so he blurted out, "Three weeks, why so long." She looked at him impatiently and said, "These things take time."

On the drive back home the sky was clear and the sun was shining, the roads were dry except for the snow piled up on the sides from the snow plow. The sunny weather made for a beautiful drive back and Alex felt good as he realized that once the paperwork was finished he was going to go to America. When Alex pulled into the parking place by his parent's apartment, his mother was standing on the balcony watching for their return. As soon as they got out of the car she yelled down to them, "We need to go to the hospital the baby is about to be born." They both went upstairs to change their clothes and get ready for the drive to the hospital. Josephine paced as she waited for them; she was excited and wanted to get to the hospital as soon as possible.

Alex helped his mother into the back seat of the car and his father jumped into the passenger side of the car. Alex drove the hour drive to the hospital where Ralph was with Brigitte during the birthing process. By the time they arrived to the hospital the baby had already been born. As soon as they walked into the maternity ward Ralph came up to his family beaming with joy and said, "We have a baby girl and we are going to call her Sabine." Josephine said, "How is Brigitte doing? And where is my new granddaughter?"

Ralph led the way to the nursery as he answered his mother's questions, "Brigitte is fine, just resting now and baby Sabine is this way." Josephine looked through the nursery window and bragged about her new grandbaby, while Alex wrapped his arm around Ralph's shoulder and said, "I am very happy for you and Brigitte." Karl looked at his granddaughter and said, "Thank you Ralph, this is the best gift you could have ever given us."

After seeing the baby, they all went in to see Brigitte. Alex drove his mother and father home. It was late when he pulled into the parking area by his parent's apartment. Josephine said as she got out of the car, "I will make us a quick supper." Alex was hungry and tired so he replied, "Thank you mother, do you mind if I spend the night, I am too tired to drive back home tonight." Karl wrapped an arm around Alex's shoulder and said, "Sure son anytime you are always welcome."

The first of March was a beautiful spring day; the sun was out and the first flowers were pushing their tops out of the ground reaching for the sunlight. Alex drove to work that morning; he would give his notice to his manager. All he could think about for days now is that on March 20th he would leave for America. Everything was falling into place, the week before he had purchased his airline ticket and made all the arrangements with Otto and his wife in Portland, Oregon USA. It was after he gave his notice at work that he felt like it was really true that he would be leaving for America in just a few short weeks. Excitement filled Alex as he drove home from work that evening.

The week before Alex was to leave for America he drove up to his parent's house to pick them up and take them to the church where baby Sabine would be baptized. Sabine was now six weeks old and Alex had not seen her since the day at the hospital in January when she was born. When Alex pulled into the parking area by his parents' apartment his mother had been watching from the balcony for his arrival.

By the time Alex got to the apartment door both his parents were coming out the door with their arms full of gifts. Josephine talked non-stop about baby Sabine all the way to the church. It had been some time since Alex had been in a church and it felt a little strange. Ralph and Brigitte stood by the door waiting for them. Josephine pulled out the christening gown from one of the boxes she brought with her. All her children had worn a similar gown for their baptisms. She handed it to Brigitte to Sabina to wear. Brigitte thanked Josephine as she took the gown to put it on Sabrina.

The pastor of the Lutheran church stepped over to Ralph and said, "The guests are arriving are you almost ready?" Ralph said, "It will be just a couple of minutes more, we are waiting for Brigitte to return with the baby." Sabine cried as the pastor poured the water over the top of her head to baptize her. Renate and Alex stood as godmother and godfather for Sabine. After the ceremony Ralph was busy taking pictures.

Alex looked over at his brother and then back to the rest of his family, his heart became sad at the thought of leaving them, he promised himself he would come back and visit often. The pastor waited at the door as everyone was leaving. Ralph asked the pastor if he would take a picture of the whole family on the church steps. The pastor was happy to and took the picture. They all went over to Ralph's and Brigitte's home to eat lunch and open the gifts. Sabina slept in Josephine's arms as they sat and talked. Alex stood to get ready to leave and asked Ralph if he could get him a copy of the family picture on the church steps. Before departing, they all hugged and Alex drove his parents back home.

This was Alex's last day at his job; he only had a couple of days left before getting on the airplane to go to America. That night his friends had a going away party to wish him well on his new adventure. After the party, he walked the couple of blocks back home; the March evening air was brisk as he walked. Alex looked up at the trees swaying in the breeze and his thoughts went to how happy he was to fulfill his childhood dream of going to America. As he climbed the steps to his apartment he said to himself, "I need to get up early tomorrow and take my car to my father, it is nice that he is purchasing my car so that I would have money for the trip." The next morning early, he cleaned out and washed the car before heading up north to his parents' home.

As Alex drove, it was a bitter sweet drive. He thought about leaving his family and everything he had known to begin a new adventure in his life. He would miss his family but in his heart, he knew going to America was the right thing to do. He did not know that the whole family would be there at his parents to have a farewell celebration. Alex did not see his brother or sister's cars when he pulled into the parking area to park his car. He rang the bell and the apartment building door buzzed open.

He slowly climbed the spiral stairwell to the door and knocked. Alex was surprised when his brother opened the door with baby Sabine in his arms. Ralph gave him a hug. Alex took Sabine from his brother and said, "What are you doing here?" Ralph chuckled and said, "I needed to make sure I harassed you before you go to America." Sabine snuggled her little head on Alex's shoulder, he thought to himself, "I am sure going to miss this little one." Josephine came up and gave him a hug before she took Sabine and said, "Go and sit down, lunch will be ready soon."

When Alex walked into the living room Renate and Brigitte were sitting on the sofa talking. He just smiled as he looked at them feeling happy to see all his family again. Karl came into the room and Alex walked over and pulled the car keys from his pocket handing them to his father. The time passed quickly as he visited with his family. It was time to say goodbye, his father thanked him for letting him purchase his car, Alex was more thankful than his father.

Josephine held back her tears as she hugged Alex a little tighter and longer than normal. He needed to take the train back home, so Ralph agreed to take him to the train station in the next town. Ralph talked to Alex in a big brother tone, "Be careful over there in America and make sure you write to mother often, she is having a hard time with your leaving you know." Alex answered, "I will be safe and I know mother is sad that I am leaving."

On the train ride back to his apartment Alex's heart felt heavy as he thought about leaving everything he knew and going to a new land. The hardest part was leaving his family. By the time he got back home the sadness had turned into excitement and adventure as he thought about leaving in the morning for America.

Alex's neighbor got up early to take him to the airport. While he sat waiting for his plane he watched all the people passing by him. Then he heard over the loud speaker, "Pan Am flight 1298 to Portland, Oregon is now boarding." Alex's heart skipped a beat as he picked up his carry-on bag and walked to line up. His thoughts were filled with much expectation as he boarded the plane and found his seat. He was going to America with only two suitcases and a hundred dollars in his pocket. He still did not know how to speak English; the only English word that he knew was "coke." Alex had no idea what this adventure that he was taking to America would be like.

Epilogue

The sound of the distant train brought Alex back to reality. He looked away from the window and down at his now cold coffee. He thought to himself, "I have been in America for over fifty years now and so much has happened. I got drafted into the US Army and became a drill sergeant!" Alex enjoyed being in the American Army. Learning a new trade of making rod iron and later he had built his own rod iron business that he had for fifteen years. As his thoughts continued he said to himself, "My where has the time gone?"

Alex turned as he heard the footsteps of his wife walking towards the kitchen; he smiled at his wife as she entered said, "Good morning Alex." He had been married for over forty-seven years and could not be happier. His wife poured herself a cup of coffee and said, "You remember the children and our grandsons are coming over today for lunch?"

Alex just sat there for a moment staring at his wife as he took stock of his life's journey. He had lots of hopes and dreams for a twenty-year old when he came to America. He was drafted into the US Army in 1964 and served his new county where so many years before the American soldiers were kind to him in Germany. In 1969, he married his wife and they have two children and four grandsons. As a man now who is over seventy-five years old, it is Alex's family that brings him the greatest joy in life. Because sometimes in life family is all you have.

About the Author

 **Sherry Malunat** visited Germany several times to interview the family members of Alex Herman. She recorded the detailed events of Alex's family during World War II over a five-year period. She speaks German and has a love for the German people.

Right after the Berlin wall and all the barb wire came down in 1990 Sherry travel to where Alex lived until he was thirteen years old. On the train ride to Suderode she saw watch towers empty but still standing at the borders, it gave her an eerie feeling as she saw them passing by the train window.

Walking through Alex's town was as if time stood still. Many of the buildings that were still standing had visible bullet hole in them and there were still a few Russian soldiers walking around the train station with guns slung over their shoulders.

The stores shelves were still mainly empty. She met with Alex's cousins and a few of his school friends. Sherry writes this book to share the stories of her dear friend, Alex, so that people would know the truth about what the children of Germany went through during World War II.

48080194R00170

Made in the USA
San Bernardino, CA
15 April 2017